National Cowboy Hall of Fame Chuck Wagon Cookbook

National Cowboy

Hall of Fame

Chuck Wagon

Cookbook

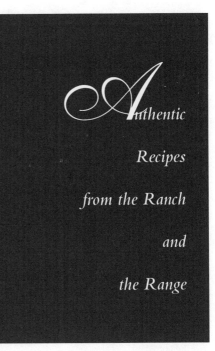

Authentic

Recipes

from the Ranch

and

the Range

B. Byron Price

HEARST BOOKS

NEW YORK

It is the policy of William Morrow and Company, Inc., and its
imprints and affiliates, recognizing the importance of preserving
what has been written, to print the books we publish on
acid-free paper, and we exert our best efforts to that end.

Library of Congress Cataloging-in-Publication Data

Price, B. Byron.
    National Cowboy Hall of Fame chuck wagon cookbook : authentic
recipes from the ranch and the range / B. Byron Price.
        p.   cm.
    Includes index.
    ISBN 0-688-12989-7
    1. Cookery, American—Western style.   2. Cowboys—West (U.S.)
I. National Cowboy Hall of Fame and Western Heritage Center.
II. Title.
TX715.2.W47V57   1994
641.5978—dc20   94-18568
                                                        CIP

Printed in the United States of America

First Edition

1   2   3   4   5   6   7   8   9   10

BOOK DESIGN BY PETER A. DAVIS

For Mother, who can cook with the best of them

$\mathcal{A}$cknowledqments

$\mathcal{W}$hen producing a cookbook there is no such thing as too many cooks in the kitchen. The spirit, wisdom, and example of several of today's finest contemporary cowboy cooks have certainly left their distinctive brand on this volume. In recent years, Garnet Brooks, Bill Cauble, Guy and Pip Gillette, Horace Hatfield, Jimbo Humphries, Tom Perini, Red Steagall, and Cliff Tienert have shared generously of their time and experience, not to mention their skillets and Dutch ovens, to help make this work a reality. Dedicated to the preservation of the history and traditions of cow camp cooking, these individuals also have figured prominently in the annual National Cowboy Hall of Fame Chuck Wagon Gathering and in the recent formation of the Western Chuck Wagon Association.

I also wish to thank Stephanie Qualls, registrar at the National Cowboy Hall of Fame, whose research contacts with museums and archives throughout the West immeasurably enriched this work, and Janice Pinney, who conducted invaluable investigations in the collections of the Center for American History, the Harry Ransom Humanities Research Center, and the Texas Memorial Museum, all at the University of Texas at Austin.

The always helpful Claire Kuehn, archivist at the Panhandle Plains Historical Museum, Canyon, Texas, provided photographic assistance and access to the XIT Ranch papers. Tai Kreidler, assistant archivist at the Southwest Collection at Texas Tech University, furnished important documents from the papers of the Spur and Matador ranches. Carol Williams, coordinator of the Cattleman's Museum of the Texas and Southwestern Cattle Raisers Association, at Fort Worth, Texas, also supplied key information and illustrations. The gracious and incomparable Tom Ryan added a special artistic touch by providing the wonderful jacket illustration, *The Long Day*.

Special words of thanks are due John Eggen of Lebanon, Oregon, for permission to include some of the remarkable photographs of Frank Sherman from his collection and Edith Bolt for making available some of the recipes of her late husband, Richard, for more than four decades an outstanding West Texas roundup cook. My profound appreciation also extends to the many other ranch cooks from all over the West who took the time to share their favorite dishes and lore for this cookbook.

Thanks also are due my long-suffering colleague, Richard Rattenbury, curator of history at the National Cowboy Hall of Fame, whose editorial suggestions have again saved me many embarrassments. My gratitude also extends to my assistant, Judy Dearing, whose extra hours and myriad contributions to the production of this volume deserve singular recognition. Many thanks also to Rick Rodgers for testing the recipes and making certain that home cooks achieve the same great taste as our chuck wagon chefs.

I owe my greatest debt, however, to my wife, Jeannie, who rearranged her life in order to share me with this project. Her unfailing encouragement sustained me along the trail.

—B. Byron Price
National Cowboy Hall of Fame

ONTENTS

ACKNOWLEDGMENTS   6

INTRODUCTION   10

PART ONE

CHAPTER 1
Cooking on the Range and Trail   14

CHAPTER 2
"Pot Rasslers" and "Belly Cheaters": Cow Camp Cooks   62

CHAPTER 3
"Everything but the Hide, Hooves, and Bawl": Meat   78

CHAPTER 4
Staples of the Range: Fresh, Dried, and Canned   90

CHAPTER 5
"Sinkers" and "Splatter Dabs": Bread   100

CHAPTER 6
"Spotted Pup" and "Shiverin' Liz": Desserts   110

CHAPTER 7
"Belly Wash": Coffee and Tea   116

PART TWO

CHAPTER 8
Appetizers, Soups, and Salads   126

CHAPTER 9
Bread and Rolls   144

CHAPTER 10
Beef, Pork, and Game   164

CHAPTER 11
Poultry and Fish   186

CHAPTER 12
Stews, Casseroles, and Mexican Inventions   200

CHAPTER 13
Beans, Vegetables, and Potatoes   222

CHAPTER 14
Desserts   238

CHAPTER 15
Sauces, Salsas, and Beverages   262

NOTES   277

BIBLIOGRAPHY   281

INDEX   291

INTRODUCTION

Feeding nomadic cowboys in the often rugged and sometimes inhospitable American West, far from convenient sources of supply, called for ingenuity, perseverance, and sacrifice. As the frontier moved ever westward, cattlemen ranged far from established towns and tended their herds in remote regions miles from the nearest road, farm, or commissary. In the years immediately following the Civil War, as cattle ranching reached the vast open range of the Great Plains, chuck wagons began to serve ranchers and their cowboys as traveling kitchens during roundups and long drives to market. An integral part of American ranching for nearly a century, team-drawn chuck wagons eventually gave way to motor vehicles, only to rise again as sentimental symbols of a bygone era.

Rich traditions evolved around cowboy cooks, their chuck wagons, and their foodways. Embellished through story and rhyme and brought to life in the work of countless artists, writers, actors, and musicians, this legacy has become a staple of American folklore. Such larger-than-life portrayals, however, frequently overshadow, simplify, or romanticize the genuine hardships that ranch cooks faced in pursuing their livelihoods. Over the years few historians have caught more than a whiff of the reality of the ranch cook's experience and none has been hungry enough to follow the scent. The enticing aromas of saddle leather, gunpowder, and rotgut whiskey have frequently steered investigators into more exciting arenas.

Apart from scant references in a handful of case studies of individual ranches, topics like cow camp cooking and supply have yet to arouse much scholarly interest. And while it is true that museums and private collectors have preserved scattered remnants of cowboy culture, including a relative handful of chuck wagons, Dutch ovens, and other artifacts, few have attempted to relate such collections to larger themes like nutrition, logistics, and food processing and preparation.

The legacy of ranch cooking survives and even flourishes in many quarters. Its memory burns brightest in the ever-thinning ranks of cowboys and cooks who once followed chuck wagons on their annual spring and fall rounds. Their vivid recollections, in turn, have enabled succeeding generations to share vicariously in the culinary heritage of the West through authentic recipes and colorful reenactments.

PART ONE

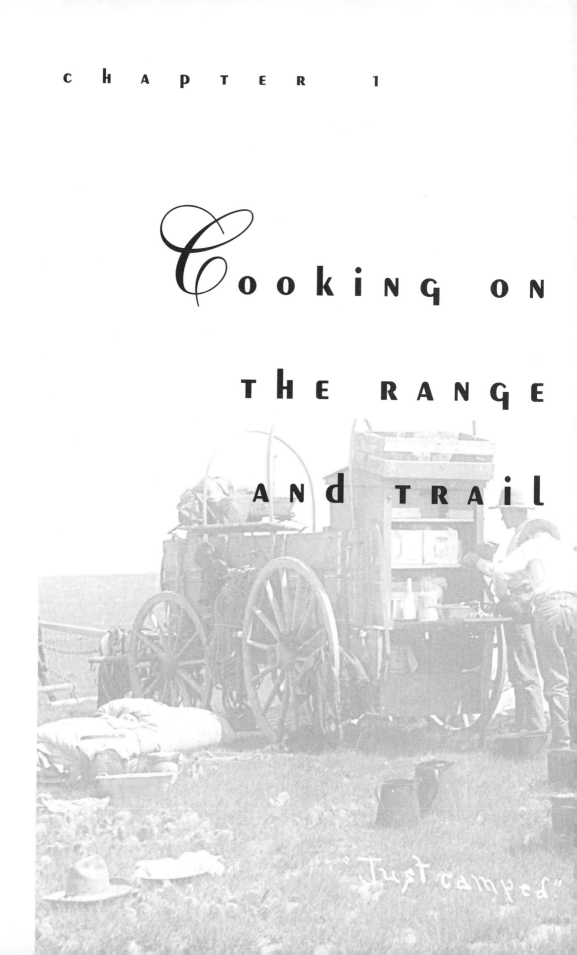

Cooking on the range and trail

"Just camped"

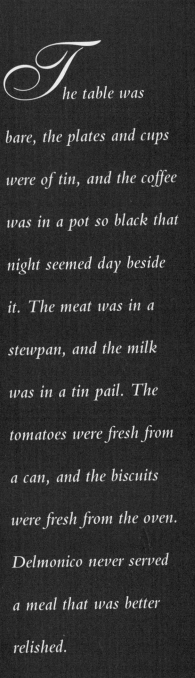

*T*he table was bare, the plates and cups were of tin, and the coffee was in a pot so black that night seemed day beside it. The meat was in a stewpan, and the milk was in a tin pail. The tomatoes were fresh from a can, and the biscuits were fresh from the oven. Delmonico never served a meal that was better relished.

"The Cowboy as He Is,"
Democratic Leader
(Cheyenne, Wyoming),
January 11, 1885

$\mathcal{L}$ong before the great roundups and trail drives of the late nineteenth century, small squads of cow hunters working cooperatively fanned out each spring and fall to gather their herds for branding or market. Participants in these events carried meager provisions with them on their saddles, either slung over the horn, stuffed in saddle pockets, or rolled in a coat or slicker and tied behind the saddle cantle. Most men packed a few days' rations in a "wallet," a cloth or canvas sack with two compartments separated in the middle by a wide mouth.

An early cow hunter's fare was simple: a little flour or cornmeal, chunks of corn bread or biscuits, some salt, perhaps a little sugar, and coffee. Many also carried a hunk of salted side meat whose fat tended to discolor wallets, thereby earning their owners the colorful, if unappetizing, label "greasy sack outfits."

A typical cow hunter of the period carried enough biscuits to last about three days. Rarely, however, did the original supply suffice, and stock hunters often stopped unannounced at isolated ranch houses for resupply. Settlers usually welcomed the wandering herders, baked them fresh bread, and sometimes provided other food, usually without fee, but occasionally charging ten cents a dozen for biscuits.

Most days each cowboy cooked for himself. Utensils were sparse, generally confined to a communal coffeepot or, more commonly, individual tin cups holding a quart or more. Shunning weighty iron skillets, the cow hunters almost always cooked their meat and bread dough on sticks over a fire.

During longer roundups, cow hunters often lashed more extensive provisions, cooking utensils, and bedding on pack animals, forming a train of mules and horses. While in the field, roundup outfits often entrusted their packs to neophyte cowhands, some of them as young as ten years old. The use of pack trains for feeding trail and roundup crews persisted in rough, isolated regions of the West well into the twentieth century, especially in those areas where dense vegetation, broken terrain, narrow passages, and the absence of roads and bridges discouraged the use of carts or wagons.

But by the 1850s, two-wheeled, ox-drawn supply carts or wagons, most patterned after the Spanish *carreta*, already were supplanting pack animals in open country along the Texas Gulf Coast. Easier to manage than mule trains and with greater carrying capacity, these lumbering vehicles also accompanied a few trail drives from Texas to distant markets in Louisiana, Missouri, California, and other points before the Civil War. The era of the ox-cart was short-lived, however, with few lasting beyond the 1870s. They were soon replaced by heavy-duty freight wagons pulled by teams of two to six horses or mules, depending on the weight of the load and the difficulty of the trail.

Historians credit freighter-turned-rancher Charles Goodnight with creating the prototype chuck wagon in 1866. His model was simply a wooden cupboard made of *bois d'arc* (Osage orangewood) that was bolted to the rear of an army wagon. The design of this "chuck" or "grub" box, as it became known, perhaps drew inspiration from the portable writing desks of the period and the compact mess chests then popular with travelers, campers, and soldiers for cooking and dining in the field. The diary of trail driver Richard Dallam, who accompanied a cattle herd from Texas to California in 1853, for example, speaks of buying lumber in San Antonio "to make a mess chess [*sic*] for the road."[1] More elaborate cabinets, such as those produced by T. Morris Perot and Company of Philadelphia in the 1860s, featured felt linings and iron mountings and, when opened, formed tables with legs.

Chuck boxes, by contrast, were usually much larger, standing about four feet tall, and were made to a cook's or rancher's specifications. Some were rectangular and of uniform depth, while the backs of others sloped rearward from top to bottom to give the cook maximum access to their contents. Whatever its shape, a chuck box usually housed a labyrinth of shelves and compartments.

Within the upper reaches of the box the cook stowed a variety of tin cans and wooden containers bearing items in more or less constant use—staples, spices, tableware and other small utensils, and perhaps medicines. Larger and heavier items like earthenware crocks, wooden kegs, and iron pots and pans were kept on the lower shelves of the unit.

Most chuck boxes also accommodated several often ill-fitting drawers that opened by means of finger and hand holes or metal, leather, or ceramic pulls. The drawer containing tableware was sometimes called the "layout box," while that holding a few personal belongings of the cook and crew was often termed the "cowboy box" or "roundup drawer." Some chuck boxes also boasted a lockable "business drawer" in which the wagon or trail boss kept important documents.

A hinged lid, secured by a hasp, covered the face of the chuck box while in transit. The lid unfolded into a work counter supported by chains, ropes, rods, or, in most cases, a single wooden leg, also on a folding hinge. A storage crate or trunk sometimes crowned the grub box, and a coffee mill and a rack for butcher knives were nailed to its sides. Pinups and decorative metal signs also sometimes adorned its walls and drawers.

Below the chuck box on many wagons hung a wooden storage compartment known as the "boot," containing heavy pots, skillets, and Dutch ovens. Suspended like a hammock between the wheel axles dangled the *cuna* (cradle), or "coonie," a green cowhide usually jammed full of kindling wood or cow chip fuel.

Stakes and picket ropes, used to tie the horses, were hanked and double half-hitched to an iron bar along the side boards of the chuck wagon. Quarters of fresh beef often cooled on nearby meat hooks. A tool box, sometimes known as a "jewelry chest," also found a place along the side boards of most chuck wagons, as did one or more thirty-five-gallon water barrels positioned on wooden platforms braced by strap iron. In areas where water was plentiful, a ten-gallon keg for incidental needs usually sufficed.

Some cooks preferred to secure the water barrel inside the wagon and extend a faucet through the side board. At least a few placed the barrel under the seat with the spout facing out the front of the wagon so that, according to one experienced trail boss, "it didn't get broken so much."[2]

The wagon itself held bulk quantities of flour, beans, sugar, molasses, coffee, lard, canned goods, and dried fruit, carried in an assortment of crates, cartons, lugs, bags, boxes, and kegs. Also stored there were bacon and fresh beef wrapped in cloth or canvas tarps. An occasional banjo or guitar might find its way into the wagon box, along with extra horseshoes, a shoeing outfit, branding irons, and other implements, all covered by a stack of bedrolls and a protective canvas sheet pulled across wagon bows of wood or iron or tightly laced directly over the cargo. Cooks often stowed a sack or two of corn or oats for the chuck wagon team beneath the driver's seat.

Although local blacksmiths usually fashioned chuck wagons from various farm, freight, and military vehicles, market demand in the mid-1880s led the Studebaker Brothers Manufacturing Company of South Bend, Indiana, to produce the "Round-up Wagon," especially designed for feeding hungry cowboys in the field. Priced at two hundred dollars, the sturdy 1888 model was equipped with zinc-lined mess boxes front and rear.

Trail driving reached its zenith between 1866 and the mid-1890s because of unprecedented demand for beef and the absence of adequate and economical railroad transport from Texas to northern markets. At its height it involved millions of cattle, thousands of cowboys, and hundreds of chuck wagons. Drove contractors and their professional crews handled most of the trade. An average outfit consisted of eleven men, including a trail boss, eight drovers, a horse wrangler, a cook and chuck wagon, sixty horses, and twenty-five hundred to three thousand head of cattle. It was these large crews that first made regular use of mess wagons.

As settlers pushed west, turning grazing land into farmland, the cattle trails became more logistically challenging. Drovers could no longer depend upon the availability of regular supply points, a day's drive apart, as they had on more easterly courses before the Civil War.

Drovers normally carried thirty days' worth of food, or at least enough to get to the next resupply point. On well-traveled and now legendary paths like the Chisholm and Great Western trails, drovers secured fresh provisions at such outfitting centers as Fort Worth and Fort Griffin, Texas, Dodge City, Kansas, and Ogallala, Nebraska. In fact, supply centers large and small rarely were more than one hundred miles apart at any point along these routes.

Nevertheless, mishaps and miscalculations could place drovers in jeopardy. After running short of food in Indian Territory in 1877, for example, one crew subsisted on beef, salt, and coffee for eight days before finally locating a buffalo hunters' camp fifty miles distant in Texas.

River crossings, especially when waters were high and turbulent, also took their toll on crews. There were only a few rivers and streams along the main cattle trails where chuck wagons could cross on bridges or ferries. Without such conveniences trail crews were sometimes forced

to float their wagons across on log rafts. Keeping bedding and perishable food dry while fording difficult rivers often tested the cook's ingenuity, skill, and luck. An imaginative cook for the 101 Ranch solved the problem by caulking his wagon box and placing critical supplies atop a crude cradle of ropes criss-crossed between the wagon's side boards.

But as Frank Simpson's trail outfit discovered at the South Canadian River on their way to the Osage country in Indian Territory, no method of crossing was foolproof. After forfeiting their wagon and supplies to the raging waters, Simpson and his men endured three days of hunger and bitter cold until a party of soldiers came to the rescue with clothing and enough food to tide them over until they could refit.

At the end of the trail many outfits sold their remudas and chuck wagons to drovers headed farther north and, with their saddles in hand, boarded trains home. Or a skeleton crew might return the wagons and horses to Texas. The enterprising Mark Withers, who reached Abilene in charge of a herd in the summer of 1868, sold his old gear, purchased new wagons and harnesses, and, detouring by way of Arkansas, returned with a load of apples.

The cattle industry took off in the mid-1870s, and ranchers from the Cross Timbers region of Texas pushed north and west onto the virgin grass of the rolling and high plains. Pack trains accompanied some outfits; chuck wagons traveled with others. Frequently several ranchers shared the expense of fitting out a chuck wagon, each cowman taking responsibility for supplying a portion of the food and other supplies. But south of San Antonio, where thick mesquite brush discouraged the use of chuck wagons for several years, cowboys still brought and prepared their own grub.

Immense open-range roundups, many of them lasting from the coming of new grass in mid-April or early May until December, replaced the relatively small local gatherings of the past. So-called "stray men" would come from other ranches, often more than doubling the size of the roundup crew from ten or fifteen men to twenty-five, thirty, or more. Although the number

varied according to local conditions and the amount of range to be covered, a half-dozen wagons or more were common, while the largest gatherings drew a dozen or more. The general roundup of a fifteen- to twenty-mile stretch of the Canadian River in the eastern part of the Texas Panhandle in the spring of 1889, for example, included fifty to seventy-five riders and eight to ten mess wagons. During this same period, ten chuck wagons served ninety hands at a Slaughter Ranch roundup in Texas, and an even larger gathering held in nearby Borden County attracted one hundred cowboys, eight hundred horses, and a dozen chuck wagons. Some thirty to forty wagons worked the lower Pecos River ranges in West Texas and eastern New Mexico during the 1880s, while a single mammoth roundup near Ford, Kansas, in 1885 attracted seventy-five wagons with an average of five men and six horses per wagon.

Although accustomed to cooking for ten or fifteen men at a time, cooks hustled to keep pace with the increased demand for steak, biscuits, and coffee brought on by a larger congregation of hungry cowboys. On one occasion a lone cook fed seventy-five punchers in one day and eighty-five hands on another. O. E. Brewster, the "belly cheater" of the Miller 101 Ranch in Oklahoma, claimed to have cooked for no less than forty-five men a day over a twenty-one-day period during a roundup near the Salt Fork of the Arkansas River. When a host of extra men arrived at the cook fire, Brewster attempted to economize on chuck by placing the food pots on the side of the fire pit opposite the chow line. As the cowboys reached across to fill their plates, the heat of the campfire caused them to dip faster and not overload their plates.

With so many hands in camp, the amount of food a cook might use was staggering. At roundup time on the Long S Ranch in Texas, for example, longtime cook Jeff Amburgey often used a

full sack of flour in making a day's worth of biscuits, cooked four water buckets full of beans daily, and slaughtered a steer for meat every other day. One cook estimated that a crew of thirty-five or forty required at least five Dutch ovens of biscuits and a proportionate amount of beef at every meal.

Despite the demand for food, cooks were sometimes handicapped by a lack of utensils. The cook for the Texas Land and Cattle Company's Indian Territory ranch during the early 1880s was expected to make do with only two sixteen-inch Dutch ovens. A Wyoming counterpart complained that baking pies for a large outfit took all morning because he could allot only one Dutch oven at a time. And a German cook for another outfit was fired because, lacking a bread pan, he mixed his sourdough in the same feed box used by the chuck wagon mules. In a pinch, however, an expert cowboy cook could prepare a hearty soup or a delicious "son-of-a-bitch stew" without so much as a single pot by digging a hole, lining it with a cowhide (hair side toward the ground), and heating the ingredients with rocks warmed in a nearby fire.

Cow camp cooks were up and at their tasks long before the roundup crew awakened at 3:30 or 4:00 A.M. The early hour in one camp prompted one sleepy puncher to complain that "a man didn't need a bed. All he needed was a lantern to catch a fresh horse."[3]

Many cooks awakened to alarm clocks, the louder the better. One even set the clock inside a dish pan for maximum effect. "The cook had to guard his timepiece," said one Panhandle cowpuncher, "for the boys . . . wanted to make a target of it."[4] Cowboys swore that cooks took perverse pleasure in singing, whistling, and rattling pans so as to disturb their slumber even before the chow call. Other cooks thought the heavens more reliable than clocks. The rising of the eastern star known as El Lucero, for example, guided many Hispanic cooks in their breakfast preparations.

At the cook's call, the camp began to stir. Be it breakfast, dinner, or supper, range cooks summoned diners with a shout sometimes punctuated by the clang of a metal triangle or perhaps two Dutch oven lids rubbed together to create "sounds calculated to wake the dead."[5] Mess calls ranged from the straightforward to the creative to the obscene. Simple calls included the familiar "Come and get it" or its Spanish southwestern counterpart, *"Vengan a comer"* ("Come to eat"). The bark "Chuck!" or "Chuckaway" or its variants "Grub" or "Grub p-i-l-e" beckoned diners from Texas to Montana.

To hurry the outfit along, cooks often threatened to "throw it out" or "on the ground" or to "spit in the skillet." "If you can't get up," crooned an African-American cook in the Texas Panhandle in the 1880s, "there are men in Dodge [City] that can."[6]

Now and then a cook added variety to the customary chow call by hollering "Grab a root an' growl" or "Roll out and bite the biscuit!" A bespectacled Montana cook in 1906 cried out, "It's a-l-lright with m-e-e!" or "B-o-n-e-h-e-a-d-s, b-o-n-e-h-e-a-d-s, take it away," depending upon his mood.

James H. Cook recalled a particularly praiseworthy South Texas trail cook in the 1870s who opened the morning with "Roll out there, fellers, and hear the little birdies sing their praises to God!" or "Arise and shine and give God the glory!"[7] More likely the call came, "Here is Hell, come and get it."

The poetic among the West's chuck wagon cooks often called the crew to chow with simple, sometimes crude ditties:

> *Bacon in the pan,*
> *Coffee in the pot,*
> *Get up and get it,*
> *Get it while it's hot.*[8]

> *Wake up, Jacob!*
> *Day's a-breaking.*
> *Peas in the pot,*
> *Hoecakes a-baking.*[9]

> *Piss ants in the butter,*
> *Flies in the meat,*
> *If you bastards are hungry*
> *Get up here and eat.*[10]

Although most outfits provided three meals a day, some ranchers and trail bosses served only breakfast and supper. King Ranch roundup crews, however, skipped breakfast in favor of dinner and supper. Cowpunchers afraid of missing a meal sometimes carried cold biscuits and perhaps a pickle or onion to keep their bellies satisfied and a piece of bacon to keep their mouths moist until they returned to camp.

There was little time for idling on the range, and both breakfast and dinner were served and consumed at a businesslike gait. At the Matador Ranch wagon, said one range veteran, when the boss finished his last bite and headed for his horse, the other cowboys had to be ready to ride or risk "a chewing."[11]

Some outfits finished breakfast as early as three or three-thirty in the morning and by daybreak were already in saddle and beginning their morning circle. Before riding away, however, the cowboys would have rolled and tied their bedding and placed it in or near the chuck wagon or risked the cook leaving it behind, or worse. "If you don't want to roll your own blankets," one Texas boss warned errant punchers, "you can get your check."[12]

By about 5:00 A.M., even earlier in some camps, the cook and his helper would have washed and stored their dishes, loaded the bedrolls and other gear, and harnessed their teams for a move of several miles. "It was a sight to see those outfits breaking camp," remembered a veteran of the

Montana range in the 1890s. "The first wagon to the next water got the best location on the water, and it was a regular wagon race from one camp to another. I have seen the lines handed up to the cook fifteen minutes after breakfast was over."[13]

Most roundup camps moved at least daily, but some moved twice a day, and in a few cases, as many as three or four. In later years, however, ranches like the King, Kenedy, and Matador found it easier to park their wagons at a strategic point on the range for several days before moving again. If work got too far from the chuck wagon and no change in camp was ordered, the cook delivered dinner to cowboys at the herd.

Remaining in one location for several days had its advantages. Cooks were not so rushed and were able to prepare more complex or time-consuming dishes, especially desserts. Such hiatuses allowed Juan Lerma, a tireless cook on the Norias Division of the King Ranch, time to clear a circular windbreak and food preparation area from the surrounding mesquite. Standing forty feet in diameter and four feet high, the enclosure contained Lerma's cooking fires and an *aparato,* a crude table built on the spot out of flat boards supported by forked sticks. When the camp was moved, both the *aparato* and the windbreak were left behind for reuse on another trip.

A fully loaded chuck wagon moved with a discordant symphony of clanging pots and pans and creaking wagon wheels. The cook and his wagon generally traveled in the company of the outfit's remuda and the horse wrangler, who acted as the pilot to the next campground. At times rough roads, unmanageable teams, and occasional wrecks played havoc with the contents of even the sturdiest of chuck boxes and the best-laid meal plans.

Upon reaching the new campsite, the cook quickly unharnessed his team and, with the assistance of the wrangler and perhaps other helpers, began to pitch camp and prepare the next meal. After digging a trench for his fire, the range cook was likely to erect a pot rack (two tall iron stakes connected by an iron crossbar) hung with several pot hooks. In later years the term

Horse heard.

"Just camped"

Evans Colman
Thatcher
Arizona
1942

"pot rack outfit" came to distinguish roundup crews that still cooked in the open, without benefit of mess tents and wood-burning camp stoves.

Most cowboy cooks relied upon the versatile Dutch oven, better known in ranch country as a "skillet and lid," for browning, baking, steaming, boiling, stewing, and frying. The classic cast-iron Dutch oven featured three or occasionally four stubby legs and a tight-fitting, slightly domed lid with an outer ridge or lip designed to support coals. When turned over, the lid doubled as a grill. Around the fire, cooks handled hot lids and ovens with bails and pot hooks.

Dutch ovens heated best on coals shoveled from the bed of the cook fire and spread on the ground or perhaps onto a sheet of tin. Some cooks also set vessels atop pieces of strap iron or branding irons, forming a grill of sorts over the fire pit. Beef tallow was melted in the flat bottom of the Dutch oven to prevent food from sticking.

Meal preparation involved an assortment of pots, kettles, skillets, and ovens made of cast and galvanized iron, tin, brass, copper, and bell metal, a tin and copper alloy.

The Griswold Manufacturing Company of Erie, Pennsylvania, the Bluff City Stove Works of Memphis, Tennessee, and other prominent foundries produced cast-iron cookware in a wide range of sizes. In the mid-1890s the trade catalogs of retailers Sears and Roebuck and Montgomery Ward offered Dutch ovens in four sizes ranging from ten to fourteen inches in diameter. The Sears models ranged in weight from eleven to twenty-seven pounds and in price from 65 cents to $1.15. A 1910 catalog offered seven sizes of deep ovens ranging up to fourteen inches in diameter, four inches in depth, and twenty-three pounds, plus an equal number of shallow ovens.

Because cowboy cooks invariably were called upon to serve a considerable number of hands,

The XIT Ranch outfitted J. Ealy Moore's crew, bound for Montana with a trail herd in April 1892, with the following cooking and eating utensils purchased from a Channing, Texas, merchant:

7	Oven @ .80	$5.60
1	Stew Kettle	.75
1	Camp Kettle	1.50
1	Coffee Pot	1.50
1	Fry Pan	.60
1	Dipper	.10
2	Dish Pans	1.20
1	Wash Pan	.20
1	Small "	.25
1	Doz. Cups	1.00
1	Doz. Plates	1.00
2-3	Doz. Knives/Forks	1.00
1	Doz. Spoons	.40
1	Bu. Steel	1.50
1	Bu. Knife	1.50
1	Large Spoon	.10
1	Large Fork	.10
2	Buckets	1.00
1	Coffee Mill	1.00

they usually selected the largest Dutch ovens. A cook for a Cherokee Strip outfit in the 1880s reported using Dutch ovens sixteen inches in diameter and five inches deep, and an Arizona "dough puncher" had ovens ranging from ten to twenty inches across.

For roasting coffee and frying meat, cooks used cast-iron skillets with protruding handles and all-purpose mess pans made in various sizes of heavy tin and sheet iron. Beans and dried fruits were boiled or stewed in cylindrical kettles or buckets.

The most accomplished chuck wagon chef could generally prepare a meal in about an hour once a fire was started. Drew People, considered one of the finest and fastest roundup cooks in New Mexico in the 1880s, is said to have required a mere forty-five minutes to unharness his team and cook a meal from scratch.

Experience, preparation, and versatility were the keys to a roundup cook's success. After supper the prudent "pot-rassler" prepared the breakfast meal as far as possible. He ground the coffee, sliced the beefsteak or bacon, and peeled and sliced the potatoes, placing them in a bucket of water so that they would not turn black. If the crew was large, he might also cook the bread before going to bed; otherwise, he banked the evening fire under a layer of dirt so that the next morning he would have coals for cooking. Careful cooks always baked a few extra biscuits and stored them in a tin in case a change in plans or an emergency delayed their bread-making chores.

Sometimes the cook also started a pot of beans while in evening camp, letting them simmer all night in the hot ashes of the fire and finishing them off when he struck the noon camp. More often the cooks began roasting meat and boiling beans or dried fruit at breakfast. If loaded into the chuck box or wagon bed at the last minute, the steaming dishes continued to cook in transit and were practically done when they reached the next camp.

Shortages of water and fuel posed serious problems to range crews. Roundup and trail bosses

Boiling and preserving kettles holding from one to several gallons ranged in height from a few inches to a foot.

therefore sought campsites convenient to freshwater lakes, creeks, reservoirs, or windmill tanks from which the chuck wagon water barrels could be replenished. A typical thirty-five-gallon barrel of water would last an outfit only about two days.

Because mineral salts tainted much of the surface water in the dry regions of the West, chuck wagon cooks often stocked canned tomatoes and Jamaica ginger by the case to stave off thirst. They also mixed soda and vinegar into a bubbling concoction as a preventative against diarrhea and other problems associated with drinking stagnant alkaline water.

At times cowboys even shared the juice of canned tomatoes with their horses to prevent the horses from cramping after imbibing the bitter water from "gyp" holes. Alkaline water also played havoc with cooking and cleaning and had to be treated with lye or sal soda before being used to wash clothes or dishes. To conserve freshwater supplies while working the salty reaches of the Pecos River in 1885, one astute wagon boss directed his cook to scour his pots with sand and wipe them with a rag.

STOKING THE FIRE

Wood, like water, was scarce on the western range, particularly on the Great Plains and in the desert Southwest. Although stands of mesquite, cedar, and shinnery usually could be found in the breaks along rivers and creeks, the incessant demand for campfire fuel often meant the harvesting of cow or buffalo chips from the prairie. Also known as "prairie coal," "bull shit coal," and "compressed hay," cow chips were a plentiful and renewable source of fuel. They produced intense

heat, but the odorous fires were hard starting, quick burning, and required constant attention, even under the best conditions. One cowboy claimed he wore out three hats one season fanning reluctant cow chips into flames.

Once the fuel was ignited, the slightest wind could carry cow chip cinders into the surrounding grass, causing fires. One such blaze started by a careless range cook in November 1885 consumed fully seventy-five miles of range between the Beaver and Canadian rivers on the Llano Estacado of northwestern Texas. In a similar but apocryphal occurrence with more humorous consequences, a hungry cowpuncher claimed to have followed an accidental prairie fire for eleven and a half miles with a coffeepot and bacon-laden skillet in hand. Although the flames eventually cooked his victuals and boiled his coffee, the storyteller deadpanned, both were cold by the time he returned to camp. As a safety precaution against fires real and imagined, cooks usually shielded their coal beds from the wind and carefully burned away the prairie immediately around their fire pits.

Sustaining a simple cook fire might require half a wagon load of cow chips daily. Many plains roundup crews therefore brought along a "chip wagon" or cart to ensure an adequate supply. Otherwise, an outfit might forage a mile or more from the wagon in order to fill enough tow sacks to satisfy the demand. After a few such forays cowboys came to appreciate cattle that "stacked their chips" rather than spread them far and wide.

Cow outfits caught in rainstorms or on the snow-covered prairie in winter had an especially difficult time finding usable fuel. Careful cooks therefore carried a supply of dry chips or kindling

for emergencies in the "coonie" under the chuck wagon. The LFD Ranch in New Mexico and perhaps others went so far as to build tin sheds at windmills for storing an emergency reserve of cow chips.

When traditional fuels were scarce or wet, ranchers and drovers resorted to a variety of substitutes, including sacks of corn, sides of bacon, and parts of the chuck wagon itself. Railroad cross ties and fence posts topped just above the barbed wire also were favorite targets of kindling seekers. A Cross L Ranch hand from New Mexico told of liberating every other post of a neighbor's fence for ten miles to provide cooking fuel during an emergency.

"GRUB'S UP"

With the arrival of the crew at mealtime, the cook usually lined up his pots in front of the fire, at times in the shade of a canvas "fly" extended from the rear or side of the wagon. When holding a herd, the men ate in shifts, forming a "chuck line" and filling their plates and cups directly from the pots, ovens, and skillets.

On some outfits there was a wild scramble for food; others approached the cooking fire at a more leisurely pace, taking care not to stir up dust around the food or otherwise rile the cook. At the "layout box," cowboys picked up iron (later stainless steel) tableware, called "reloading tools" by some, in reference to firearms. As with food and cookware, many ranchers and trail bosses were sparing with dishes and eating utensils. One frugal Texas manager provided his men only spoons with which to eat. In another case a shortage of cutlery prompted a Cherokee Strip branding crew to replenish the stock with a supply of knives and forks purloined from a Caldwell, Kansas, restaurant.

Even when ranches did provide sufficient tableware, some cowboys still preferred to use their pocketknives, spearing pieces of meat from the pots and devouring them between the halves of a biscuit to save dish washing. Or they'd use the flats of their knives to eat helpings of beans, corn, and hominy, and chunks of bread to scoop beans from the plate or sop gravy from a skillet.

Although a visitor to the Matador Ranch about 1889 noted the presence of pewter plates and mugs, cowboys generally ate and drank from cheap tin dishes or lightweight, inexpensive enameled ware in widespread use from the late 1830s on. Granite ware, also known as glazed ware and agate ware, came mottled in pink, gray, blue, white, and brown. The American brands, made of iron, did not withstand heat, wear, and food acids as well as the imported varieties, which had steel bases.

Once they had filled their plates, the cowboys squatted on their heels or sat on their bedrolls

Cow ... going

At Dinner

or cross-legged on the ground. Those too stiff with rheumatism to assume any of these positions stood or knelt.

Breakfast and dinner were eaten quickly, with little fanfare or conversation. Supper was a more leisurely affair. When they finished eating, cowboys scraped their plates into a garbage pit and deposited them in a washtub, usually called a "round pan" or "wreck pan," which was located at the rear of the wagon beneath the chuck box lid. The cook carefully saved any edible leftovers to serve as a snack or at a future meal. With scraps from the noon meal on the menu, an African-American cook from the coastal country of South Texas described his evening offering as a "wedding o' dinner and supper."[14] Another called dishes made of recycled remnants "clean up the kitchen" or "homogeneous mass."[15]

THE SOCIAL ROUTINE

Some observers found camp life dull and routine. While on the roundup, cowboys spent their few free hours engaged in such mundane tasks as washing clothes, patching equipment, or perhaps braiding leather or horsehair into serviceable, often artistic gear. Gambling offered a diversion for

---

Whatever the rate, a proficient cook was always orderly and ready to feed the crew on time.

some, though after about 1880, wagers and sidearms were forbidden in most cow camps.

The cowboy's social life on the range and trail centered on the campfire or cook stove, where the talk usually turned to work, horses, and women. Behavior and language varied considerably from camp to camp. While some crews quietly conversed, according to a Wyoming newspaper correspondent writing in 1885, "without swagger or bluster, horse play or boisterousness,"[16] the cowboys that writer Hamlin Garland observed around a Colorado campfire a decade later "sang and boasted and told stiff yarns and exploded in obscenity till time to turn in."[17]

Music was often a part of camp life. Many hands, including cooks, were proficient musicians, playing such instruments as guitars, banjos, fiddles, jew's harps, and accordions. In later years the cook for a northern plains roundup outfit once wagged along a Victor talking machine and two cylinder records, which he played repeatedly for an enchanted cowboy audience each night after supper.

Outfits camping in close proximity often got together for storytelling and poetry sessions that featured their most gifted "augurs." John K. Rollinson told of one occasion in Wyoming when the cooks from two nearby outfits displayed their culinary talents for each other's crews. One cook served fresh beef, red beans spiced with chili and onions, biscuits and gravy, a mixture of rice and raisins known as "spotted pup," and dried apple pie. The Two Bar wagon cook offered fried steaks, tomato-flavored white beans, yellow hominy, hot rolls sprinkled with brown sugar and cinnamon, and a steamed pudding with blackberry sauce. Although both outfits seemed to enjoy the occasion, they were careful not to compliment the other cook in front of their own.

Besides entertaining other crews, chuck wagons also hosted meals for absentee owners, corporate officials, and even female guests from time to time. On the JA Ranch, the cook alerted cowboys returning to camp to the presence of female callers by tying a dish towel to a nearby mesquite tree. Neighbor women sometimes brought pies, cakes, and dance invitations to the cowboys. When the wagon worked near the LX Ranch headquarters in the Texas Panhandle at the turn of the century, the wife of the ranch manager often visited the wagon in a surrey loaded with butter and eggs and, if the outfit was not too large, cakes and pies.

Visitors notwithstanding, cowpunchers usually turned in early, some by 8:00 P.M. In camps where night herders worked three- or four-hour shifts, cooks kept a fire going and the coffeepot boiling all night.

ROMANCE OR HARDSHIP?

Although the cowboy life on the open range seemed adventuresome and romantic to most casual observers, knowing critics like Joseph McCoy, a cattle trader instrumental in establishing Abilene, Kansas, as a principal shipping point for Texas longhorns, disparaged many prevailing practices. "It would cost little effort or expense," wrote McCoy in his classic 1874 treatise, *Historic Sketches of the Cattle Trade of the West and Southwest,* "to add a hundred comforts, not to say luxuries to the life of the drover and his cowboys. . . . They sleep on the ground with a pair of blankets for bed and cover. No tent is used, scarcely any cooking utensils and such a thing as a camp-stove is unknown."[18]

But as ranching expanded into the farthest reaches of the northern and western plains in the late 1870s, climate and terrain, coupled with new corporate attitudes toward investment and labor, contributed to improvements in shelter and provisions. Finally, larger outfits were equipped with mess and bed tents, portable cooking and heating stoves, and even dining tables, chairs, and sleeping cots.

Forced to endure extended periods of cold weather, ranches on the northern plains pioneered many of these improvements. North of the Platte River, for example, the average southern plains bedroll, known as a "suggan" or "hot roll," consisting of a pair of blankets, perhaps a quilt,

and a canvas tarp, proved wholly insufficient to protect a cowboy from the weather. The need for thicker bedding led not only to a bulkier bedroll but also to sleeping tents and heating stoves.

Cook tents and portable wood-burning cook stoves, better suited to cooking in bad weather and more sanitary than open cook fires, were not far behind. Some wagons also began to carry portable mess tables equipped with folding legs and even a chair or two. Longtime drover Jack Potter observed his first such outfit in 1882 on a drive between Greeley, Colorado, and the Big Horns of Montana. By 1890 they were widespread from Colorado to the Dakotas.

Upon breaking camp, cooking stoves were dismantled and their lids and cross pieces removed and stored away. An inventive wagon cook on the Diamond-A Ranch in New Mexico devised a hinged stove table that folded up like the chuck box lid during transit.

When a single chuck wagon could not carry all of a cow outfit's gear, ranches added a second wagon, known variously as a "bed wagon" or "hoodlum wagon." Generally lighter and more maneuverable than the standard chuck wagon, hoodlum wagons also carried extra wood and water and sometimes were used to deliver food to the roundup when the chuck wagon remained in one place for several days.

Texas ranches establishing finishing ranges for steers in the 1880s were not long in discovering the amenities used in the north. When, for example, an XIT outfit appeared on the Yellowstone with a "pot rack outfit," Montanans hazed the new arrivals so unmercifully that the manager threatened to quit unless the company allowed him to buy a $150 mess tent and a stove. Some of these luxuries eventually found their way back to the Southwest, where they became standard on many spreads. Cowboy George Bedo recalled that hands working along the Pecos

River in New Mexico and Texas during the 1890s lived in tents during the winter and in the open during the summer.

On some of the more conservative spreads, however, tents did not surface until the 1920s. The Matador Ranch and perhaps other southwestern outfits did not embrace bed tents and wood-burning stoves until poor visibility caused by the encroachment of mesquite brush forced management to run their wagon almost year round. According to one West Texan, even after such improvements had been introduced, dangerous static electricity generated by periodic wind and

*D-shaped swivel handles on both sides of the stove facilitated loading and unloading.
Some outfits mounted their stove on a shelf behind the chuck box, others on a
short-tongue, two-wheeled cart pulled behind the chuck wagon. A stout chain secured
both the stove to the cart and the cart to the wagon.*

dust storms in the region dissuaded some cooks from using their iron stoves. During such times, canned goods were consumed directly from the can in lieu of a cooked meal.

Prior to 1870 a few basic staples dominated the menu in all cow camps. These included coffee, bread (in the form of biscuits, cornmeal, or hard crackers), meat (bacon, salt pork, beef—fresh, dried, salted, and smoked—and game), salt, and some sugar and sorghum molasses. The quality and quantity of cowboy food varied considerably from north to south depending upon such factors as tradition, culture, region, sources of supply, the attitude of management, and the ability of the cook. Over the years southwestern ranches gained a reputation as unimaginative and miserly in their fare, and those on the northern plains became known as more progressive and generous. "Those Texas outfits," recalled "Teddy Blue" Abbott with characteristic candor, "sure hated to give up on the grub."[19] Some supplied only flour, salt, and coffee, but most also allowed some salt pork or beef along with cornmeal and sorghum molasses. Mexican culinary traditions, including tortillas, fried beans, chiles, *chorizo* (sausage), and rice, dominated the range fare in South Texas and parts of New Mexico, Arizona, and California.

Abbott claimed that superior food, including cane sugar, wheat flour, canned fruit, and other "luxuries," induced many Texans to remain on the northern plains to work on the ranches of large eastern and foreign syndicates, long after their less particular comrades had departed for sunnier climes. Contrasting the lot of the Montana-based cowhand with that of his southern plains counterpart in 1885, a Dodge City, Kansas, newspaper correspondent concluded: "Live! Why, these cowboys [in Montana] live higher than anybody. They have every thing to eat that money can buy, and a cook with a paper cap on to prepare it. The cook is so neat and polite that you could eat him if you were right hungry."[20]

In 1877, a Colorado newspaper, the Las Animas Leader, commented: The cowboy works for a man who has capital, is making great profits, and is naturally liberal in the use of money. The result is that there is plenty of food and a great enough variety. . . . Fresh meats of the best quality they can have at any time, and canned fruits and vegetables are found at almost every camp. Coffee, syrup, sugar and tea are among the comforts found, while of the more substantial kind of food there is no lack in either quantity or quality.

[July 27, 1877]

Exaggerations aside, such sterling conditions were far from universal, even in Montana. The stingy fare of the R L outfit on the Musselshell, for example, led to the resignation of the range chef, who declared that the ranch needed no cook, only a teamster.

The influx of capital from the East and abroad, which made such improvements as tents and stoves possible, also improved the diet of the average cowboy. By 1877 canned goods were common on the Colorado range and within a decade were available to even the most remote ranching outposts throughout the West. The flourishing American food-processing industry continually expanded its offerings, so that by 1885 a typical Spur Ranch supply order included not only canned tomatoes and peaches but also cinnamon, nutmeg, cayenne pepper, Colman's mustard, vanilla, and lemon extract. Meanwhile, the steady advance of the farmer's frontier brought fresh fruits and vegetables to ranch country, particularly to the largest and most progressive ranches.

In some remote areas, supplies still had to be hauled a hundred miles or more by wagon, at great expense, from railroad supply points. The freight rate from Colorado City on the Texas and Pacific railroad in West Texas in the mid-1880s, for example, was seventy-five cents per hundred pounds. The difficulty and cost of transportation encouraged ranchers in remote regions to purchase from one to six months' worth of supplies at a time. Large spreads ordered enormous quantities of food. In 1901, for example, the Spur Ranch required 30,000 pounds of flour, 6,000 pounds of sugar, 6,000 pounds of bacon, 2,500 pounds of coffee, 5,000 pounds of lard, 3,500 pounds of beans, and 3,000 pounds of dried fruits.

Ranch provisions arrived from suppliers in tin cans, ceramic jugs, wooden boxes and barrels, and sacks of paper and cloth. Not all of the stores reached their destination in first-class condition. In 1892 alone, A. J. Majoribanks, owner of the Rocking Chair Ranch in Texas, struggled with spoiled flour and dried fruit, substandard molasses, and two cases of "very sorry" bacon, "about four-fifths being pure fat and waste."[21] In August he complained to a supplier about rotten prunes:

> *The 53 pounds of prunes you lately sent us were more wormy than prunes; it is an outrage to try to put off such filthy stuff on us; we utterly refuse to receive or pay for such stuff and the said sack of prunes and worms have been left . . . to be returned to you. . . . It will save you a good deal of trouble if you will bear in mind that we will only receive and pay for articles that are good.*[22]

In order to purchase bulk supplies at wholesale prices and ensure quality, larger ranches often opened their own commissaries. Besides providing regular rations, these company stores also offered ranch employees food and sundries on credit, charged against wages. And while some ranches

Texas folklorist J. Frank Dobie enjoyed recounting an oft-told tale illustrating the average cowboy's aversion to cooking. Dobie's rendering held that a crew without a cook agreed to rotate the duty among the remaining cowpunchers and to bestow the honor permanently on the first man to complain about the food. One day one of the cowboys bit into the bread and exclaimed, "This bread is burned on the bottom, burned on the top, raw in the middle, and salty as hell—but I sure like it that way."

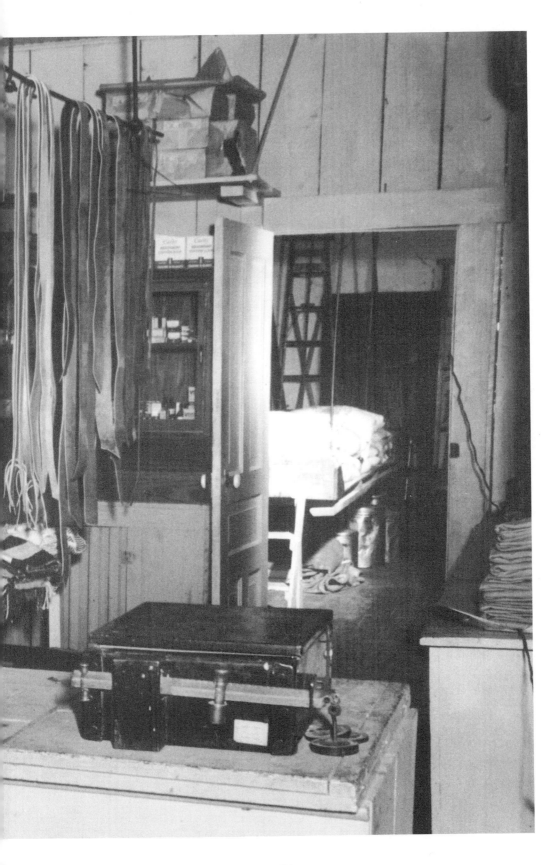

sold to their hands at a discount, a few unscrupulous types engaged in price gouging and other monopolistic practices.

In most areas, local stores and occasional traveling peddlers also competed for cowboy customers. In addition to tobacco, ammunition, and clothing, these prairie oases often stocked such delicacies as canned sardines and salmon, potted chicken, deviled ham, cheese, crackers, and other victuals.

Although expenditures for food usually comprised the largest entries on ranch supply ledgers, the cost of feeding cowboys in the late nineteenth and early twentieth centuries appears nominal. William Curry Holden's survey of the records of the well-supplied Espuela Land and Cattle Company, for example, revealed that a single twelve-man cow outfit in 1889 devoured 19.2 pounds of food per day costing only $1.32—or less than 4 cents per man for a meal. This figure seems consistent with a 1901 estimate that placed the cost of comfortably sustaining a cowboy at $1.00 per week or 14.3 cents per day. By 1916 inflation had pushed the cost as high as 53.5 cents per man per day in some places.

Even with improved supplies of food, chuck wagon fare continued to vary enormously, from excellent to awful. A cowboy working near the Red River in northern Texas during the 1880s perhaps spoke for the majority when he reported, "Our 'chuck' is substantial, but not aristocratically cooked."[23] Most considered range cuisine repetitious and bland, and some wondered how cowboys maintained their health with such "unvaried fare." One frontier settler speculated that outdoor work and riding the range helped keep cowboy digestive tracts in order. One recent study of the cowboy diet pronounced it deficient in vitamins A and C, calories, and calcium, facts that no doubt accounted for the lean look that has always characterized the cowboy breed. Calcium deficiencies, the result of a lack of milk, were blamed for bowlegs and bone decalcification, although long hours in saddle surely also contributed to these conditions.

OFF SEASON

The chuck wagon was home to a cowboy only about seven months of the year, and on the northern plains sometimes only about half that time. After the fall roundup cow outfits usually cut their labor force by more than two thirds. A few hands who were willing to work only for room and board were kept busy hauling fuel and doing odd jobs around headquarters. Ranchers sent the rest of the holdovers, usually in pairs, to outlying winter camps thirty miles or more apart to keep watch over their herds.

Crude dugouts, shacks, and tents sheltered most of these cowboy campers. Furnishings were

as meager as the housing—a chair perhaps, more likely a crate, but rarely a table. A wall-mounted chuck box often served as a cupboard. Kerosene lanterns provided light.

The camp men generally shared the chores, including cooking, although a few larger ranches also provided a cook for each line camp. Freight wagons sent from the commissary kept them supplied with food and other necessities. Campers butchered beef as needed and hunted wild game to supplement their provisions. If a line camp had a fireplace or stove, cooking was done inside; otherwise, cowboys prepared meals outdoors over an open fire. Such primitive conditions persisted well into the twentieth century. In fact, most outlying camps and a few headquarters were without electricity, refrigeration, stoves, and indoor plumbing as late as the 1940s.

Cowboys laid off over the winter drifted back to their families, trapped and freighted, sought work in towns, or simply "rode the chuck line," depending upon the hospitality of area ranchers for food and shelter. Floyd Bard, whose family settled on Mead Creek in the cattle country of Wyoming in 1883, recalled that a cowboy or two partook of the noon meal at Bard Ranch almost every day. "No one seemed to consider it necessary to be invited for a meal," agreed an Oklahoma homesteader, "but considered it proper to drop in when convenient." Cowboys enjoyed the company as well as the vittles, especially if women were present.

Corporate ranch policy often was less hospitable. XIT Ranch rules, for example, allowed for feeding and sheltering employees from neighboring ranches so long as they transacted their business promptly. Bona fide travelers were expected to pay company prices for provisions and feed but could be housed for an evening, if convenient, without charge. Company practice, however, prohibited employees from selling or giving "loafers or dead beats feed or provisions."[24]

OCCASIONS

A well-equipped corporate ranch headquarters usually had more amenities than chuck wagons and line camps. Besides a substantial headquarters building, most also had a kitchen, a bunkhouse, and a mess hall where cowboys dined around a long table with benches. Although while visiting their properties a few wealthy ranchers savored such rare delicacies as capers, oysters, truffles, cheeses, ice cream, and even fine wine and champagne, served on fine china and in crystal, few cowboys ever enjoyed such benefits. The Square and Compass Ranch in West Texas, whose owners were wholesale grocers, was certainly one of the few ranches in the West to supply their hands regularly with pickled pig's feet and other "fancy eatables."[25] Most had to await special events before consuming such luxuries.

In a land of few social diversions, ranch folk naturally greeted holidays, picnics, weddings, and dances with special enthusiasm and cuisine to match. Sometimes lasting for two or three days, such events often attracted guests from several counties and never failed to bring forth a cornucopia

of food. Mary Jacques, an Englishwoman, recalled one memorable Christmas dinner in Texas ranch country about 1890. With the temperature at 90 degrees, guests feasted upon turkey, roast pig, plum pudding, mincemeat, and chocolate cake with pecan icing and sugar plum designs. An equally bountiful Matador Ranch Christmas dance during the same era featured barbecued beef, boiled beans with ham, roasted turkeys, venison steaks, and antelope stew with dumplings, along with doughnuts, cakes, fried pies, and several gallons of home-canned wild plum jelly and preserves.

BARBED WIRE

The introduction of barbed wire in the 1870s unleashed a host of technological and social changes on ranch life. And as ranching changed, forever altering the cowboy way of life with it, traditional foodways changed as well. By the mid-1890s an expanded rail network had ended trail driving, spawned towns, and hastened the arrival of farmers in ranch country. The invasion of these "hoe men" not only broke up countless large ranches into smaller stock farms but also introduced a

Reily and Cree's Outfit.

large number of women, who would profoundly affect the social and culinary fabric of the cattle country.

Enclosing the open range with the "devil's rope" facilitated the upbreeding of livestock and eroded traditional cowboy skills and eventually the cowboy population itself. As huge open-range roundups became a thing of the past, chuck wagons also began to disappear, and few mourned their demise. However, many sentimentalists came to regret the loss of the traditions and camaraderie of life around "the wagon."

Although rough and remote sections of the West would not be affected for decades, the invention of the automobile and improved roads in rural America in the early twentieth century foreshadowed fresh challenges to the unstable tenure of chuck wagons. By the 1920s, for example, many ranches were feeding their hands from chuck boxes mounted on a truck, pickup, or automobile chassis.

Even in Texas, the bastion of old-time ranching traditions, horse-drawn chuck wagons were a rarity by the mid-1930s. By 1932 only two ranches, the Reynolds Long X and the Kokernot

Although motor vehicles and paved roads
eventually supplanted freight wagons and dusty trails, easing the isolation
of ranch life, the full impact of this mechanized revolution would not
be fully evident until the mid-twentieth century.

06, in the vast Big Bend region, still relied upon a chuck wagon and team. All their neighbors used trucks.

Within a few years the Bell Ranch, one of New Mexico's most distinguished ranches, traded its worn-out chuck wagon for a four-wheel-drive army vehicle, equipping it with a butane-burning cook stove and refrigerator, a water tank that provided running water to a double sink, and sleeping quarters for the cook. A motorized hoodlum wagon ferried beef, groceries, and fresh water to the roundup from headquarters daily.

Traditional horse-drawn chuck wagons persisted longest on the largest ranches. Some operated more than one wagon. The JA Ranch, in the Texas Panhandle, for example, often ran separate chuck wagons for the roundup and fencing crews, and as late as 1933 the Matador Ranch, in West Texas, operated three chuck wagons to feed the cowhands required to gather and brand more than 15,000 calves annually. Such gatherings still covered several sections of pasture.

During the Depression, in 1931, Virgil Parr, manager of the Pitchfork Ranch, neighbor to the Matador in West Texas, attempted to abandon the chuck wagon as part of a money-saving measure. Instead of hiring an extra cook, he planned on returning his men to headquarters each evening. His cowboys, however, rebelled at the notion of riding several miles on horseback between the bunkhouse and the range twice a day, and Parr restored the wagon to the range shortly thereafter.

POSTWAR COWBOYS

World War II brought an acute labor shortage across the country, one that was felt on the ranches as well. By this time pickups and horse trailers were transporting hands and their mounts between the roundup ground and the bunkhouse in many areas. Ranches that still operated wagons in the field faced a dearth of experienced cooks and cowboys willing to endure the hardships of nine months in the field for relatively low pay.

Nevertheless, a few "dough punchers" of the old school remained on the job. Among them was Joseph Bailey "Cap" Warren, cook for the half-million-acre Waggoner Ranch near Wichita Falls, Texas, who began as a range chef in 1912. In the early 1950s, after more than forty years on the job, Warren still arose at 4:00 A.M. each roundup morning to prepare breakfast for more than three dozen hungry cowboys. He considered modern ranch hands "a bunch of sissies" and declared that only a few were left "that would make a wart on a good old-time cowpuncher." The bed tent and army cots that stood in infuriating disarray near his cook stove and chuck truck reminded Warren more of a "gospel camp meeting" than an orderly roundup outfit. Why, a helicopter even helped the Waggoner cowboys gather their cattle![26]

Chalma Pitts Reid, the "biscuit shooter" for the 232,000-acre Pitchfork Ranch in nearby King County, shared Cap Warren's contrary opinions about contemporary ranch life. Interviewed

in 1958 at the age of sixty-seven, Reid noted that his once simple cow camp fare of bacon, beef, beans, sourdough biscuits, canned tomatoes, and coffee now included daily servings of eggs, chicken, fresh fruits and vegetables, and ice tea. "I might as well be cooking in one of them Dallas hotels," he snorted with disdain.[27]

By 1960 cooks of Cap Warren's and Chalma Reid's ilk and chuck wagons of any type were rarities on the range, and the horse-drawn types were virtually museum relics. Old-time cowboys, however, venerated and perpetuated their memory through organizations like the Old Time Chuck Wagon Trailers, the Sweetwater Chuck Wagon, and the Texas Cowboy Reunion. Rodeos, dude ranches, and countless advertisements for products from cigarettes to chili also celebrated cowboy and chuck wagon life, as did motion pictures and television. *Rawhide,* a popular western television series of the late 1950s and early 1960s, even featured a cantankerous cook known as Wishbone in a strong supporting role.

Meanwhile, many ranches retained their chuck wagons for entertainment and ceremonial purposes long after their usefulness on the range had passed. In recent years a renewed interest in America's western heritage and lifestyle has brought others out of mothballs and a few into the field again as active participants in modern roundups. An even larger number of original and reproduction chuck wagons congregate at a growing number of chuck wagon gatherings held in connection with museums, rodeos, and re-enactments. Such assemblies authentically re-create a part of cowboy life of the late nineteenth and early twentieth centuries for participants and visitors alike. Each Memorial Day weekend the National Cowboy Hall of Fame and Western Heritage Center in Oklahoma City hosts one of the most authentic of these gatherings. The Cowboy Hall also is home to the Western Chuck Wagon Association, an organization dedicated to the perpetuation of the history and lore of one of the most colorful chapters in America's history.

CHAPTER 2

"POT RASSLERS" AND "belly cheaters":

COW

CAMP

cooks

Your occupation vanished, your guild is as extinct as the buffalo hunter and the cow puncher, and while the short-story writer and the movie picture actor keep alive the memory of the latter, in their own quaint fashion, I fear the memory of you is as dead as your old Dutch oven.

—*Anonymous*[1]

xperienced and competent ranch cooks were always in demand and rarely looked long for a job. Top hands sometimes chose their outfits according to the reputation of the cook, whose importance and influence at times rivaled even that of the roundup or trail boss. Prudent foremen, knowing how crucial a cook was to the crew's health and morale, usually deferred to the cook in all matters of camp operation.

The specialized position of cow camp cook was largely a post–Civil War phenomenon. Even then cooking for a roundup or trail drive remained seasonal work. Many cooks laid off during the winter freighted supplies, trapped wild game, or performed odd jobs to make ends meet until the spring, when their services were again in demand at the chuck wagon.

Culinary critics are not a phenomenon of today's "lifestyle" sections. In fact, back in the 1800s, critics were busy praising and damning the abilities of the men who cooked for

the trail drives and roundups. A reporter covering a roundup in southwestern Colorado in 1877, for example, partook of pot rack meals that "would shame the cookery of many a farmer's wife."[2] Almost a decade later a Wyoming writer favorably compared cowboy cuisine to that served at the Manhattan Club in New York, an opinion disputed by the author of an 1883 Trinidad, Colorado, newspaper article that read in part: "But little can be said to the credit of the average cook. In crossing the plains fifteen years ago, I thought the race of bad cooks then at work must surely die out in this age of progress, but some of the same school are on the roundup this summer."[3] Drover A. W. Capt agreed, proclaiming the cook on his 1871 drive to Kansas "the only man in the outfit that everybody could cuss."[4]

Good or bad, cooks were well paid, their wages varying according to responsibility and working conditions. Invariably they drew higher wages than the rest of the outfit, except for the trail boss or range foreman. A few of the best commanded twice as much as the average cowboy, and even the least drew wages comparable to those of top hands. During the late nineteenth century the wage scale of cooks ranged from $30 to $50 a month, depending on time, location, and general economic conditions.

The headquarters cook, considered the "aristocrat" of his profession, often got $10 to $15 more than cooks in the field. Spade Ranch head cook Perry Bracey, for example, earned $1.50 a day in 1907, equivalent to the $45 monthly salary of the wagon boss, $15 higher than the normal monthly stipend for a camp cook, and $20 a month more than the regular cowboy wage. Despite his exalted position and the amenities available at the headquarters kitchen, Bracey insisted on serving the ranch owner's family from a campfire and chuck wagon parked outside their quarters.

If cooks drew higher pay than the average rider, they earned it by working incredible hours with little rest. Up to make breakfast long before daylight, they rarely finished their work-

day before 10:00 P.M. The chief cook of the T5 Ranch in the Cherokee Strip in the 1880s, for example, cooked for thirty men, cut wood for the manager's fireplace, looked after the store room, milked ten cows, and tended one hundred chickens and turkeys and a garden.

Besides cooking two or three meals a day, often in different locations, wagon cooks also expected to serve their outfits as teamsters, barbers, bankers, dentists, and doctors. If not too far past their limber years, cowboy chefs even shucked their aprons occasionally to "top off" a rank bronc or help gather a stampeded herd.

As healers, cooks treated disorders from diarrhea to broken bones to the rare gunshot wound (most outfits banned the carrying of sidearms in camp). A well-stocked chuck box carried a multitude of purgatives and other medicines, including Epsom salts, calomel, arnica salve, Mustang liniment, quinine, blue vitriol, slack lime, castor oil, and turpentine. Cooks doctored cuts and bruises on men and horses alike with time-tested home remedies that included kerosene oil, flour paste, and fresh cow manure.

To ease rheumatism—and a host of other ills—cowboy cooks sometimes dispensed doses of medicinal whiskey from a carefully guarded bottle kept in the chuck box. Despite strict prohibitions against drinking on most ranches, alcoholism still plagued many cooks and cowboys. One puncher recalled that a cook who became drunk on a bottle of lemon extract, normally used only sparingly to make the dried apples more palatable, "ran us all off from the wagon and had to be roped and hogtied before he would behave." The tipsy cook, observed the cowboy, "was only mortal after all."[5]

"A damp evening."

One or more assistants usually aided a range chef in his myriad field duties. On most outfits the horse wrangler not only looked after his remuda, but also helped the cook pitch and break camp, load the chuck wagon, harness the team, and secure water and fuel. When the size of the roundup crew called for an additional wagon to haul bedding and equipment, the driver, known variously as the "flunkie" or "hoodlum," also helped with the camp chores. Cooks willing to forgo an assistant sometimes received higher pay. At one time the Miller 101 Ranch in Oklahoma paid cooks $1.50 a day if the ranch furnished a helper and $2.50 without.

Helpers and higher wages notwithstanding, few cowboys were attracted to cooking before their horseback days were done, although some cooked on a temporary basis in winter line camps or during emergencies. "To a real cowhand," observed longtime Texas cowboy Fat Alford, "the offer of a ranch cooking job is pretty much of a shock and insult, even lower than hole digging or windmilling."[6]

Some cooks plied the cowboy trade for two or even three decades before donning an apron for a second career that might last just as long. One celebrated Montana roundup cook took up the trade when he was past fifty and cooked for the same outfit for thirty years. Oak "Colie" Owens fed rancher Burk Burnett's clan for thirty-six years, quitting only when he became, according to a family member, "so blind he couldn't tell a tarantula from a fly in a batch of sour dough."[7]

Other cowboy cooks came to the trade after injuries ended their riding careers. Bell Ranch manager George Ellis recalled "an old saying—greatly exaggerated—that Bell horses made cooks out of lots of cowboys."[8] Far more punchers took up cooking as the number of riding jobs on ranches dwindled with the spread of barbed wire.

Desperate for a job, some candidates fabricated or embellished their cooking experience. When asked if he could cook, a former Texas Ranger and sheriff who applied for a job on the Atarque Ranch replied, "I'm the fastest and nastiest cook in New Mexico." The ranch manager would later recall with a wry grin that the job seeker had been at least "half truthful."[9]

Some cooks were drafted when the former cook quit or was run off. One self-effacing draftee allowed that he "could not boil water without burning it."[10] Although most rookies could "tan a steak," as frying meat was sometimes called, preparing such delicacies as mountain oysters (testicles) and marrow guts (entrails), not to mention pies and cakes, soon separated the seasoned cooks from the greenhorns.

The ranks of range cooks were filled by men of many cultures and backgrounds. "It made no difference to us who a man was or where he came from," wrote former cowboy H. V. Whitlock, "just so he could cook the grub and plenty of it."[11]

The LFD outfit had an able cook called Curley the Crow, who claimed to be a member of the Crow tribe and former scout for General Custer. Indian or not, Curley pursued his cooking duties barefoot, and the soles of his feet were "like cowhide." He often used them to smooth the coals of the cook fire before placing his Dutch ovens. "The smoke," one observer marveled, "would boil up from his old bare feet as if some one was branding a calf."

Numerous Hispanics and African Americans, including former slaves, cooked for western cattle outfits, especially those originating in South and Gulf Coast Texas. In some regions blacks and Hispanics made up entire roundup and trail-driving crews. Traditionally these ranches paid the lowest wages, cooks included. In 1890, for example, Rincon Ranch cooks earned only 50 cents a day, the same wage as members of the cow crew but a bit more than fence riders, who were paid only $12 a month. Little wonder that some of those who traveled north with Texas trail herds remained to ply their trade on the higher-paying ranches of the northern plains.

A good-humored cook on any outfit always improved morale, and according to some reports, black and Mexican-American cooks tended to be more congenial and better cooks than many of their white counterparts. Dillard Fant, a prominent droving contractor, proclaimed one of his mulatto trail cooks the "cleanest and best cook he ever saw."[12] African American Jim Perry, for two decades a master of roping, riding, and "son-of-a-bitch stew" on the XIT Ranch, became a local legend. In different times his leadership, hard work, and common sense might have earned him a position of greater responsibility. "If it weren't for my damned old black face," he once lamented to a friend, "I'd have been boss of one of these [XIT] divisions long ago."[13]

In a region where many cowboys, for secrecy or other reasons, went by names other than

their own, given names were rare and nicknames flourished. Cooks were no exception. In the Southwest, where Spanish was nearly as common as English, variations of *cocinero,* the Spanish term for cook, were frequently heard. The Anglo corruptions "coosey" or "coosie" were among the most prominent variants. Generic references included "pot-rassler," "grub-spoiler," "dough-puncher," "doughbelly," "beanmaster," "belly-cheater," and "biscuit-shooter."

In some instances a single incident might saddle the cook with a nickname that stuck forever. The 66 Ranch cook known as Piebiter earned his name after an ill-fated wager that he could bite through as many as ten thin pies at once. Personal idiosyncrasies or physical characteristics accounted for names like Rickety Bob, Sourdough Jack, Cooty Slim, Coonskin Sam, Rawhide Bill, and Whistling Jake. A Matador Ranch cook who griped all the time was known as Bellyache Charley Colic.

Whatever they were called and wherever they toiled, cow camp cooks presided over their chuck wagons as czarlike autocrats. Their domain extended sixty feet in every direction from the chuck wagon, and the space between the fire and the chuck box was as sacred to them as was Mecca to a Moslem.

The cook also generally appropriated the shelter of the wagon box for sleeping, and the jealous sort were even known to throw water underneath the chuck wagon to prevent a cowboy from napping in the coveted shade. Although he alone slept dry in foul weather, the protection that the wagon afforded the cook sometimes backfired, as occurred when a stampede jarred one sleeping "beanmaster" awake. Bolting upright at the first sound of thundering hooves, the cook cracked his skull on the rear axle of the wagon. He asked for his pay the next morning.

"Goin' to quit?" queried the boss.

"Done quit," the sore head replied.[14]

Often hurried in their tasks, cooks brooked no interruptions while preparing meals. Eating on the chuck box lid or leaving one's plate and cup there instead of in the "round pan" invited the cook's wrath, as did looking in the food pots, rummaging through the chuck box for snacks, or even taking a cup of coffee without permission. Such breaches of camp etiquette were sometimes tried by kangaroo courts and the guilty offender whipped with leather leggings.

From Canada to the Rio Grande, cowboys remembered most wagon cooks as cranky. According to John Arnot, a cowboy on the LX and Frying Pan ranches during the 1880s, the cook's very efficiency "was gauged by his contrariness."[15] Said one careful observer of range chefs, "They act like they are mad at everybody and everything all the time, and they usually are."[16] Con Price of Montana remembered one particularly crabby "belly-cheater" named Big Nose George, "so mean that I think he hated himself."[17]

Some cooks were known for their quick tempers and fists, and ill-advised criticism of either the "biscuit-shooter" or his menu could incite a sudden explosion of curses and flying pots and pans. Evan G. Barnard, one-time cook for the W.B.G. outfit in the Cherokee Strip, recalled throwing a coffee mill at one critic and cursing the rest of the outfit in both Spanish and Cheyenne before quitting his post. On another occasion the cook for a northern plains ranch pummeled his boss alternately with a frying pan and coffeepot when he dared complain about cold food after showing up late for the meal. The cook kept his job, and the incident was never mentioned as long as he remained with the outfit. In still another instance, when a drunken cowboy accidently turned over the cook's cherished sourdough keg, the furious chef drubbed the man's head in a puddle of dough, then, apparently feeling remorse, helped his victim wash off the mess in a nearby stream.

Poor working conditions, onerous duties, and long hours certainly contributed to the sour disposition among ranch cooks of the West. Most cowboys understood this and were willing to endure the cook's surly demeanor and personal idiosyncracies as long as he turned out good grub, especially if the reigning beanmaster was a former cowboy.

Adaptable and often ingenious, cow country chefs prepared their dishes without the aid of written recipes or even a knowledge of how many hands they might have to serve at a given meal. They relied instead on tradition, experience, and intuition—the look and feel of the mixture. Even when cookbooks became available, they were no guarantor of success to neophytes. Rancher and raconteur J. Evetts Haley told of two aspiring twentieth-century "coosies" who were completely stymied by a cookbook in which every recipe began, "Take a clean pan . . ."[18]

When supplies were scarce and ingredients lacking, resourceful cooks often pressed unconventional recipes into service. Almost out of flour, Cherokee Strip cook Oliver Nelson mixed sourdough and cornmeal together, fried it in lard, and served it with molasses and the cooked meat of freshwater turtles. Roasted liver, heated until completely dried out, made a passable substitute for bread.

Ranch cooks compensated for the usual shortage of butter on the range by adding hot water to lard in which breaded steak had been fried to produce a concoction known as "Texas butter." A similar blend of sorghum syrup and bacon grease resulted in a combination called "Charley Taylor." Out of cinnamon for a waiting apple cobbler, a Spade Ranch cook once substituted Copenhagen snuff with apparent success.

Although true culinary artists undoubtedly were in short supply in the western cattle range, at least one remarkable cook emerged in the memoirs of *vaquero*-author Joe Mora. Mora encountered this *cocinero,* a native of Spain, cooking for a roundup crew in the San Juan country of southern Colorado. The man was a former ship's cook who had taken leave in New York and eventually made his way to the kitchens of New Orleans. Driven by wanderlust to Texas, he landed a job as a chuck wagon cook and later a chef in the mining camps of the Rockies.

The vicissitudes of high-altitude cooking did not suit him, however, and he soon returned to ranch cooking.

Besides the traditional staples in his chuck box, this Catalonian chef, known to his associates only as Carl, kept a private stock of imported olives, fish, sausage, chocolate, olive oil, and Spanish and Cuban pastas and a cache of red wine locked in a wooden box under the wagon seat. When he discovered that Mora was a fellow Catalonian, he prepared for the whole crew an unforgettable campfire feast that included shredded codfish flakes, sliced raw onions with wine vinegar and oil dressing, *langoniza* (a pork sausage) with garlic and herb seasoning, *calamar con tinta* (squid packed in ink) cooked in rice, *olla podrida,* and an eclectic stew that included beef, ham bone, salt pork, sausage, pasta, potatoes, carrots, onions, and saffron. For dessert the cook fixed light crepes rolled and sprinkled with sugar and filled with Cuban guava.

Not every fancy cook, however, could produce culinary masterpieces under such primitive conditions. Participants in a Green River, Wyoming, roundup in 1918, for example, recalled that rancher Abner Luman's longtime Salt Lake City house cook, who also cooked for the Lumans on their European tour, never quite got the hang of Dutch oven cooking and was relegated to washing dishes.

Colorful nicknames, crabby dispositions, and innovative
cooking styles aside, most cooks were nondescript in appearance.
For the most part they dressed like other hands, although rarely as flamboyantly—
a flannel shirt, broad brimmed hat, overalls or jeans, brogan shoes more often than boots or spurs.
Many "dough bellies" used a flour sack for an apron and at least one snappy Arizona type
sported a Derby while doing his chores.

A similar fate befell a famous New York City restaurant chef who, looking for fresh air and a change of scenery, signed on with the Pitchfork Ranch in Texas in the 1960s. When the cowhands of the "Forks" tired of soufflés and boiled beef, and the cook wearied of the Lone Star State, he headed for greener pastures in Wyoming and a cooking job with a haying crew.

At least a few cooks tended their fires while "packing iron." One inebriated Montana cook stirred a pot of navy beans with the barrel of his Colt six-shooter, expelling those beans that clung inside by firing at a nearby rock. The "grub-spoiler" informed a bystander that he was testing the beans to see if they were soft enough to eat!

A pistol also came in handy when Frank Walden, the cook of the Yokley Ranch in New Mexico, played host to a band of hungry desperadoes. As his rowdy guests began to brag about their evil exploits, Walden is said to have suddenly drawn his weapon and opened fire indiscriminately, hitting plates, pots, and furniture and sending his startled company scurrying for their horses.

Still, many cooks also displayed a tender side. One aging hand recalled his days as a young horse wrangler and the sympathetic cook who always had a snack ready when he arrived in camp and, although it was not his job, even helped the wrangler build his rope corral. A few cooks were also fond of pet horses or mules that, upon retirement, were allowed the run of camp and liberties around the chuck box that no cowboy would dare take.

In intellect, ranch cooks ran the gamut from ignorant to educated. One enterprising latter-day cook earned extra money by composing letters to the families and sweethearts of unlettered crew members on a second-hand typewriter. Certainly one of the most literate of the lot was Bob Simpson, cook for C. C. Slaughter's famous Long S Ranch in Texas. Simpson's phenomenal memory and knowledge of Shakespeare and Tennyson enabled him to quote long passages from two volumes he always kept close at hand. Slaughter cowboys constantly called for recitations of their favorite poems and plays, even though they had heard some of the texts many times before. When his days as a cowboy and cook were done, Simpson retired to more mundane pursuits as a bank cashier and a postmaster.

Other cooks of Simpson's stripe were accomplished storytellers, and still others were musically inclined. Boss Neff, a noted drover, recalled with pleasure one fiddle-playing *cocinero* who enlivened otherwise dreary evenings around the campfire with renditions of such standards as "Old Mother Blair," "Cotton-Eyed Joe," "Saddle Old Spike," "Mississippi Lawyer," and "Turkey in the Straw." Dickey Ranch cowboys likewise praised Paddy Walsh, whose thunderous singing voice and prompt vittles earned him admiration throughout Colorado.

Appreciative cowhands who wanted to stay in the cook's good graces fetched him extra

firewood, cow chips, or wild fruit. Obliging chefs often returned such favors by preparing special desserts or providing an extra can of peaches or perhaps a doughnut stored away for a special occasion. Cowboys were always eager to help the cook grind the Arbuckles' coffee in exchange for the stick candy included in each package.

Whatever the situation, a good cook could always hold his own with a crew. At times his humor could be cutting and sarcastic, as one cowboy discovered when sent as a "rep" to a distant roundup. Arriving at the new camp, he encountered the cook alone, toiling over a pot of stew.

"Well, I see you're going to have a son-of-a-bitch for supper," the new man ventured.

"Yes," growled the cook. "We've been having seventeen regularly. Now we'll have eighteen."[19]

The cook, too, endured teasing and practical jokes and retaliated in kind with rocks in the beans, dishwater coffee, and worse. One evening an awful cook known as Big Hank quit a cow camp under the cover of darkness for parts unknown, but not before he threw away the alarm clock and poured molasses in the cowboys' boots.

Asked by a cowboy to prepare a pie, another devilish "doughbelly" baked up a tin of potato skins, onion peelings, and other waste, leavened it with clay, and served it to the unsuspecting hands. When they discovered the trick and tried to make the cook eat the pie, a scuffle ensued and guns and knives were drawn in anger before order was restored.

Occasional practical jokes aside, cooks usually ran harmonious, orderly, and sanitary camps. Bill Sims of the Chiricahua Cattle Company in Arizona, for example, not only prohibited Three C punchers from wearing their leggings into camp but even dressed down one of the ranch's owners for spearing dried apples out of the pot with a dinner fork. Cowboys on horseback took care to approach any cow camp from downwind of the chuck wagon, and when on foot they treaded lightly around the cooking pots so as not to stir up dust. After observing an open kettle full of stewed raisins and breeze-born dirt, the good-humored cook of the Hat X Ranch in Montana estimated that the dish would "assay 80 per cent."[20]

Not every cow camp cook was a stickler for etiquette and cleanliness. A former camp man on the LX Ranch admitted that he and his partner "never washed dishes as long as we could remember what was in them last."[21] The flies and filth were so terrible in another locale that a cowboy asked the cook for some screw worm medicine with which to "doctor" the chuck box. In another instance the cook of an Arizona crew permitted a hog to root about in the cooking pot, then allowed the crew to partake of the dish as if nothing happened. And in still another case a cowboy observed a cook seasoning a pudding with dishwater.

Nor did all ranch cooks measure up in the way of personal hygiene. One observer remembered early West Texas cooks as mainly Irish and "generally dirty,"[22] while Texas cowboy Rollie Burns recalled a particularly filthy specimen called Soggy:

> He was a dirty, filthy fellow. He never washed his hands (or any of the rest of his person for that matter) unless he got them wet by accident when he was mucking out the pots and pans. He chewed tobacco, and the juice had a way of running down his chin from the corners of his mouth. I often saw him spatter amber in the sourdough, but cow punchers were not very finicky about their victuals in those days.[23]

Contrary to Burns's statement, cowboys rarely suffered an unsanitary cook for long and the poor reputations of misfits usually followed them, often making it difficult to find employment in the same region.

If succeeding generations of ranch folk showed more appreciation for life's amenities, for sanitation, and for the general quality of cooking, part of the reason surely lay in the ever-increasing number of women drawn to ranch country. As chuck wagons began to fall victim to mechanization, so, too, male ranch cooks began to give way to females and, on occasion, husband and

wife teams. Mr. and Mrs. Bill Corder, for example, hired out to the XIT Ranch in 1902 to cook and do general chores at headquarters in northwestern Texas. Women being scarce, Mrs. Corder did not see another female for three months. None of the cowboys had seen a woman in quite some time, and they avoided her at first out of shyness. Another wife and mother, whose husband received $20 a month as a line rider for ranches near Lone Wolf in Indian Territory, cooked for cowhands in exchange for room and board for their family.

While most ranches would not hire married cowhands during the late nineteenth century, by 1900 progressive ranchers began to take a more enlightened view of married employees. Although more costly to maintain, married cowboys represented the stability and responsibility of a new order compared to their footloose single counterparts. A letter from Frank Hastings, manager of the Swenson SMS Ranch, to his employers regarding the hiring of top hand John Selmon in 1915 beautifully summarized the cow country in transition:

> *Scandalous John is one of the best punchers in the country, and has worked for Half Circle S people a number of years. They, however, will not keep anyone for range work if he marries and John bowed to cupid to the extent of giving up his job to take the girl of his choice, and he is treating her to a grand honeymoon in the shape of making her cook for a cow camp, which only goes to show how the course of true love runs on the Western range. . . .*
>
> *I think he will prove to be one of our most valued men. He is true blue in every way. We don't know much about the girl yet, but you can form your own views after you eat one of her biscuits.[24]*

"Everything but the hide, hooves, and bawl":

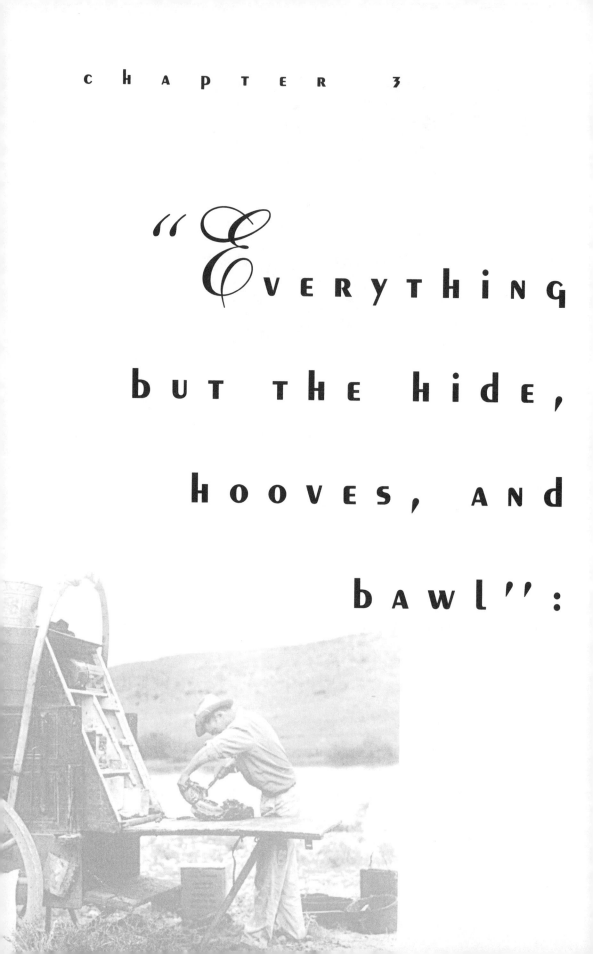

MEAT

There's a beef

in the herd

And the boss says kill it

And we'll all eat beef

From the same old skillet.

Anonymous[1]

$\mathcal{L}$ ike coffee, meat was a mainstay of the cowboy diet and often the only fresh food on the menu. According to one cowboy, as long as the cook served beef, "nobody cared whether there was anything else or not." Yet for many years bacon, salt pork, and wild game rivaled fresh beef in importance at mealtime. Nowhere was this more true than among cattle drovers, whose consumption of fresh meat usually was confined to wild game or strays from other

herds. After all, trail bosses expected to arrive at market with the same number of cattle with which they started and not slaughter them for food along the way.

Bacon, sometimes known as "overland trout," along with salted beef and pork, therefore comprised the bulk of drovers' meat rations. Civil War veterans among the cowboy population were all too familiar with beef impregnated with saltpeter. Troops detested the foul-smelling stuff, calling it "embalmed beef," "salt horse," and the "vilest ration distributed to the soldiers."

Salt pork could be equally unappetizing. Both military critics and cowboys labeled the poorest qualities "salt junk" or "sow belly." One African-American "grub-spoiler" dubbed it "Kansas City fish."[2] A versatile food, salt pork could be eaten raw, fried, broiled, or boiled, and was used in soups and in the preparation of beans and other vegetables.

In the absence of refrigeration, roundup crews enjoyed fresh fat beef only a few months of the year. Until about mid-June, when grass-fed animals finally became fat enough to slaughter on the plains, roundup crews subsisted mainly upon bacon and salt pork. A former cowboy recalled that the first fresh beef of the season usually played havoc with cowboy digestive systems attuned to "a diet of sow-belly and beans for a month or so."[3]

More than a few stingy ranchers preferred that their cowboys dine on wild game, unbranded mavericks, or stray cattle from the herds of others. Those outfits that did furnish their men beef from their own herds stressed strict accountability and did not condone waste.

DINING OFF THE HERD

Most ranches kept records of "beeves" (the word used for beef at the time) slaughtered by their hands for local consumption. One of the famous "General Rules of the XIT Ranch," issued by ranch manager Abner Taylor in 1888, prohibited the killing of ranch beef except as directed by division managers and then only if it could "be distributed and consumed without loss."[4]

Reluctant to engage in the wasteful slaughter of large steers, many smaller outfits preferred killing fat calves weighing only three hundred to four hundred pounds, or tasty yearling heifers. When a crew could not consume all the meat of a slaughtered animal, they usually shared the excess or bartered the less desirable cuts to local farmers for butter, milk, fruit, or vegetables. One such trade during the fall of 1894, for example, netted a Wyoming roundup outfit part of a wagon load of juicy watermelons. On another occasion cowboys on an Indian Territory ranch freely shared excess meat with nearby settlers who repaid their kindness by nursing sick or hurt cowboys in their homes.

The typical plains cow outfit slaughtered beef every two to four days, depending upon the

number of men in camp and the climate for preservation. The Spur Ranch, for example, consumed from sixty to one hundred steers a year during the late nineteenth century. During the same period, XIT roundup crews butchered a fat calf about every other day. During the 1930s, the JA Ranch roundup crew devoured as many as two hundred such calves annually, while the employees of the nearby Pitchfork Ranch ate an average of two hundred pounds of fresh beef per person annually, nearly three times the national average.

Cowboys on the Gulf Coast and in the Southwest enjoyed fresh beef less often, sometimes only once weekly. At the turn of the century a single cow or steer fed four families on the Kenedy Ranch for a month. Supplemented by wild game, the meat intake averaged about one hundred pounds per month per family. As late as the 1950s, weekly fresh beef rations on the King Ranch ranged from six to ten pounds, depending upon the size of the household.

Beef usually was butchered in the late afternoon so that the carcass could chill in the night breeze and also because the flesh of animals killed in the morning was often bug infested by sunset. In the field those cowboys detailed to slaughter an animal for meat drove it to a point near the wagon, roped it by the neck and hind legs, and struck it on the head with an ax. An ax blow was preferable to shooting, which produced internal bleeding. The dead animal was then bled at the jugular vein, skinned, and quartered on the fresh hide, operations that required only a few minutes to accomplish.

After selecting a hind quarter for the next meal, the cook hung the remainder on hooks attached to the side boards of the chuck wagon, from the wagon's brake lever, or suspended the meat from a tent pole, nearby tree, or windmill away from predators. The next day the carcass was wrapped in a tarp or slicker to ward off flies and stored in the wagon, where bedrolls acted as insulation against the heat. In a high, dry climate, meat could be kept fresh for two or three days and sometimes longer. The carcass became more tender with the passage of time, but it also became green around the edges.

CURING THE REMAINS

In the arid and semiarid Southwest, where the warm nights and often torrid days spoiled meat quickly, much was dried in the form of jerky, a term derived from the Spanish *charqui,* also called *carne seco, carne asada,* and *tasajo,* or its English corruption, "tasso." To prepare jerky from beef or wild game, cooks typically immersed slices three inches wide and an inch thick into hot brine or a layer of salt, then hung them to dry for a few hours on racks and ropes and over doorways, gutter pipes, and corral fences.

Deer, antelope, and buffalo also made outstanding jerky. The granular structure of venison particularly lent itself to drying, and deer meat was usually better appreciated cured than fresh. Dried buffalo meat was cheaper than bacon, and some thought it better tasting. During the 1870s, buffalo hunter J. Wright Mooar and perhaps others supplied salted and smoked buffalo humps, hams, and tongues to merchants at Fort Worth and Fort Griffin, Texas, who then sold the meat to trail drivers on their way north to shipping pens at Dodge City, Kansas, and to area ranchers who used it for steaks during the winter.

Packed in boxes or bags, jerky was easily transported and could be eaten plain or fried in tallow. Some cooks also prepared a tasty dish known as "jowler" by boiling pieces of tasso in water thickened with flour or an egg (if available) and seasoned with plenty of salt and pepper.

COOKING FRESH CUTS

The cut and quality of the meat usually determined how fresh beef was prepared. Lesser-quality meat ended up in stews, while the better cuts were almost always roasted or covered with flour and fried in skillets greased with beef tallow or pork fat. When asked in 1883 "why it was that the fine steaks were spoiled by being cut up into little bits and fried in black grease, when they could be just as easily broiled," a Colorado cowpuncher "said he doubted if the cooks knew what a broiled steak was, but if the steaks were broiled a cowboy might walk off with a whole steak, eat of it what he could and throw the rest away."[5]

Fresh beef was rarely boiled or seasoned with anything more than salt and pepper. Until the 1950s most cowboys also desired their meat well-done. In the West rare steak still invites comments like "I've seen cattle hurt worse than that live" or "That beef's cooked just enough not to hook you."

Some cooks served beef with pan gravy made from the hot fat and a dash of water. Others insisted on "compounding the sop" by stirring a couple of tablespoons of flour into the fat and adding salt and water to produce a thicker mixture. Occasionally range chefs also added a little milk. Brown or brindle gravy was made when chefs poured water into a skillet of hot grease in which slices of bone-cured ham had been fried.

Barbecued meat took longer to cook and was generally reserved for special occasions or times when the chuck wagon remained in one place for several days. A side of barbecued or pot-roasted ribs or tasty marrow bones never failed to earn the cook high marks from the cowboys.

Skillful *cocineros* also knew how to prepare meat underground. A favorite method involved stuffing a clean paunch with beef and roasting it overnight, Indian style, in a bed of hot coals. Pit-roasted wild turkeys were prepared in a slightly different fashion. After removing the bird's entrails and adding salt and pepper, the cook placed the whole turkey—skin, feathers, and all—into a pit from which hot coals had just been removed. He then covered the fowl with hot earth, over which he built a fire, and cooked it for hours until the meat became savory and tender.

Cow-boys Skinning a Beef

MOUNTAIN OYSTERS AND MARROW GUTS

Among connoisseurs of ranch cooking, no delicacy surpassed "mountain oysters" in favor. Sometimes known as "prairie oysters," the skinned testicles of castrated bull calves were often tossed immediately into the coals of the branding fire, where they roasted and burst open to reveal a rich, yellowish center. One inexperienced "biscuit-shooter" who did not yet appreciate the virtues of the sumptuous morsels drew the wrath of his crew by discarding the organs into a nearby creek. No matter—a large branding might yield enough of the delicious snack to last a crew for several weeks.

Calf entrails, better known as "marrow guts," rivaled mountain oysters in the estimation of cowboy epicures. An integral part of many early ranch recipes, the "guts" were chopped into pieces three or four inches long and roasted in live coals or fried in a skillet with sage, salt, and pepper. Not everyone, however, appreciated their look and tang, which one critic characterized as a "low-down, cow lot flavor—sort of a hound dog relish."[6]

Marrow guts were an essential ingredient in son-of-a-bitch stew, certainly the most famous dish in the cow cook's repertoire. To make sure that no edible beef was wasted, parsimonious cooks put a pot of son-of-a-bitch on the fire every time a steer was killed and did not remove it as long as any of the mixture remained.

No one knows who named this most celebrated dish or why. One story says that a visitor to a roundup camp asked the cook what was in his pot and he replied, "I'll be a son-of-a-bitch if I know!" In later years, of course, the name was refined to "son-of-a-gun" in deference to more polite sensibilities.

Experienced chuck wagon chefs believed that unweaned calves or "short" yearling heifers provided the best ingredients, which included the tongue, heart, kidneys, liver, sweetbreads, marrow gut, and tenderloin. These elements were first chopped into one-inch pieces, rolled in flour, and browned in tallow in a Dutch oven. Then the meat was thickened with brains, flour paste, and occasionally eggs. One cook claimed to have put "everything into it but the animal's hide, hooves, and bawl."[7] Some likened the stew's taste to that of Mexican *menudo*. Authentic cowboy son-of-a-bitch was usually made without vegetables, although potatoes, canned tomatoes, onions, and chiles were sometimes added for bulk, variety, and flavor.

Cooks seasoned the concoction to taste with salt and black pepper and sometimes a little sage. Range chefs in the Southwest almost always added fiery *chilipiquines,* tiny wild peppers, to the mix, while those farther north poured on chili powder until the brew "was almost hot enough to blaze."[8] "I almost burned down the first time I tried it," admitted one-time XIT cowboy Frank Shardleman, "but learned to tone it down with rice or beans until I got seasoned to it."[9]

When all the ingredients had been added, the cook placed the pot on the fire to simmer a half day or longer, until the meat became tender. All the while the cook watched the stew closely

to see that it did not boil and stirred it occasionally to prevent it from sticking. Some cooks also delayed adding the chunks of liver until the other meat was nearly done to avoid cooking them up into puffy balls. A grilled version of son-of-a-bitch that required only about thirty minutes to cook used the same ingredients chopped fine and scrambled together on a thick sheet of iron or tin set over mesquite coals.

As surely as they loved son-of-a-bitch stew, most cowboys loathed mutton. In the cattle country of the late nineteenth century, "cooking mutton" more often than not meant setting fire to a sheep range. Among Hispanic *vaqueros* and those ranches that pastured both cattle and sheep, however, strictures against eating mutton, lamb, and goat were less severe than on strictly beef operations. In fact, many cowboys actually enjoyed roasted or stewed *cabrito* (kid). The Daugherty Ranch cook in Frio County, Texas, for example, butchered a goat every evening and served it with beans, corn bread, and molasses.

HUNTING AND FISHING

Many ranches allowed their employees to supplement their meat rations through hunting. In fact, wild game large and small, including deer, elk, antelope, javelina, squirrel, buffalo, and bear, lent both variety and substance to the larder of most ranches and trail wagons. During the winter of 1881, for example, the occupants of one line camp in the Texas Panhandle dressed and hung a variety of game outside their dugout, where, according to one, "it would freeze and stay froze until it was eaten up. You could take a hatchet and chop off a chunk of that meat then take it to the fire and thaw it out. . . . It was the tenderest and sweetest meat I ever ate."[10]

Cowpunchers on the JAL Ranch in southeastern New Mexico probably could not say the same for the flesh of the many jackrabbits they consumed during scarcer times. Still, rabbit meat appeared so often on their menu that neighbors began to refer to the ubiquitous long-ears as "JAL beef."[11]

The rivers and creeks on the plains also yielded delicious softshell turtles that could be harvested with a small-caliber rifle. The meat was soaked in salt water, then fried to perfection in an iron skillet. By serving white and dark turtle meat on alternate days, one clever "coosie" kept the hands guessing as to what flesh they were eating.

Western waters also produced a bounty of fresh fish, although the finned creatures did not figure significantly in the menu of open-range cowboys. On at least one occasion, however, a couple of cowpunchers took leave of a roundup long enough to bag two gunny sacks full from a generous creek by dragging a borrowed seine behind their swimming horses. Cowpunchers on the LX Ranch, on the other hand, so detested the salted codfish and mackerel that owners dispatched from Dodge City in the early 1880s that some of the offending fish remained packed in containers in the store room for years. Finally, a resourceful cowboy is said to have used sixteen buckets full to mark a path between headquarters and an outlying camp.

Properly prepared, prairie chickens, geese, ducks, quail, and wild turkey made delicious eating and were especially sought after for Thanksgiving and Christmas feasts. A parboiled Franklin grouse and sourdough dumplings was a favorite pairing of one Montana ranch cook. Like beef, a plump fowl, be it wild or domesticated, made a better repast than a skinny one, as R. B. Masterson's ranch hands discovered when the boss decided to add chicken to the menu:

> The age of the fowl, an old rooster, had not been considered at the time of his purchase, but soon developed after he had been skinned and placed in the pot. No teeth in camp could penetrate his sinews. . . . Therefore a council was held and decision reached to convert him into soup. This process was continued from day to day by the simple addition of creek water until only the bones remained. What disposition was finally made of the bones is not recorded.[12]

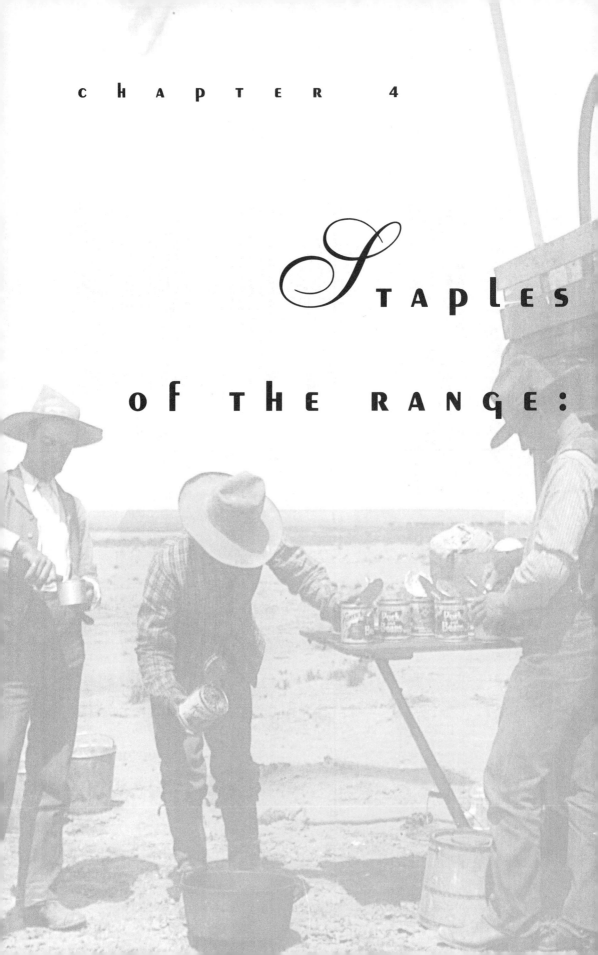

CHAPTER 4

Staples of the range:

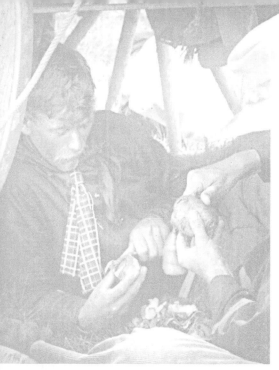

fResh, dRiEd, And CANNEd

*H*is food is largely of the "regulation" order, but a feast of vegetables he wants and must have, or scurvy would ensue. Onions and potatoes are his favorites, but any kind of vegetables will disappear in haste when put within his reach.

Joseph G. McCoy, Historic Sketches of the Cattle Trade of the West and Southwest[1]

ne contemporary observer estimated that vegetables and fruit made up less than 10 percent of the open-range buckaroo's diet. Until refrigeration and automobiles were common, time and distance kept fresh produce from reaching cowboys on the open range. Punchers usually encountered only dried or canned products, such as beans, rice, hominy, prunes, currants, and apples, with a few fresh potatoes, onions, pickles, and wild fruit added at times for variety. The limited nature of this fare would not measurably improve until the early twentieth century, when the increased availability of farm produce and improvements in transportation and distribution finally reached the most remote regions of the West.

Beans were by far the most common food in western cow camps. Although navy and lima beans and perhaps other varieties periodically appeared on the chuck wagon menu, Mexican red beans or *frijoles,* also known as pinto beans, "Pecos strawberries," or "prairie whistles" in honor of their gaseous qualities, were the standard.

Ranches near the Mexican border served beans both boiled and fried in lard. The boiled variety were sometimes called *charros a pie* (*charros* on foot), an allusion to the colorful gentlemen horsemen of Mexico; the fried type, *charros a caballo* (*charros* on horseback). Most cow camps, however, served pinto beans boiled with salt pork, either as a separate dish or combined with meat and other ingredients in soups or stews. When asked about the countless beans he had consumed over a long cowboy career, a grizzled West Texas range veteran responded that he had "liked the first carload or two pretty well."[2]

Beans challenged a cook's ingenuity. They took a long time to cook and, coupled with frequent moves of camp, posed a significant challenge to chuck wagon chefs in the field. Many cooks compensated by soaking their beans overnight to soften them and by boiling two meals'

Pickles and laundry

worth of beans at one time. Seasoned range chefs also put a pot of beans on the fire while making the evening camp and let it simmer all night. After draining off the excess water the next morning, the cook finished boiling the beans at the noon camp to ensure sufficient liquid, or "pot liquor."

Cooking beans at high altitudes or in alkaline creek water presented an even greater challenge. William A. Baillie-Grohman, a British travel writer, noted that it took "a week to boil them, a fortnight to chew them and eternity to digest them."[3] On a trip from San Antonio to the mountains of far West Texas, two friends once wagered on the probability of beans cooking in brackish Pecos River water. After two hours of boiling, the beans were still "hard as brickbats,"[4] and after ten hours, only barely edible and still not soft. According to an old Pecos River hand, "It was hard to cook beans. They would rattle when they would hit the tin plate."[5]

To help neutralize alkali and hasten the cooking process, cooks added citric acid or baking soda at the boiling point. Although quickly skimmed from the surface of the pot, such treatments tended to give the beans a flat taste.

SPUDS AND RICE

The sheer size of potatoes and the difficulties of transporting them limited their presence in

"Pelling Spuds"

the chuck wagon larder. When potatoes were available, cowboy cooks served them boiled and fried, the former in their skins, the latter usually peeled. A Spade Ranch chef fried thick slices he called "Saratoga chips,"[6] while an Indian Territory "pot-rassler" soaked sliced potatoes overnight in salt water and vinegar, then served them raw, like cucumbers. At least some hands in the Texas ranch country exhibited a fondness for sweet potatoes, whose taste resembled that of parsnips.

Rice, which some "coosies" renamed "John Chinaman,"[7] often could be found boiling in a kettle beside the beans. The starchy dish was served both plain and in tandem with tomatoes or with raisins as a dessert. As often occurred with beans, many a rookie cook overestimated the amount of rice required for a meal. A half gallon of boiled rice prepared by an inexperienced cook on the 22 Ranch, for example, overflowed two Dutch ovens and a small bucket. "We had rice for three days," recalled a cowboy who was present, "and were pretty well caught up on that cereal by the time we finished the batch."[8]

Cal Polk endured a similar experience in his first attempt at line camp cooking with beans and rice:

> I built up a big fire and put on a pot full of beans and rice with a little water in each one. . . . About that time I saw the beans was coming out of the pot. I grabbed a half gallon

cup and dipped out a cup full and carried it to the door and threw it away. When I got back the rice was doing the same way. I got a cup of it out. I looked and saw the beans was coming over again. It kept me dipping out of one and then the other and throwing them away, until I had carried at least two potfuls of each out and then had a pot of each left. . . . I then walked to the door and saw what a mess of beans, rice and dough was there. To keep Jim [his partner] from seeing them I got a spade and dug a hole in the ground and put it all in there and covered it up. About that time Jim come riding up. He asked me had I got supper. I told him yes.[9]

DRYING AND CANNING

The closest most cowboys came to fresh fruit was when dried apples or apricots were shipped into camp. Like beans and rice, "evaporated" fruit tended to swell with the addition of water. When the first batch of desiccated apples that one Texas outfit had ever seen began to boil out of its kettle and into the fire, someone ventured the opinion that "Yankees" had poisoned the fruit before it was shipped. None would eat it until the owner arrived and explained the nature of dried fruit soaked in water. His point was further illustrated by the distended stomachs of some hands who ate the shriveled apples raw, then drank copiously from the coffeepot. Nevertheless,

95

by the 1880s major ranches stocked several thousand pounds of dried apples, prunes, apricots, peaches, raisins, and currants annually to be eaten raw or used in sauces, cobblers, puddings, and pies.

Following the invention of the tin can in the United States in 1823, expensive canned meats, poultry, fish, vegetables, fruit, and milk began to appear on the market. As food processors thrived during and in the wake of the Civil War, the price of canned food became more affordable. By 1900, H. J. Heinz of Pittsburgh, the largest food processor in America, bottled and canned more than two hundred different products, including catsup, pickles, and baked beans.

As late as the 1880s, however, canned food was still uncommon around many western chuck wagons, particularly on the southern plains. Former cowboy Harry Ingerton, for example, did not recall seeing canned goods in northwestern Texas until 1883, while inspecting an LS Ranch supply dugout. Within a year, however, merchants at the nearby town of Tascosa, Texas, were stocking canned victuals obtained from Dodge City wholesalers. Although progressive ranchers furthered their spread, canned goods were far from universal for many years. As late as 1902, for example, a married couple who cooked for the Buffalo Springs Division of the XIT Ranch were not allowed to order canned food. Their first request for "canned goods" resulted in a crate of axle grease.

Thanks to cheap canned goods, sometimes called "air tights," corn and tomatoes appeared on chuck wagon menus with greater frequency. Cowboys also toted the handy tins in their saddle bags for between-meal snacks.

Canned tomatoes became a particular favorite among cowboys, who preferred them to the

fresh variety. In camp, cooks combined tomatoes with cold biscuits to produce a dish known on the Spade range as "pooch." Cooks in many states flavored beans with tomatoes, and on the King Ranch, *cocineros* mixed them with red rice cooked to a paste.[10] In the hands of a master chef and in lieu of other fruit, canned tomatoes spiked with sugar produced a decent Dutch oven cobbler.

Perhaps their most important value, however, lay in the thirst-quenching juice, whose acidic qualities helped neutralize the bitter alkali in the dust and water ingested by cowboys in many regions. On hot days the juice of canned tomatoes, combined with sugar or lemon extract, made a delicious beverage. Montana outfits devoured cans of the Blue Hen brand by the case, and New Mexico cowboys placed such great stock in food tins that when the new manager of the Prairie Land and Cattle Company ceased providing canned tomatoes and corn at the 1886 roundup, the crew erupted in protest. Each afternoon, until their wrath was exhausted, aggrieved hands slaugh-

tered a $10 company heifer, taking only one hindquarter and leaving the rest, two or three days' worth of meat, for the wolves.

Cowboys were equally fond of the tins of peaches and pears that some outfits provided. According to a New Mexico rancher, canned food, especially peaches, ranked second only to pie in the "average puncher's idea of luxury."[11] With printed matter in short supply, some semiliterate cowboys even sharpened their reading skills on the labels of canned goods.

FARM FRESH

Before 1890 only a few cattle ranchers bothered to plant a garden, and then usually only to supply the table at headquarters. Skeptical cowboys from the WS outfit ridiculed the attempts of their boss, William French, to plant shade and fruit trees and a garden near Silver City, New Mexico. "Fresh vegetables on a cow ranch," recalled French with amusement many years later, "were considered a desecration"[12] fit only for grangers. Many buckaroos shared such opinions.

The coming of railroads and permanent farm settlements increased the availability of fresh vegetables and fruit, as did ranchers' own experiments with crops. Farmers often were eager to trade produce for meat, while ranchers hoped not only to become more self-sufficient but also to demonstrate the agricultural potential of their land. The Matador and Spur ranches and the Franklyn Land and Cattle Company, all of Texas, began notable farming programs, as did the three-million-acre XIT Ranch. The most vigorous experimenter of all, the XIT cultivated nineteen different fields and invested in expensive farm machinery.

The XIT and at least a few others also instituted small-scale irrigation projects that produced fruits and vegetables. A few counties away, gravity-fed water delivered from a nearby well nourished an extensive garden plot on the RO Ranch and, according to historian Laura V. Hamner, produced "such abundance that never did a ranch wagon pass that it did not go filled with vegetables. The Shoe Bars and Quitaques passed that way often."[13]

Irrigation caused the plains to bloom with all sorts of new food crops, including fruit trees and corn. By the 1870s the Craig Ranch in Colorado and the Munger spread in the Kansas Flint Hills maintained pioneer irrigation projects and produced bumper harvests of fruits and vegetables.

Ranchers began to store potatoes, onions, squash, and other produce in root cellars for winter use, and corn and green beans often were dried as well as canned. A vigorous canning program that filled about one thousand half-gallon jars annually and produced enough dried fruit to fill ten sacks enabled an Oregon ranch family to limit store purchases to coffee, sugar, salt, and a few other staples.

By the 1930s many large ranches and smaller stock farms raised all or most of their food needs. The Pitchfork in Texas, for example, annually produced four thousand pounds of bacon, five thousand pounds of home-canned vegetables, and the same amount of canned meat while maintaining five hundred laying hens and twenty-five dairy cows for eggs, milk, and butter. Thanks to refrigeration, fresh beef was available every day of the year.

Although cowboys enjoyed a greater variety of foods than ever before, their attitudes toward food and nutrition had not kept pace. As late as the 1940s most Pitchfork cowboys and undoubtedly many others throughout the West still scoffed at the notion of eating green vegetables. Mamie Burns, wife of the Pitchfork Ranch manager, thought otherwise and felt that the typical chuck house fare of beans, potatoes, rice, corn, and bread was too starchy. She strove for better balance and variety, but the stubborn and conservative cowboys, with attitudes rooted in the nineteenth century, resisted her efforts—that is, until a respected top hand took the lead and began to partake of the leafy green dishes. At least on the Pitchfork range, most of the rest of the cowboy tribe soon put aside their reservations and followed suit.

"Sinkers" and "splatter dabs":

bRead

There is something more to it than just stirring up flour and water. You get to know your dough just like a mechanic knows cars. You can't make sourdough bread unless you have the right attitude of mind.

Fred Graven, XIT Cook[1]

*D*uring the heyday of the open range in the late nineteenth century, most ranch cooks served hot bread, usually sourdough biscuits, at every meal. Neither sourdough nor biscuits, however, laid exclusive claim to the cowboy's taste buds. Bread baked as thick loaves, as well as thin tortillas, competed for his attention in some regions, as did pans of hot corn bread and boxes of bland soda crackers.

Packing light and often forgoing weighty skillets or Dutch ovens, early-day Texas cowboys often brought along small sacks of flour in which they made up their dough by mixing in water, a little lard or other grease, and saleratus (baking soda). After fashioning a wad of dough perhaps the size of a fist, the hungry cow hunter either wound it in a ribbon around a short stick and toasted it over a fire or else baked it in a cloth under hot ashes.

If cooking was inconvenient or supplies were short, cowboys munched on ship's bread, flour-and-water crackers about three inches square and half an inch thick. Also called sea biscuit, pilot's bread, and a host of unseemly epithets, the crackers were perhaps best known as "hardtack." Compact and solid, these "tooth dullers" were tough to chew, which scarcely deterred the weevils and maggots that often infested them. Some cowboys crumbled the crackers in coffee or soup or combined them with water and fried them in meat fat to make them more palatable.

In much of South and East Texas, cornmeal was more plentiful than wheat flour. After interviewing many old-time trail drivers and cowpunchers, writer J. Frank Dobie concluded that early-day South Texas outfits rarely, if ever, saw sourdough. Rancher-historian J. Evetts Haley agreed that sourdough cooking "was essentially a product of range life on the High Plains. The extremely hot weather of South Texas, and the rigidly low-pitched standard of its fare, did not encourage its use in the cow camps there."[2]

"Yaller bread," as cornmeal was known, appeared in many forms and under many names, including corn pone, hoecakes, johnnycakes, corn dodgers, and hush puppies. Although few cowboy *cocineros* ever mastered the light and fluffy corn breads produced in fine southern kitchens, their rough outdoor variety mixed well enough with meat, beans, molasses, and the rest of the cowboy's fare.

Not everyone appreciated corn bread, but few detested it with the passion of Ab Blocker, one of the most famous of all Texas trail bosses. Blocker's brother, John, once made the mistake (or perhaps a joke) of including a sack of cornmeal in Ab's trail wagon bound for Deadwood, South Dakota. After the drive Ab returned with both the chuck wagon and the unused sack of cornmeal. "Here, Johnny, is your damned mule feed!" said Ab with disdain. "We didn't need it."[3]

Texas cowpunchers arriving in Montana, Wyoming, and the Dakotas were sometimes amazed at the absence of corn bread among the northern outfits. After partaking of hot cakes and "light" bread at breakfast and dinner on Granville Stuart's Montana ranch, a Texas-reared puncher confronted by a plate of biscuits at supper is said to have exclaimed with astonishment: "Jesus Christ! Do you fellows have white bread three times a day?"[4]

Cooks leavened their loaves and biscuits with either baking powder or tangy sourdough. Although baking powder was invented in 1856 and commercial yeast cakes were available by 1868, many cooks continued to produce their own homemade leavening by combining cream of tartar with bicarbonate of soda, flour, or cornstarch.

Sourdough was created from a starter that included warm water, potato pulp, sugar, flour, and yeast, combined to produce a batter thick enough to rise. As the mixture began fermenting ("workin'," as cowboy cooks referred to the process), the batter thinned naturally and began to

bubble. Left in a warm place for about two days, the starter swelled to about twice its original mass and became sour. Accomplished sourdough cooks suggested stirring the starter from time to time, with a paddle of white rather than yellow pine so as not to impart the taste of rosin.

Most cooks stored their sourdough in earthenware crocks holding from one to five gallons, depending upon the amount of dough required. Cooking for a typical crew of ten to fifteen cowboys demanded a five-gallon container.

To encourage the fermentation process, cooks took great pains to keep the starter from getting cold. On the move between camps, they usually carried the crock under cover in the wagon box. In the cool of the evening and in the early morning hours, they often set the keg near the fire, turning it periodically to assure even heating. On especially cold evenings, cautious "biscuit-shooters" were known to sleep with their sourdough crocks to keep the starter from freezing.

Many sourdough cooks considered themselves artists and had distinctive methods that were not easily distilled into formulas or recipes. If short a bread pan, a cowboy cook might mix his dough right in the sack by hollowing a depression in the top of the flour and adding a gallon or more of the pungent contents of the sourdough crock along with "a liberal pinch of salt . . . a dash of sugar . . . a small handful of baking powder and a great gob of lard" or bacon grease.[5]

Some cooks also added a teaspoonful of soda dissolved in a little lukewarm water. The addition of this latter ingredient spelled disaster for one crew whose "belly-cheater" mistook the wide-mouthed pickle bottle containing calomel for a jar of baking soda. The batch of bread not only tasted peculiar but also induced diarrhea in all who consumed it. Cooks took care to replenish the starter with flour and water equivalent to that poured off.

The cook then kneaded the mixture into a flexible sphere of dough from which biscuits were pinched or "choked" off by hand and rolled in melted lard or bacon fat at the bottom of the Dutch oven until thoroughly coated. An oven full of bread had to be cooked at one time or the bread would not rise.

Masters of Dutch oven biscuits rarely kneaded their sourdough except by hand. When asked to pose for a photograph with a rolling pin, Cap Warren of the Waggoner Ranch spoke

for the majority of cooks when he replied that he had "no more use than a hog has for a rolling pin."[6]

When the biscuits had risen for half an hour or more and doubled in size, the cook shoveled some mesquite coals from the fire, scattered them on the ground, and set the Dutch oven on top. Lifting the lid from the cook fire with a pot hook, he tapped it against his shovel to jar off any clinging coals that might accidentally fall into the bread, eased it into place, and covered it with a thin layer of live coals.

The biscuits baked slowly, usually for about forty-five minutes or until a light brown. When baking sourdough bread in a stove rather than a Dutch oven, some experienced cooks added a pan of water to provide the moisture that the Dutch oven naturally provided.

Most cowboys demanded piping-hot bread at every meal. "To ask a [cow]boy to eat cold bread is nearly insulting," remarked Scottish businessman Alexander Mackay after a visit to the Matador Ranch. An exception to the rule, a wagon cook known as "Cold Bread Phil" never endeared himself to hands by serving hot bread only once a day.

Cherokee Strip cook Marion Hildreth, on the other hand, regularly delighted the crew of the T5 Ranch with "biscuits about the size of a silver dollar, five inches high, real light, crusted over with sugar" at every meal.[7] Many cooks, however, made their biscuits larger so that the outfit's dirty hands would not have to reach in the Dutch oven so often.

In keeping with the general tendency to avoid waste, fearless "doughpunchers" like Frank Smith, who accompanied Ab Blocker's trail outfit many times, made the cowboys he served eat every last bite of bread they took from the oven. If any was left on a plate, he saved it for that cowboy at the next meal and would not give him anything else to eat until he finished the leftover.

A British traveler wrote that a sourdough biscuit was "neither more nor less than an inferior and heavier French roll."[8] And while most cow camp cooks and many cowboys could, according to one nineteenth-century rancher, "turn out biscuits of some degree of edibility,"[9] stories of heavy, hard, and inedible bread abound in the folklore of the range.

One of George Asa's cowboys, for example, once marveled at how a chuck wagon cook "could take a 25 lb. sack of flour and make it into a ton of bread."[10] The cook for the W.B.G.

outfit in the Cherokee Strip produced bread heavy as lead, solid as a rock, and streaked yellow with soda. His biscuits, he laughed perversely, were of the "stick to their ribs" variety.

Still, some cowpunchers were not sure that such bread could even be chewed, much less swallowed. Writing of the early 1870s, cowpuncher John Young commented that the well-known solidity of hardtack was "nothing compared to the hardness that a big supply of home-baked bread would sometimes attain before the last of it was consumed."[11] Another cowboy once requested an ax from the cook with which to break his biscuit. Still another was sure that succeeding generations would "pick up petrified pieces of bread around where we have camped, and preserve them as curiosities."[12]

According to conventional wisdom, even wolves avoided stale and inedible cow camp bread. Droll hands report finding an occasional piece of bread bearing the marks of a wolf's teeth, thus demonstrating conclusively to their comrades "that the bread was not as hard as some people said it was."[13] One outfit did nickname its cook Jesus because he could turn bread into stone.

Buckaroos held sourdough biscuits in such esteem that they sometimes called them "dough gods." Resourceful cooks created sourdough masterpieces in other forms, including cakes, dumplings, pie crusts, and pancakes (called "splatter dabs" or "saddle blankets" by one imaginative West Texas cook[14]). At least a few "coosies" preferred loaves to biscuits. Uncle Johnnie Patton, an Arkansas native ranching on the northern plains, made Dutch oven loaves of "salt-rising bread" that, according to one contemporary, "tasted mighty good but smelled something like old dirty socks."[15] Juan Lerma of the Norias Division of the King Ranch also made round loaves the size and shape of small grindstones, which he stacked like poker chips on his cooking table.

Old-time cowpunchers proclaimed sourdough bread, whatever its form, superior in every way to the baking powder variety, except perhaps in the critical arena of convenience. But as the deliberate and artistic sourdough bakers of the open range slowly died off, their craft also began to decline. By the First World War sourdough cooking already was a lost art in some regions of the West, and within another three decades all but a few die-hard traditionalists fed their hungry cowboys straight baking powder biscuits. The sourdough guild, however, never completely disappeared and in recent times has experienced a revival that promises to keep it alive both on the range and in town for many years to come.

CHAPTER 6

"Spotted pup" and "shiverin' liz":

desserts

ost-conscious ranchers did not always cater to the cowboy's well-known sweet tooth. Milk and eggs, essential ingredients for many desserts, were scarce on the open range, at least until some chuck wagons began to carry canned milk and hens became more plentiful around ranch headquarters. Critics blamed the shortage of dairy products in a land of cattle on the rank disposition of wild longhorns, the laziness of owners and hands, and unavoidable spoilage.

"The signs of a great 'cow country' are these," wrote *The New York Times* in 1881:

> *That milk for your coffee is a rarity and a luxury to be remembered; that butter is seldom to be seen, and when seen, except during a few short weeks of Summer, it has been brought 150 or 250 miles from the railway, is rather fit for wagon grease than for greasing the palate of mankind, and is extravagantly dear of price.*[1]

Within a few years of that article, some of the more dynamic ranches began to maintain dairy herds and build water-fed milk and meat coolers, but until that time eggless cakes, puddings, and pies were the norm. Only seldom did a nest of wild turkey eggs and the prospect of a custard pie two inches thick convince a cowboy to attempt milking a wild bovine.

Cane sugar also was a rarity in many cow camps, especially in Texas. "Teddy Blue" Abbott told of a cowpuncher from the Lone Star State who, when offered sugar at a Montana chuck wagon, refused, thinking it salt. Texans were far more familiar with sorghum molasses, better known as "lick" or "long sweetnin'." The sticky substance rivaled even coffee in Texans' estimation, said one British traveler, who sat amazed when a cowboy dining at a hotel eatery in ranch country casually mixed canned oysters with molasses and hot corn bread.

Around the chuck box molasses also came in handy as fly bait in wire cage traps. Since molasses had a similar effect on cowboys, one waggish cowman suggested that the manager of the LFD Ranch might easily fill his quota of hands for the spring branding simply by soaking a stake rope in molasses, tying it behind his mess wagon, and dragging it through the cow town of Roswell, New Mexico.

The sorghum molasses supplied to most cow outfits was the cheapest syrup on the market, less than half the cost of maple syrup and only about two thirds the price of ribbon cane. These factors came into play when one trail crew was delayed en route to the railroad by heavy rains. While shopping for supplies at a nearby town to replenish the chuck box, one of the partners decided to buy a couple of cases of expensive maple syrup as a reward for the men's faithfulness in the face of adversity. His associate, a frugal Scot, objected so strenuously to the "extraordinary" expense that his equally insistent colleague bought him out on the spot and ordered the maple syrup. Later, when the storekeeper asked the drover how his herd had fared at market, the cowman replied with grim humor, "Well, I guess that maple syrup cost me about a thousand dollars."[2]

If an outfit ran short of "lick," experienced "grub-spoilers" sometimes prepared a passable substitute by browning melted sugar in a skillet, adding water and perhaps vanilla or orange flavoring, and bringing the whole mess to a boil. On other such occasions cowhands garnished their sourdough biscuits with stewed fruit, homemade jelly obtained from local settlers, and even Eagle Brand condensed milk.

If sugar was not available, molasses could also be used to sweeten "spotted pup," one of the most popular of all chuck wagon desserts. Although it was usually a simple mixture of boiled rice and raisins, some recipes called for eggs, milk, and a dash of cinnamon. In another version, cold biscuits replaced the rice, and stewed prunes, the raisins. Lee Proctor, a "coosie" on the Spade Ranch, called this concoction French dish, "to make it more mysterious."[3]

Gelatin, too, was unfamilar to buckaroos when it made its debut on the range. Intrigued by its quivering qualities, buckaroos christened it "tremblin' jelly" and "shiverin' Liz."[4]

Most chuck wagon desserts combined sourdough with some type of dried or canned fruit. Puddings, pies, and cobblers made with apples, prunes, apricots, peaches, currants, and even to-matoes topped the roster of cowboy favorites.

A newspaper correspondent on the Colorado range for the spring roundup in 1877 reported having eaten puddings "which, to put it mildly, are seldom surpassed for excellence in our city hotels."[5] One type, known as "sucamagrowl," featured sugar, water, vinegar, flour, cinnamon, and sourdough.[6] A boiled pudding of some repute bore the nickname "lumpy Dick,"[7] while a steamed cousin carried the even more colorful moniker "son-of-a-bitch in a sack." To concoct the latter, "doughbellies" combined diced suet, dried fruit, flour, and water into a malleable dough and wrapped it in a cloth sack or bag, which was steamed until moist in a large kettle on the pot rack. The pudding was then served with a hot sauce of stewed blackberries or other fruit, or perhaps "buttery brandy" or Mexican mescal.

Inexperienced cooks often loaded their confections with extra ingredients in hopes of making them more palatable. In creating a particularly unsuccessful English pudding, James Emmit McCauley of the XT Ranch in southern New Mexico claimed, with typical frontier exaggeration, to have "put very near everything they was in from a latago strap to bear marrow." Having omitted baking powder, McCauley observed that his creation "didn't swell any" and, after two days of boiling in a deer hide, became hard as rock and inedible. According to McCauley, the dish served as a footstool and a doorstop known as "Old Rough and Ready" before it finally melted when placed too near the fireplace.

McCauley believed that the positive reception among the cowboys for his lumpy-crusted Christmas pies resulted more from a cowpuncher's universal appreciation of pie than his amateurish efforts to invigorate the dried apple filling with "all kinds of flavorings." "But you can fix up any sort of stuff and call it pie, sink it in the Rio Grande River, and every cowboy in New Mexico would be drownded [sic] diving after it. Anything a cowboy likes is pie and 'tis something hardly ever crosses their path."[8]

When camped near wild fruit thickets, cowboys eagerly gathered grapes, plums, blackberries, gooseberries, and other varieties in their pockets and shirt fronts in hopes that the cook would

"build" a pie or cobbler. Some of the more artistic of the *cocineros* ornamented the tops of their fruit-filled specialties with "fantastic strips of dough, with cunning little designs," often in the shape of their outfit's brand. A successful Colorado cow camp chef also added "emblematical little cupids" as decorations along the edge of the crust but still depended upon "great gobs of apples" and "a God's quantity of sugar" to convince the palate of the discriminating cowboy diner.[9]

Sourdough appeared not only in pie crusts and puddings but also in cinnamon rolls and in doughnuts deep-fried in Dutch ovens. On one West Texas ranch, fried strips of sourdough were dubbed "houn' ears" or "whirlups," and another distinctively shaped lump, a "bear sign."[10]

By 1900, thanks largely to the influence of the women who had joined the ranks of ranch cooks and the availability of more diverse ingredients, the repertoire of desserts, particularly those served at the headquarters mess hall, broadened considerably. The variety was almost endless, from cookies to tea cakes to cream puffs to gingerbread to rich pies with fillings of chocolate, lemon, egg custard, pecan, and banana cream. If desserts were heaven to a cowboy, by now he was certainly approaching paradise.

"Belly wash":

coffee and tea

offee, strong and black, was the universal beverage of choice in western cow camps. Cowboys consumed prodigious quantities of the robust black drink, rivaling soldiers in their fondness for the brew. A typical trail crew of ten or eleven men consumed about a pound of coffee at every meal. From August 1882 to August 1883, the T5 cook exhausted 2,080 pounds of coffee beans to satisfy his outfit's craving for the beverage.

A British traveler estimated that cowhands typically consumed "one or more quarts of the strongest coffee imaginable, without sugar or cream," with each meal.[1] The amazed cook for the Miller 101 Ranch in Oklahoma observed a burly trail guide and commission agent consume an entire gallon pot of boiling coffee straight from the fire at a single sitting.

To accommodate such prodigious thirst, cooks usually kept a two- to five-gallon pot brewing almost constantly, a broom weed stalk sometimes across the lid to keep the contents from boiling over. The larger containers being too heavy for pouring, punchers simply dipped their cups in instead.

"Were an Easterner who leads a sedentary life," said writer George Pattullo, recalling his own experiences on southwestern ranges, "to drink the beverage one of these men consumes he would be a nervous wreck in six months, yet they thrive on it. Nerves? They don't know the meaning of the word."[2]

Understanding the average cowhand's liking for coffee, Hal Mangum, a rancher on the Texas Gulf Coast, never allowed his cooks to serve the beverage before breakfast, believing that it spoiled the appetites of his hands. Mangum feared, not without reason, that forgoing breakfast on account of a belly full of coffee weakened the stamina and mental alertness during a long and hard day's work.

In the 1880s ranchers bought factory-roasted coffee beans in hundred-pound sacks that cost twenty-five to thirty cents a pound. The roasting of the beans in a mess pan or skillet required time, patience, and skill that apparently few cooks possessed. While stirring a single layer of beans with a stick in an often futile attempt to achieve an even roast and keep them from burning, some cooks also added spices to obtain a better flavor. Although overroasting spoiled the aroma of the coffee for connoisseurs, such fumes, wrote one traveler through cattle country, were "loved by the Texan as fondly as his molasses."[3] Even so, the difficulty of roasting coffee beans prompted some cooks to boil the same grounds again and again while claiming that they "flavored" the next day's batch.

Once the beans were roasted, the cook crushed them in a flat-sided, hopper-style coffee grinder that was bolted to the side of the chuck wagon. Attempts to mill coffee beans in fierce plains winds sometimes led to disaster. The cook on one 1889 cattle drive, for instance, lost most of twenty packages to a stiff northerly gale that spread the beans for fifty yards around the chuck wagon. The ground beans that the cook did manage to salvage from the mill were put in tins until needed.

Coffee processed by the Arbuckle Brothers Company, wholesale grocers of Pittsburgh, dominated the coffee market in the American West. In 1865, John Arbuckle began to package

roasted coffee in one-pound bags while it was still warm in order to preserve the freshness. Three years later the company developed a sugar-egg white glaze that preserved the flavor and aroma of roasted coffee beans.

In August of 1873, Arbuckle Brothers introduced their soon-to-be-famous Ariosa brand with its flying angel trademark, and concentrated their sales efforts in the West. Ironically, the company eventually invested some of the revenue from this highly profitable enterprise in two Wyoming ranches. Between 1889 and 1901 a post office at the Arbuckle headquarters ranch was officially listed by the U.S. Postal Service as Ariosa, Wyoming Territory.

Arbuckle coffee came in burlap bags holding one hundred one-pound packages of whole beans. After the turn of the century, the company perfected a method of packaging ground coffee that soon eliminated the venerable coffee grinder from kitchen shelves and chuck boxes.

As part of their marketing strategy, Arbuckles' included a stick of peppermint candy in each package and, beginning in 1893, collector's trading cards featuring animals, countries of the world, U.S. states, and recipes. Two years later they began to offer coupons redeemable for any of dozens of premiums, ranging from lace curtains and wedding rings to Torrey razors and small-caliber revolvers. During the 1890s the company exchanged 108 million coupons annually for some 4 million premiums, including 100,000 wedding rings, 819,000 handkerchiefs, and 186,000 razors. Cowpunchers and range cooks redeemed their share.

Normally the cook appropriated the coveted coupons, or signatures as they were sometimes known, and awarded the candy to the hand who helped grind the beans. For 284 coupons and 18 cents' worth of postage, one Turkey Track Ranch cook acquired a wedding ring, several handkerchiefs, and three pairs of lacy curtains. J. E. Russell, a longtime Matador Ranch cook, was said to have clipped enough coupons during his tenure in a cow camp to acquire almost everything in Arbuckles' substantial premium catalog.

The coupons were so universally recognized that some western merchants began substituting them for change and thieves began stealing them. Coupon theft became so widespread that vigilant western storekeepers often refused coffee shipments that arrived without them and railroads sometimes added special guards to protect them.

In time Arbuckles' flying angel trademark became nearly as ubiquitous in the West as mesquite. Customers converted the company's sturdy Maine fir shipping crates into all sorts of serviceable items, from furniture to chicken coops. The firm's roasting plant, pictured on each coffee bag, inspired the design of many ranch homes. Veteran cowpunchers even referred to neophytes as "Arbuckles," the implication being that the cow boss had purchased their services with coupons.

Reviling weak coffee as "dishwater" or "belly wash," cow cooks generally added a handful of ground coffee to the pot for every cup of water to ensure a strong brew. Such a blend was sometimes called "six-shooter" coffee, that is, strong enough to float a pistol. Others used the buoyancy of a horseshoe as a test of the strength of properly prepared coffee.

Although most cowboys consumed their coffee black, a wagon boss at La Parra Ranch added milk supplied by an obliging Hispanic cook who kept a cow with his wagon. Others wished for something stronger. Frank Smith, an obliging Irish cook who was known to give night herders a drink of whiskey when they returned to the camp, from time to time also laced trail boss Ab Blocker's morning coffee with liquor.

Besides milk and alcohol, other foreign objects sometimes frequented the camp coffeepot—ashes from the campfire, tobacco, even small varmints. To the chagrin of a careless wagon cook, a live "vinegaroon," or scorpion, once emerged from coffee grounds during an 1884 roundup in West Texas. "Biscuit-shooters" on the Pecos River in New Mexico faced a different foe when they attempted to make coffee in the aftermath of a frightful winter in 1886. So many cattle had perished of cold and malnutrition along the river that in some places its banks were littered with carcasses to a height of four feet. Worse, the dead and dying animals attracted swarms of worms, flies, and maggots that saturated the surface water, which had to be strained through a gunny sack before it was used to make coffee.

If coffee beans were in short supply, an acceptable substitute could be concocted from parched maize, wheat, chicory, meal bran, or even the parings of sweet potatoes. Tea, however, was the most common if not popular substitute, especially on British-owned ranches, which stocked it regularly. Oliver Nelson told how the manager of the T5 Ranch in the Indian Territory in the early 1880s attempted to reduce his outfit's excessive and expensive coffee habit by serving the cheaper drink—or so he thought. But when the cook used up a twenty-five-pound box of tea in only four days in an attempt to attain a brew robust enough to satisfy the finicky crew, the boss relented and sent for more coffee.

PART
TWO

Appetizers,

soups, and

salads

Modern cowboy cooking blends past traditions with current tastes into a style that retains a distinct western flavor. Whether interpreting classic cowboy favorites or the avant garde in western cuisine, these recipes from contemporary cooks demonstrate the breadth and vitality of ranch-style cooking at its best.

Hot stuff:

how to wrangle

chile peppers

Not all chile peppers are created equal. A small, innocent-looking chile can be hotter than Hades, and a big fella can be as tame as a calf.

FRESH HOT CHILE PEPPERS, usually the familiar *jalapeño* variety, are now found in most supermarkets. Depending on what ethnic group is most prominent in your neighborhood, you may also find the thinner *serrano,* the long, twisted *cayenne,* or tiny Thai peppers. Every pepper, even of the same variety, has its own heat level. The best way to deal with this problem is to mince the whole pepper (remove the stem, ribs, and seeds) and add to taste. The heat is stored in the chile pepper's ribs and seeds, so if you like hot foods, don't remove them before chopping. If you have sensitive skin, wear rubber gloves. Be careful not to rub your eyes or touch any other mucous membranes for at least a couple of hours after handling the chiles. Rinsing your hands with water and rubbing with salt may help to remove some of the irritating chile oil. You can substitute *canned green chile peppers* for fresh, using about 3 tablespoons of canned for each fresh chile. Check the can's label to see how hot the canned peppers are to avoid surprises; all canned chiles used to be on the mild side, but as the American palate has come to accept spicier foods, hotter varieties are now being processed.

LARGE, MILDLY HOT FRESH CHILE PEPPERS such as *poblanos* and bell peppers, are treated more like vegetables than seasonings. They are best if roasted until their skins are blackened and removed before using. The most efficient way is to broil or grill them, turning occasionally, until the skins are scorched. (This method is particularly handy when you have to peel a whole batch of peppers, as in the Green Chile Stew on page 208.) Take care just to scorch the skin—don't cook until a hole is burned through the flesh. Place the blackened chile into a paper bag and let steam for 10 to 15 minutes. Using a small knife, scrape the skin from the pepper. You may rinse the chile briefly under cold water to help remove stubborn areas. Again, remove the seeds and ribs unless you like incendiary foods.

DRIED CHILE PEPPERS need to be soaked in hot water to soften before using in sauces and stews. Ranch cooks mostly use dried chiles from New Mexico. You will often find them for sale at roadside stands (although they are now available at many supermarkets), usually gathered into decorative ropes called *ristras*. If you buy a *ristra,* be sure that it is for cooking and hasn't been coated with inedible lacquer to discourage critters, rendering it suitable only for interior decoration. Tear the chiles open and *reserve* the seeds. Rinse the chiles under cold water to remove any dust. Soak them in boiling water to cover just until softened, about 20 minutes, depending on the dryness of the peppers. Drain and *reserve* the cooking liquid. Most recipes will direct you to puree the soaked peppers in a blender with a bit of the soaking liquid. Taste the puree, and if you like it hotter, add some of the hot little seeds that you set aside to taste.

Always store chile peppers in the refrigerator. Even dried peppers keep better in the refrigerator, which keeps out the little insects that seem to love to use them as low-maintenance housing.

QUESA-dillas RiCAS

Clyde Nelson,
The Home Ranch, Clark, Colorado

Makes 6 to 8 servings

Here's a good example of the new cowboy cooking, where some grub cooks are sometimes trained chefs who bring a distinctive flair to their kitchens. Clyde Nelson makes these delicious appetizers with ripe Brie cheese (rind removed and thinly sliced), but Monterey Jack is a fine substitute.

1 medium onion, chopped

1 fresh poblano chile pepper, roasted, peeled, seeded, and chopped into ½-inch pieces (page 129)

1 medium red bell pepper, roasted, peeled, seeded, and chopped into ½-inch pieces (page 129)

1 ripe mango, peeled, pitted, and cut into ¼-inch pieces

2 tablespoons chopped fresh cilantro (coriander)

8 ounces barely ripe Brie, rind removed and thinly sliced, or Monterey Jack cheese, coarsely shredded

8 (7-inch round) flour tortillas

2 tablespoons unsalted butter, melted

2 tablespoons vegetable oil

1 Bring a small saucepan of water to a boil over high heat. Add the onion, cover, and remove from the heat. Let stand until the onion is wilted, about 10 minutes. Drain well and transfer to a small bowl. Stir in the chopped chile and bell peppers, mango, and cilantro. Cover and set aside.

2 Place one eighth of the cheese on the bottom half of a tortilla. Top with one eighth of the mango mixture. Fold the top half of the tortilla over to form a half moon and enclose the filling. Use a toothpick to secure the tortilla. Continue the procedure with the remaining ingredients.

3 Make a medium-hot fire in the bottom of a charcoal grill according to the instructions on page 166.

4 In a small bowl, combine the melted butter and oil. Lightly brush both sides of the quesadillas with some of the butter mixture. Grill the quesadillas for 30 seconds. Rotate them 90 degrees and grill for another 30 seconds. Turn over and continue grilling until the cheese begins to melt, about 1 minute. Transfer to a cutting board, remove the toothpicks, and cut each quesadilla into 3 wedges. Serve immediately.

# Chile

CON QUESO

Clyde Nelson,
The Home Ranch, Clark, Colorado

Makes 8 to 12 servings

What to serve with cold beer while watching a Broncos game on television.

2 tablespoons unsalted butter

2 tablespoons all-purpose flour

¾ cup half-and-half, scalded

⅓ cup beer

1 tablespoon vegetable oil

1 small onion, finely chopped

1 fresh hot chile pepper (such as jalapeño), seeded and finely chopped, or
    1 (4-ounce) can chopped green chile peppers, drained

1 clove garlic, minced

1 cup drained canned tomatoes, chopped

½ teaspoon ground cumin

2 cups (8 ounces) shredded sharp Cheddar cheese

2 cups (8 ounces) shredded Monterey Jack cheese

Salt to taste

Hot red pepper sauce to taste

Tortilla chips, for dipping

1 In a medium heavy-bottomed saucepan, melt the butter over medium-low heat. Whisk in the flour and let bubble without browning for about 2 minutes.

2 Whisk in the half-and-half and beer. Bring to a simmer over medium heat. Reduce the heat to low and cook until thickened, about 5 minutes.

3 Meanwhile, in a medium skillet, heat the oil over medium heat. Add the onion, chile pepper, and garlic and cook, stirring often, until the onion is softened, about 3 minutes. Add the tomatoes and cumin and cook until the excess moisture is evaporated, about 3 minutes. Stir the vegetables into the sauce. (This sauce base can be prepared up to 1 day ahead, cooled, covered, and refrigerated. Reheat over low heat.)

4   Gradually stir the cheeses into the sauce. Cook until the cheeses are melted, but do not boil. Season with salt and hot sauce to taste. Transfer to a serving bowl (a small electric slow cooker or a thick ceramic soup bowl works best to hold the heat) and serve warm, with the tortilla chips for dipping.

Spicy Pecan Pinwheels

Betty Price,
Lubbock, Texas

Makes 8 to 12 appetizer servings

Make-ahead appetizers are always popular, and these are doubly welcome because they are so easy to prepare.

1 (8-ounce) package cream cheese, at room temperature

⅓ cup sour cream

½ cup finely chopped pecans

2 tablespoons bottled picante sauce

1 teaspoon finely chopped fresh hot chile pepper (such as jalapeño), or to taste

1 small clove garlic, crushed through a press

4 (8-inch) flour tortillas

1   In a medium bowl, using a hand-held electric mixer at medium speed, beat the cream cheese and sour cream until smooth and combined. Beat in the pecans, picante sauce, chile pepper, and garlic.

2   Spread about 6 tablespoons of the mixture on a tortilla and tightly roll it up. Wrap in plastic wrap. Continue the procedure with the remaining ingredients. Refrigerate the rolls for at least 4 hours or overnight.

3   When ready to serve, remove the plastic wrap from the rolls. Cut into ½-inch-thick slices and serve immediately.

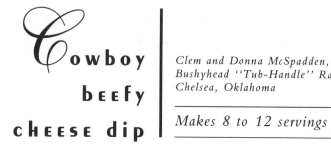

Cowboy beefy cheese dip

Clem and Donna McSpadden,
Bushyhead "Tub-Handle" Ranch,
Chelsea, Oklahoma

Makes 8 to 12 servings

This is a simplified version of *chile con queso* that uses processed cheese spread, sidestepping the need to make a sauce to melt the cheese in. It also gets "beefed up" with the addition of ground round.

8 ounces ground round

1 medium onion, finely chopped

1 fresh hot chile pepper (such as jalapeño), seeded and minced, or
    1 (4-ounce) can chopped green chile peppers, drained

1 clove garlic, minced

1 (15-ounce) can chopped stewed tomatoes, undrained

1 teaspoon dried oregano

1 teaspoon Worcestershire sauce

1 (16-ounce) jar processed cheese spread (such as Cheez Whiz)

Tortilla chips, for dipping

1 In a medium nonstick skillet, cook the ground round, onion, chile pepper, and garlic over medium-high heat, stirring often with a spoon to break up the meat, until the meat has lost its pink color, about 5 minutes. Stir in the tomatoes with their juices, oregano, and Worcestershire sauce and cook until tomato juices are almost completely evaporated, about 5 minutes.

2 Gradually stir in the cheese spread. Reduce the heat to very low and cook, stirring often to blend the flavors, about 20 minutes. Transfer to a serving bowl (a small electric slow cooker or a thick ceramic soup bowl works best to hold the heat) and serve warm, with the tortilla chips for dipping. (The dip can be made up to 1 day ahead, then cooled, covered, and refrigerated. Reheat in the top part of a double boiler over boiling water.)

Ranch dressing

National Cowboy Hall of Fame, Oklahoma City

Makes about 1½ cups

Cowboys were never known for their love of fresh greens. Some clever cookie invented this sensational dressing made with those cowboy favorites, buttermilk and mayonnaise (both used with a heavy hand in modern ranch cooking), and cowboys have been asking for seconds of salad ever since.

¾ cup mayonnaise

¼ cup buttermilk

⅓ cup minced celery with leaves

2 tablespoons chopped fresh parsley

1 tablespoon grated onion (1 small onion)

1 clove garlic, crushed through a press

¼ teaspoon dried thyme

¼ teaspoon celery seed

¼ teaspoon salt

⅛ teaspoon freshly ground pepper

1 In a medium bowl, combine all the ingredients. Cover and refrigerate until ready to use, up to 5 days.

VARIATION: Cucumber Ranch Dressing: Peel a medium cucumber. Cut in half lengthwise and scoop out the seeds with the tip of a spoon. Grate on the large holes of a cheese grater. A handful at a time, squeeze out the excess liquid from the grated cucumber. Stir the grated cucumber into the prepared ranch dressing.

CORN
bread salad

Clem and Donna McSpadden,
Bushyhead "Tub-Handle" Ranch,
Chelsea, Oklahoma

Makes 8 to 10 servings

A good chuck cook never lets anything go to waste, even stale corn bread. Some cooks prefer to serve this salad on a bed of chopped lettuce that has been tossed with a little extra ranch dressing.

4 cups crumbled stale corn bread

2 large ripe tomatoes, seeded and chopped into
    ½-inch pieces

8 scallions, chopped

6 radishes, scrubbed and thinly sliced

1 small green bell pepper, seeded and chopped into ¼-inch pieces

1 cup fresh or thawed frozen corn kernels

½ cup mayonnaise

½ cup Cucumber Ranch Dressing (page 135)

2 teaspoons prepared mustard, preferably Creole or Dijon

¼ teaspoon salt

½ teaspoon freshly ground pepper

1 In a large bowl, combine the corn bread, tomatoes, scallions, radishes, bell pepper, and corn.

2 In a small bowl, combine the mayonnaise, cucumber dressing, mustard, salt, and pepper. Pour over the corn bread mixture and toss well. Cover and refrigerate until chilled, at least 4 hours or overnight. Serve cold.

Layered salad

Christine L. Francis,
Francis Hat Creek Ranch, Lusk, Wyoming

Makes 8 servings

Ranch cooks love this salad. It serves a crowd, can be prepared well ahead of time (making it a must at barbecues and picnics), and tossed together just before serving.

2 cups mayonnaise

1 tablespoon sugar

¼ teaspoon freshly ground pepper

½ head iceberg lettuce (about 12 ounces), chopped into 1-inch pieces

2 celery ribs, chopped into ½-inch pieces

4 hard-boiled eggs, peeled and chopped

1½ cups cooked or thawed frozen peas

1 small red onion, finely chopped

8 slices bacon, cooked crisp and crumbled

1 cup (4 ounces) shredded sharp Cheddar cheese

1 In a small bowl, mix the mayonnaise, sugar, and pepper. In a large glass bowl, arrange the following ingredients in the order given: lettuce, celery, eggs, peas, red onion, and bacon.

2 Spread with the dressing, then sprinkle with the cheese. Cover tightly with plastic wrap and refrigerate until well chilled, at least 4 hours or overnight.

3 When ready to serve, toss well and serve immediately.

Cabbage and pepper slaw

National Cowboy Hall of Fame, Oklahoma City

Makes 8 servings

Coleslaw and barbecued meat go together like Roy Rogers and Dale Evans. A dollop of barbecue sauce adds zest to the dressing.

½ large head green cabbage, cored and shredded (about 10 cups)

1 large red bell pepper, seeded and thinly sliced

1 large green bell pepper, seeded and thinly sliced

2 celery ribs, thinly sliced

6 scallions, thinly sliced

⅓ cup cider vinegar

3 tablespoons prepared barbecue sauce

2 teaspoons sugar

1 clove garlic, crushed through a press

¾ teaspoon salt

¼ teaspoon freshly ground pepper

1¼ cups vegetable oil

1 In a large bowl, toss the cabbage, bell peppers, celery, and scallions.

2 In a small bowl, whisk the vinegar, barbecue sauce, sugar, garlic, salt, and pepper. Gradually whisk in the oil. Pour over the vegetables and toss well. Cover tightly and refrigerate until well chilled, at least 4 hours or overnight.

3 When ready to serve, reseason the slaw with additional salt and pepper. Serve chilled.

GERMAN bacon and potato salad

National Cowboy Hall of Fame, Oklahoma City

Makes 4 to 6 servings

There is quite a large middle European community to be found in the heart of the Texas hill country, where German-American smokehouses produce fine bacon and wursts. Here's a potato salad like one you might find near New Braunfels, Texas.

12 small red-skinned potatoes (about 2 pounds), scrubbed

6 slices bacon, coarsely chopped

1 small red onion, finely chopped

2 teaspoons all-purpose flour

1 cup chicken stock, preferably homemade, or canned low-sodium broth

2 tablespoons red wine vinegar

½ teaspoon salt

¼ teaspoon freshly ground pepper

¼ cup chopped fresh parsley

1 In a large saucepan of boiling salted water, cook the potatoes until barely tender when pierced with the tip of a sharp knife, 20 to 30 minutes. Drain, then rinse briefly under cold water to make them easier to handle. Peel the potatoes if desired, then slice while still warm into a large bowl.

2 Meanwhile, in a medium skillet, cook the bacon over medium heat until crisp, about 5 minutes. With a slotted spoon, transfer to paper towels to drain. Pour off all but 2 tablespoons of fat from the skillet.

3 Add the onion to the skillet and cook over medium heat, stirring often, until softened, about 3 minutes. Sprinkle with flour and stir for 1 minute. Add the stock, vinegar, salt, and pepper. Bring to a simmer and stir constantly until thickened.

4 Pour the hot dressing over the warm potato slices. Add the bacon and parsley and toss gently. Serve warm or at room temperature.

RANCH
MACARONI SALAD
WITH TOMATOES
AND CORN

National Cowboy Hall of Fame, Oklahoma City

Makes 8 servings

This macaroni salad with a creamy buttermilk dressing is perhaps at its best in the summer, when tomatoes and corn are at their peak.

8 ounces elbow macaroni

1½ cups fresh or thawed frozen corn kernels

4 ripe plum tomatoes, seeded and chopped into ½-inch pieces

2 celery ribs, chopped

4 scallions, chopped

1 cup Ranch Dressing (page 135)

¼ teaspoon salt

¼ teaspoon freshly ground pepper

1 In a large pot of boiling salted water, cook the macaroni until just tender, about 6 minutes. Drain well, rinse under cold water until cool, and drain again. Place in a large bowl.

2 Add the corn, tomatoes, celery, and scallions and toss well. Add the dressing, salt, and pepper and mix gently. Cover tightly with plastic wrap and refrigerate until well chilled, at least 2 hours or overnight. Serve chilled.

Avocado and lime salad

Cecil R. Gerloff,
X-G Ranch, Belen, New Mexico

Makes 8 to 10 servings

Green as the mountain plains in springtime, molded salads like this are featured at many cowboy gatherings. Gelatin salad's popularity with cowboys can be explained by its main ingredient, which is, after all, from steers.

1 (20-ounce) can crushed pineapple in juice

1 (3-ounce) package lime gelatin

½ cup boiling water

2 teaspoons lemon juice

¼ teaspoon salt

1 ripe avocado, preferably Hass variety, peeled, pitted, and chopped

½ cup heavy (whipping) cream, chilled

½ cup mayonnaise

1 In a wire sieve set over a bowl, drain the pineapple well, reserving ½ cup of the pineapple juice.

2 In a medium bowl, sprinkle the gelatin over the boiling water and let stand for 2 minutes. Stir until the gelatin is dissolved, about 2 minutes. Stir in the reserved pineapple juice, lemon juice, and salt.

3 Place the bowl in a larger bowl of ice water and let stand, stirring occasionally, until partially set, about 10 minutes. Stir in the pineapple and avocado.

4 In a chilled medium bowl, beat the cream until stiff peaks begin to form. Fold the whipped cream and the mayonnaise into the gelatin mixture.

5 Lightly spray the inside of a 1½-quart mold with vegetable cooking spray. Pour in the gelatin mixture, cover, and refrigerate until the salad is set, at least 4 hours or overnight.

6 Dip the outside of the mold into a large bowl of warm water. Unmold the salad onto a chilled plate and serve cold.

Chuckwagon soup

National Cowboy Hall of Fame, Oklahoma City

Makes 8 servings

Many ranch meals consist of a hearty soup like this one, packed with such cowboy favorites as beans and beef, served with a big hunk of corn bread.

3 tablespoons vegetable oil, plus more as needed

2 pounds beef round, trimmed well and cut into ½-inch pieces

1 large onion, chopped

2 medium carrots, chopped

2 stalks celery, chopped

1 clove garlic, minced

2 tablespoons chili powder

1 tablespoon dried oregano

7 cups beef stock, preferably homemade, or canned low-sodium broth

1 (28-ounce) can tomatoes, drained and chopped

¼ cup chopped fresh parsley

1 (16-ounce) can pinto beans, drained

½ cup (2 ounces) elbow macaroni

1 In a large soup pot, heat 2 tablespoons of the oil over medium-high heat. Working in batches to avoid crowding, cook the beef until browned on all sides, about 6 minutes. Using a slotted spoon, transfer to a plate.

2 Heat the remaining oil in the pot. Add the onion, carrots, celery, and garlic and cook, stirring often, until the onion is softened, about 5 minutes. Add the chili powder and oregano and stir for 1 minute. Add the browned beef, stock, tomatoes, and parsley and bring to a simmer. Reduce the heat to low and simmer, partially covered, to blend the flavors, about 1 hour.

3 Add the beans and macaroni and increase the heat to high. Cook, uncovered, until the macaroni is tender, about 10 minutes. Serve hot.

Chile, TOMATO, AND RICE SOUP

National Cowboy Hall of Fame, Oklahoma City

Makes 8 servings

This is a simple hot soup from the recipe collection of Mexican ranch cooks. Its capacity to warm a cowhand's insides is increased by its use of chile peppers—use more or fewer chiles as you prefer. If you have leftover chicken or turkey, cut it into small pieces and stir it into the soup with the rice.

1 (35-ounce) can peeled tomatoes in juice, drained and chopped

1 large onion, chopped

1 green bell pepper, seeded and chopped

1 fresh hot chile pepper (such as jalapeño), seeded and minced, or to taste

2 cloves garlic, minced

2 tablespoons olive oil

2 quarts chicken stock, preferably homemade, or canned low-sodium broth

1 tablespoon dried marjoram

⅓ cup long-grain rice

¼ cup chopped fresh cilantro (coriander)

1 In a blender or food processor fitted with the metal blade, process the tomatoes, onion, bell pepper, chile pepper, and garlic until smooth. In a large soup pot, heat the oil over medium heat. Add the tomato mixture and cook, stirring often, until thickened, about 5 minutes. Stir in the stock and marjoram and bring to a simmer over high heat. Reduce the heat to low and simmer for about 1 hour.

2 Add the rice, cover, and continue simmering until the rice is tender, 15 to 20 minutes. Stir in the cilantro and serve the soup hot.

Bread

and rolls

Old-time ranch cooks would sleep with their bucket of sourdough in their bedroll so their body warmth would keep the starter from freezing.

Sourdough

cookin'

The tangy flavor of sourdough is one of the most authentic cowboy flavors, right up there with beans and beef. Sourdough is temperamental, so a few words of caution are required.

Back in the old days, in order to make a sourdough starter, all a grub cook had to do was mix some flour and water. Before long, the nutrients in the flour would combine with the natural wild yeasts in the air, ferment, and create a starter strong enough to use as a leavening. Now things are different. Modern processing methods have removed many of the essential sourdough-making ingredients from flour, and chlorinated water inhibits yeast growth. Therefore, use only un-bleached organic flour and spring water to make your starter. Also, wild yeasts have become unpredictable, and the flour and water slurry is as likely to attract some rather undesirable yeasts that cause unpleasant aromas and flavors, as well as the good yeasts that make bread rise. To counteract this problem, use dry active yeast in the starter to guarantee consistent results. Some cooks will quibble that this isn't a true sourdough, but it's better than having to toss out a starter you've nursed for days because it has attracted some malodorous yeasts.

Sourdough doughs are slow to rise. This isn't an especially bad characteristic, as the longer a bread dough rises, the more full-flavored it becomes. If you are in a hurry, you can stir ¼ to ½ teaspoon of dry active yeast into the sourdough (it doesn't have to be thoroughly dissolved). This will give your sourdough a boost and shave some time from the rising periods.

Maintained properly, according to the instructions on page 147, sourdough will literally last forever. Thank the stars for modern refrigeration; on bitter nights, old-time ranch cooks would sleep with their bucket of sourdough in their bedroll so their body warmth would keep the starter from freezing.

Sour-dough STARTER

Garnet and Helen Brooks,
—B (Bar B) Brand, El Reno, Oklahoma

Makes about 2½ cups starter

Be good to your starter by using or replenishing it every 10 days, and it will reward you with baked goods full of tangy sourdough taste. Remember, the older your starter, the heartier the sourdough flavor.

2 cups unbleached flour, preferably organic stone-ground

2 cups water

2½ teaspoons (1 package) active dry yeast

1　In a medium bowl, stir together the flour, water, and yeast until a thin batter forms. Cover tightly with plastic wrap and let stand at room temperature, stirring once a day, for at least 24 hours and up to 48 hours. If the liquid that forms on the top turns pinkish, discard the entire batch of starter and begin again.

2　Rinse a 1-quart jar with boiling water. Stir the starter well and transfer to the jar and cover tightly with the lid. The starter is now ready to use but will improve in flavor if refrigerated for at least 3 days. The older the starter is, the stronger the flavor, and the better the bread. If a brownish liquid rises to the top of the starter, just stir it back in before using. (It's only the alcohol forming as a by-product of the fermentation process.)

3　To use the starter, rinse out a metal measuring cup with warm water (this discourages sticking). Use a level measured amount. Replace the amount of starter used with an equal amount of flour and water in 50-50 proportions. For example, if you use 1 cup of starter, stir ½ cup each of flour and water into the jar of remaining starter. Cover loosely with plastic wrap and let stand at room temperature for 24 hours to ferment. Cover with the lid and refrigerate until ready to use again.

4　If the starter is not used within 10 days, it must be replenished. Discard (or use) 1 cup of the starter. Stir ½ cup each flour and water into the remaining starter, and let stand as above. If you feed your starter faithfully every 2 weeks, it should last indefinitely.

Sour-
dough bread

Richard Bolt,
West Texas ranch cook

Makes 1 (9-by-5-inch) loaf

This recipe for a simple, wholesome white loaf of bread is easily doubled.

½ cup milk

2 tablespoons sugar

2 tablespoons vegetable shortening

1 cup Sourdough Starter (page 147)

1 large egg, beaten, at room temperature

1¼ teaspoons salt

2½ cups (approximately) unbleached flour, preferably bread flour

1 In a small saucepan, heat the milk over medium heat until tiny bubbles appear around the edges, about 3 minutes. Remove from the heat, add the sugar and shortening, and stir until the shortening is melted. Cool until lukewarm (no more than 105°F).

2 Pour into a large bowl. Add the sourdough starter, egg, and salt and mix well. Stir in 1 cup of the flour to make a thick batter. Gradually beat in enough of the flour to make a dough that is too stiff to stir.

3 On a lightly floured work surface, knead the dough, adding more flour as needed to make a supple dough that isn't sticky. Continue kneading until smooth and elastic, 10 to 15 minutes. Form into a ball and place in a large, lightly buttered bowl. Turn once to coat the top of the dough with butter. Cover the bowl with plastic wrap and let rise in a warm place (in a turned-off oven with a pilot light, for example) until doubled in volume, about 3 hours.

4 Punch down the dough and let rise again until almost doubled, about 1½ hours.

5 Lightly butter a 9-by-5-inch loaf pan. Form the dough into a loaf and place, seam side down, into the prepared pan. Cover with plastic wrap and let rise until almost doubled, about 45 minutes.

6 Preheat the oven to 375°F. Using a serrated knife, cut two shallow slashes in the top of the bread. Bake until the top is golden brown and the bottom sounds hollow when tapped with a knuckle (remove the loaf from the pan to test, using pot holders for protection), 30 to 40 minutes. Unmold onto a wire cake rack and cool completely.

N O T E : The bread can also be shaped into a round loaf and placed in a greased 12-inch Dutch oven, allowing the final rise to take place in the Dutch oven. Bake according to the directions on page 203 for 50 minutes to 1 hour. Fan the coals occasionally and protect the fire with a wind guard to ensure even heat. You may also want to ignite some extra coals to have ready if the first coals die out before the bread is done.

# Cowboy's dutch oven delight

Cliff Teinert,
Long X Ranch, Kent, Texas

Makes 1 large loaf, about 12 servings

Sourdough bread dough is rolled into balls that bake up into a loaf of sugar-coated bubbles that are pulled apart to eat. See "The Dutch Oven: A Chuck Cook's Best Pal," on page 202.

> *Double recipe for Sourdough Bread (page 148)*
> *1 cup sugar*
> *1 tablespoon ground cinnamon*
> *¾ cup (1½ sticks) butter, melted*

1 Make the sourdough bread dough through step 4. Tear off pieces about the size of golf balls and roll them between your floured hands to form smooth balls. In a small bowl, combine the sugar and cinnamon. Dip the balls in the melted butter, then roll in the cinnamon sugar. Place each ball in a well-buttered 14-inch Dutch oven. Drizzle any remaining butter on top, and sprinkle with the remaining cinnamon sugar. Cover the Dutch oven with the lid and let the balls rise in a warm place until doubled in volume, about 2½ hours.

2 Build a charcoal fire with 28 briquets and let them burn until they are coated with white ash. Using a garden spade or kitchen tongs (protect your hands with oven mitts), spread about 10 of the coals in a 14-inch circle, pushing the other coals to one side. Do not place any coals in the center of the circle.

3 Place the Dutch oven over the ring of coals. Use the spade to place the remaining 18 coals on the lid. Cook until the bread is golden brown, about 45 minutes. Let stand 10 minutes, then remove from the Dutch oven. Serve warm, pulling off portions of the bread to eat.

# Sourdough orange-spice raisin rolls

Tom Christian,
Figure 3 Ranch, Claude, Texas

Makes 16 rolls

If you want to serve these spicy treats for a late breakfast, make the dough the night before and let it spend its second rising period in the refrigerator. Let the chilled dough stand in a warm place for 1 hour before rolling it out.

Recipe for Sourdough Bread (page 148)
½ *cup sugar*
½ *cup packed light brown sugar*
½ *cup raisins*
1 *teaspoon ground cinnamon*
3 *tablespoons butter, melted*
½ *cup orange juice*

1 Make the sourdough bread dough through step 4.

2 On a lightly floured work surface, roll out the dough to a 12-by-16-inch rectangle. In a medium bowl, combine the sugars, raisins, and cinnamon. Brush the dough with the melted butter, leaving a 1-inch border all around, then spread with the raisin mixture. Starting at a long side, roll up tightly into a cylinder, and pinch the seam to seal. Using a sharp knife, cut crosswise into 16 slices about 1 inch thick.

3 Butter well a 13-by-9-inch baking pan. Arrange the slices in the pan and cover with plastic wrap. Let the rolls rise in a warm place until doubled in volume, about 1 hour.

4 Preheat the oven to 350°F. Pour the orange juice over the rolls. Bake until the rolls are golden brown, 25 to 30 minutes. Invert the rolls onto a serving platter and serve warm.

N O T E : The rolls can also be prepared in a 16-inch Dutch oven and baked for about 25 minutes according to the instructions on page 203.

Sourdough biscuits

Garnet and Helen Brooks,
—B (Bar B) Brand, El Reno, Oklahoma

Makes about 2 dozen biscuits

Here's one of the staples of cowboy cooking, ready to bake for a crowd of hungry folks. Because of their long rising period, you may find it most convenient to bake them for supper rather than breakfast.

5 cups unbleached flour
2 tablespoons sugar
2 teaspoons baking powder
2½ teaspoons salt
¼ cup vegetable shortening or lard
1 cup Sourdough Starter (page 147)
2¼ cups (approximately) milk
1 tablespoon butter, melted

1 In a large bowl, combine the flour, sugar, baking powder, and salt. Using a pastry blender or two forks, cut the shortening into the flour mixture until it resembles coarse crumbs. Make a well in the center and add the starter. Mix, adding enough milk to make a stiff dough.

2 On a lightly floured work surface, knead the dough briefly until smooth and pat out to a ½-inch-thick circle. Using a 2½-inch round biscuit cutter or glass, cut out biscuits. Gather up scraps, knead briefly, and cut out more biscuits.

3 Place the biscuits about 2 inches apart on a baking sheet. Cover with plastic wrap and let rise in a warm place (in a turned-off oven with a pilot light, for example) until almost doubled in volume, about 3½ hours.

4 Preheat the oven to 400°F. Brush the tops of the biscuits with the melted butter. Bake until golden brown, 15 to 20 minutes. Serve hot.

N O T E : The biscuits can also be baked in a greased 14-inch Dutch oven. Use the cooking instructions for Dutch Oven Biscuits on page 153.

Dutch oven biscuits

Stephen Zimmer,
Philmont Scout Ranch, Cimarron, New Mexico

Makes about 16 biscuits

Cowboy cooks first stirred up their biscuit dough with water because milk was not easy to come by, and while the results were edible, they wouldn't win any prizes. When dehydrated milk became available, it was incorporated into the recipe, making much nicer biscuits. Before cooking, read "The Dutch Oven: A Chuck Cook's Best Pal" on page 202.

¼ *cup vegetable shortening*

½ *cup warm water*

2 *cups all-purpose flour*

½ *cup nonfat dry milk*

2 *tablespoons sugar*

1 *tablespoon plus 1 teaspoon baking powder*

½ *teaspoon salt*

1 Build a charcoal fire with 36 briquets, and let them burn until they are covered with ash. Place 12 of the coals in a circle.

2 Place a 12-inch Dutch oven over the circle of coals. Add the shortening to the Dutch oven and heat until melted. Using pot holders, tilt the Dutch oven to lightly coat the interior with the melted shortening. In a heatproof bowl, pour the shortening into the warm water; mix well.

3 In a medium bowl, combine the flour, dry milk, sugar, baking powder, and salt and mix well with a fork to aerate. Stir the liquid into the dry ingredients, just to make a soft dough. Do not overmix.

4 Drop heaping tablespoons of the dough into the Dutch oven. Place the lid on top and use a spade to place the remaining coals on the lid.

5 Cook the biscuits until they are lightly browned, 15 to 20 minutes. Serve hot.

Apricot Nut Bread

Cecil R. Gerloff,
X-G Ranch, Belen, New Mexico

Makes 1 (9-by-5-inch) loaf

Dried apricots have found their way into many a ranch cook's baked goods over the years. This makes a not-too-sweet loaf that can be served in the supper bread basket.

½ cup packed chopped (½-inch) dried apricots

½ cup hot water

2 cups plus 2 teaspoons all-purpose flour

1 tablespoon baking powder

¼ teaspoon baking soda

¼ teaspoon salt

½ cup orange juice

¾ cup corn syrup

½ cup sugar

1 large egg

1 tablespoon vegetable shortening, melted

1 cup coarsely chopped pecans

1 Preheat the oven to 350°F. Lightly butter and flour a 9-by-5-inch loaf pan.

2 In a small bowl, soak the apricots in the hot water for 30 minutes. Drain well, reserving ¼ cup of the soaking liquid. Pat the apricots with paper towels to remove the excess moisture.

3 Sift 2 cups of the flour, the baking powder, baking soda, and salt together onto a piece of waxed paper. In a glass measuring cup, mix the orange juice and reserved soaking liquid.

4 In a medium bowl, whisk the corn syrup, sugar, and egg until well combined. Whisk in the shortening. Alternating in thirds, mix in the flour and orange juice mixtures. Toss the apricots and pecans with the remaining 2 teaspoons flour. Stir into the batter. Transfer to the loaf pan.

5 Bake until a toothpick inserted in the center of the loaf comes out clean, about 1 hour. Cool in the pan for 10 minutes. Unmold onto a wire cake rack and cool completely.

Cinnamon buckwheat bread

Clyde Nelson,
The Home Ranch, Clark, Colorado

Makes 2 (9-by-5-inch) loaves

Few aromas can surpass that of Cinnamon Buckwheat Bread toasting. It's a great way to get cowhands out of bed when it's so early the sun hasn't risen yet!

2½ teaspoons (1 package) active dry yeast

½ cup warm (100° to 110°F) water

5½ cups (approximately) unbleached flour, preferably bread flour

½ cup buckwheat flour

½ cup sugar

2 teaspoons ground cinnamon

2 teaspoons salt

2 cups water

½ cup nonfat dry milk

¼ cup vegetable oil

1 In a small bowl, sprinkle the yeast over the ½ cup warm water and let stand until creamy, about 10 minutes; stir to dissolve.

2 In a large bowl, combine 2 cups of the flour, the buckwheat flour, sugar, cinnamon, and salt. Make a well in the center and add the 2 cups of water, the yeast mixture, dry milk, and oil. Stir to make a thick batter. Gradually beat in enough of the remaining flour to make a dough that is too stiff to stir.

3 On a lightly floured work surface, knead the dough, adding more flour to make a supple dough that isn't sticky. Continue kneading until smooth and elastic, 10 to 15 minutes. Form into a ball and place in a lightly buttered large bowl. Turn once to coat the top of the dough with butter. Cover the bowl with plastic wrap and let rise in a warm place until doubled in volume, about 1½ hours.

4 Lightly butter 2 (9-by-5-inch) loaf pans. Punch down the dough and divide in half. Form each portion of dough into a loaf and place, seam side down, into the loaf pans. Cover with plastic wrap and let rise until almost doubled, about 45 minutes.

(continued)

5 Preheat the oven to 375°F. Bake until the tops are golden brown and the bottoms sound hollow when tapped with a knuckle (remove a loaf from a pan to test, using pot holders for protection), about 30 minutes. Let cool in the pans for 10 minutes. Unmold onto a wire cake rack and cool completely.

OVERNIGHT COFFEE CAKE

Nancy E. Ferguson,
Eatons' Ranch, Wolf, Wyoming

Makes 9 to 12 servings

You'd have to walk a country mile to find a coffee cake with a lighter crumb. The batter can be tossed together the night before serving, refrigerated, and baked in the morning—just the thing to start the day off right.

Cake

 2 cups all-purpose flour

 1 cup granulated sugar

 ½ cup packed light brown sugar

 1 teaspoon baking powder

 1 teaspoon baking soda

 1 teaspoon ground cinnamon

 ½ teaspoon salt

 ⅔ cup vegetable shortening

 1 cup buttermilk

 2 large eggs, beaten

Topping

 ½ cup packed light brown sugar

 ½ cup coarsely chopped pecans or walnuts

 1 teaspoon ground cinnamon

 1 teaspoon ground nutmeg

1 If baking the cake immediately, preheat the oven to 350°F. Lightly butter a 13-by-9-inch baking pan.

2 Make the cake: In a large bowl, combine the flour, sugar, brown sugar, baking powder, baking soda, cinnamon, and salt. Add the shortening. Using a hand-held electric mixer set at low speed, beat until the mixture resembles coarse oatmeal. Add the buttermilk and eggs and mix just until smooth. Do not overbeat. Transfer to the baking pan and smooth evenly. Cover with plastic wrap and refrigerate up to 12 hours. (The cake can also be baked immediately.)

3 Make the topping: In a small bowl, combine the brown sugar, pecans, cinnamon, and nutmeg. Cover and store at room temperature until ready to bake.

4 When ready to bake, sprinkle the top of the cake with the topping. Preheat the oven if necessary. Bake until the cake springs back when gently pressed in the center with a finger, 35 to 45 minutes. Cool on a wire cake rack. The coffee cake can be served warm or at room temperature.

Buttermilk coffee cake

Clyde Nelson,
The Home Ranch, Clark, Colorado

Makes 12 servings

There is always plenty of buttermilk around ranches today, and it should be a staple in your kitchen too, as nothing makes a cake's crumb more tender. If you must, you may substitute 1 cup whole or low-fat milk mixed with 1 teaspoon cider vinegar for every cup of buttermilk, but please try the real McCoy. This cake, guaranteed to disappear from the kitchen table in record time, will easily prove buttermilk's talents.

> 2¼ cups all-purpose flour
>
> 1 cup packed light brown sugar, rubbed through a sieve to remove lumps
>   if necessary
>
> ¾ cup granulated sugar
>
> ¾ cup vegetable oil, preferably corn oil
>
> 2 teaspoons ground cinnamon
>
> ¼ teaspoon ground ginger
>
> ¼ teaspoon salt
>
> 1 cup chopped walnuts
>
> 1 cup buttermilk
>
> 1 large egg, beaten
>
> 1 teaspoon baking powder
>
> 1 teaspoon baking soda, sifted to remove lumps if necessary

1 Preheat the oven to 350°F. Butter and flour a 12-by-8-inch (2½-quart) baking pan, shaking out the excess flour.

2 In a medium bowl, whisk the flour, brown and granulated sugars, oil, 1 teaspoon of the cinnamon, ginger, and salt until smooth. Transfer ¾ cup of the mixture to a small bowl. Add the walnuts to the small bowl and mix until well combined. Set the nut mixture aside to be used later as the topping.

3 Add the buttermilk, remaining 1 teaspoon cinnamon, egg, baking powder, and baking soda to the remaining batter in the large bowl and whisk just until smooth. Transfer to the baking pan. Sprinkle the nut mixture evenly over the top.

4 Bake until the topping is browned and a toothpick inserted in the center of the pan comes out clean, about 30 minutes. Cool the cake in the pan for at least 20 minutes. Serve the cake warm or at room temperature.

Mom's cloverleaf rolls

Nell Shaw,
Stonewall, Oklahoma

Makes 20 rolls

For a Sunday supper, you might brush the tops of these rolls with a little melted butter, then sprinkle with sesame or poppy seeds.

2½ teaspoons (1 package) active dry yeast

2 cups warm (100° to 110°F) water

⅓ cup vegetable oil

⅓ cup sugar

2 teaspoons salt

4½ cups (approximately) unbleached flour, preferably bread flour

1 In a small bowl, sprinkle the yeast over the water and let stand until creamy, about 10 minutes; stir to dissolve.

2 In a large bowl, mix the yeast mixture, oil, sugar, and salt. Gradually stir in enough of the flour to make a soft dough. Knead the dough in the bowl until smooth, about 5 minutes.

3 Form the dough into a ball and place in a lightly buttered large bowl. Turn once to coat the top of the dough with butter. Cover the bowl with plastic wrap and let rise in a warm place (in a turned-off oven with a pilot light, for example) until doubled in volume, about 1½ hours.

4 Lightly butter 20 (1¾-inch-diameter) muffin tins. Divide the dough into 4 equal portions. Divide each portion into 5 equal portions. Divide these into 3 portions each, and form these into balls about the size of walnuts. Place 3 balls of dough in each of the prepared muffin tins. Cover with plastic wrap and let rise in a warm place until almost doubled, about 40 minutes.

5 Preheat the oven to 400°F. Bake until the rolls are golden brown, 12 to 15 minutes. Cool slightly, then remove from the muffin tins and serve warm.

BUTTER-milk Rolls

Clyde Nelson,
The Home Ranch, Clark, Colorado

Makes 1 dozen rolls

Cowboys love biscuits, but rolls come in a very close second.

2½ teaspoons (1 package) active dry yeast

2 tablespoons warm (100° to 110°F) water

1 cup warm (100° to 110°F) buttermilk

¼ cup (½ stick) butter, softened

1 large egg, beaten

2 tablespoons sugar

1 teaspoon salt

½ teaspoon baking soda

3 cups (approximately) unbleached flour, preferably bread flour

1 tablespoon milk, for glaze

1 In a small bowl, sprinkle the yeast over the water and let stand until creamy, about 10 minutes; stir to dissolve.

2 In a large bowl, mix the yeast mixture, buttermilk, butter, egg, sugar, salt, and baking soda. Add 1 cup of the flour and beat to form a batter. Gradually beat in enough of the remaining flour to form a dough that is too stiff to stir.

3 On a lightly floured work surface, knead the dough, adding flour as needed to make a supple dough that isn't sticky. Continue kneading until smooth and elastic, 10 to 15 minutes. Form into a ball and place in a lightly buttered large bowl. Turn once to coat the top of the dough with butter. Cover the bowl with plastic wrap and let rise in a warm place (in a turned-off oven with a pilot light, for example) until doubled in volume, about 1½ hours.

4 Lightly butter a 10-inch round springform pan. Punch down the dough. Knead briefly on a lightly floured work surface. Divide the dough into 12 equal portions. Form each into a ball and place in the prepared pan. Cover with plastic wrap and let rise until almost doubled, about 45 minutes.

5 Preheat the oven to 350°F. Lightly brush the tops of the rolls with the milk. Bake until the rolls are golden brown, about 15 to 20 minutes. Cool slightly, then remove the sides of the springform pan. Pull the rolls apart to serve.

Cheesy chile corn bread

Clyde Nelson,
The Home Ranch, Clark, Colorado

Makes 9 to 12 servings

Cheese and chiles are great additions to corn bread. If you have access to blue cornmeal, you can use it to make this bread, but you may have to use a bit more buttermilk to get the right batter thickness because blue cornmeal has a slightly stronger absorption rate than the yellow variety.

2 cups yellow cornmeal

2 cups all-purpose flour

⅓ cup sugar

2 tablespoons baking powder

½ teaspoon salt

3 cups buttermilk

4 large eggs, beaten

6 tablespoons (¾ stick) butter, melted

2 cups (8 ounces) shredded sharp Cheddar cheese

1 fresh hot chile pepper (such as jalapeño), seeded and minced, or more to taste

1 Preheat the oven to 350°F. Butter a 13-by-9-inch baking pan.

2 In a large bowl, combine the cornmeal, flour, sugar, baking powder, and salt. Make a well in the center and pour in the buttermilk, eggs, and melted butter. Stir just until combined; do not overmix. Stir in the cheese and chile pepper. Spread evenly in the baking pan.

3 Bake until a toothpick inserted in the center of the bread comes out clean, 30 to 35 minutes. Serve warm or at room temperature.

Corn and corn bread

Horace Hatfield,
Rainy Valley Ranch, Baird, Texas

Makes 6 to 8 servings

Moist and cakey, this corn bread is equally tasty served hot out of the oven or cooled to room temperature. It's irresistible spread with butter and honey.

1 cup yellow cornmeal

1 cup all-purpose flour

1 tablespoon baking powder

1 tablespoon sugar

½ teaspoon salt

1 (8½-ounce) can cream-style corn

1 cup milk

¼ cup vegetable oil

2 large eggs, beaten

1 Preheat the oven to 350°F. Butter a 10-inch round baking pan.

2 In a medium bowl, combine the cornmeal, flour, baking powder, sugar, and salt. Make a well in the center and pour in the cream-style corn, milk, oil, and eggs. Stir just until combined; do not overmix. Transfer to the baking pan.

3 Bake until a toothpick inserted in the center comes out clean, 25 to 30 minutes. Serve warm or at room temperature, cut into wedges.

Berry

OATMEAL

PANCAKES

Makes 9 pancakes

Flapjacks, hotcakes, pancakes—no matter what you call them, they disappear at ranch breakfasts. Oats and berries lift this version out of the ordinary.

1½ cups old-fashioned rolled oats

1½ cups buttermilk

3 large eggs, at room temperature

¼ cup (½ stick) butter, melted

½ cup all-purpose flour

2 tablespoons light brown sugar

¾ teaspoon baking powder

½ teaspoon baking soda

¼ teaspoon ground cinnamon

⅛ teaspoon ground nutmeg

⅛ teaspoon salt

1 pint fresh sliced blackberries (or whole blueberries or raspberries)

Honey or maple syrup, for serving

1 In a medium bowl, combine the oats and buttermilk and let stand for 10 minutes.

2 In a large bowl, whisk the eggs and melted butter. Beat in the oatmeal mixture. Add the flour, brown sugar, baking powder, baking soda, cinnamon, nutmeg, and salt and whisk just until combined; do not overmix.

3 Heat a lightly greased griddle until a sprinkle of water turns into tiny bouncing droplets upon contact. Preheat the oven to 200°F.

4 Using about ⅓ cup of batter for each pancake, pour the batter onto the griddle. Arrange a few berries on top of each pancake. Cook until the edges are firm and the underside is golden brown, about 2 minutes. Turn carefully and continue cooking to brown the other side. Transfer the pancakes to a baking sheet and place in the oven to keep warm while making the remaining pancakes.

5 Serve the pancakes hot with honey or maple syrup.

Beef, pork, and game

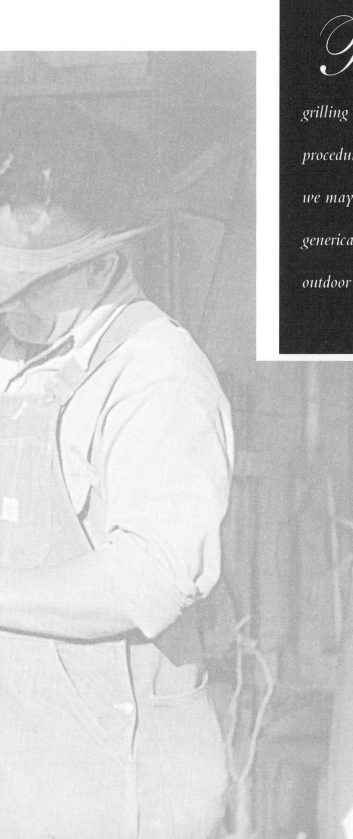

Barbecuing and grilling are two different procedures, even though we may use barbecuing generically to refer to any outdoor grilling.

Cooking in

wide open

spaces

The term *barbecue* comes from the Spanish *barbacoa,* a method of pit cooking that was very popular in colonial Mexico. As Texas was once Mexican territory, barbecuing became the state's preferred method of cooking meats. Used correctly, the term refers to *slowly* cooked meats prepared over smoldering wood coals that smoke the food as it is heated. Cowboys like to barbecue large cuts of beef such as brisket and prime rib. (Out West, beef is considered the meat of choice for barbecuing. This opposes the South's contention that pork is the king of the pit. Another argument occurs over what wood to use, with cowboys choosing mesquite and Southerners preferring hickory. Both of these choices are cultural, as beef and mesquite were more plentiful and much cheaper in the West than pork and hickory.) Rather than give instructions on how to barbecue a whole steer, we are giving more practical instructions on how to coax truly fine barbecue out of a kettle charcoal grill using supermarket cuts of meat.

Grilling is actually the *quick* cooking of meats directly over an open flame. As the food cooks, its fat can render out and drip onto the coals, causing flareups. For this reason, trim meat well and use as little oil as possible in any marinades. Grilling works best on relatively small, thin portions of meat such as steaks, burgers, fish fillets, and chicken.

Building a fire can be the hardest part of the whole job. A charcoal chimney (a vented metal cannister available at most hardware stores) is a very efficient tool, as it starts a fire in a very short time with only crumpled newspaper and a match. Electric starters are a nuisance because you must have an electric outlet nearby. Try to avoid self-starting briquets and lighting fluid, which can give an unpleasant flavor to your foods.

How many coals should you use? Before lighting them, spread a single layer of coals in the bottom of the grill to get an idea—there should be around 5 pounds, or one fourth of a 20-pound bag. If you are barbecuing and you are to bank coals on only one side of the grill, you will need only 2 pounds or so to start. If you are using natural charcoal, be warned that it starts quicker and burns faster and hotter than briquets. As far as briquets are concerned, you get what you pay for. Some inexpensive briquets are mostly petroleum-based fillers that can give off black, sticky smoke, so buy a reputable brand.

Start your fire at least 30 minutes before placing the food on the grill. Be sure that the coals have burned until they are evenly covered with white ash. Let the coals burn down to the proper temperature for the food you are preparing. For example, beefsteaks and burgers can be cooked over high heat, but fish steaks cook best over moderately hot coals. Hold your hand over the flame and start counting. If you can count only to 1 or 2 before the heat becomes unpleasant, the fire is hot. If you reach 3 or 4, it is moderate, and above 5, cool. You can control the heat of the coals by using the vents found on the best charcoal grills. Opening the vents allows more oxygen to surround the coals, so they burn hotter. Closed vents cut off the oxygen, so the coals burn cooler.

If you are barbecuing a large cut of meat that takes hours, you will need to add more hot coals every 45 minutes or so to maintain the temperature as the coals burn down. Use a small, inexpensive hibachi or even a charcoal chimney placed on a concrete surface to ignite these auxiliary coals. A garden spade works well to transfer the hot coals to the working grill.

You can get passable barbecue from a gas grill, getting the smoky flavor from wood chips in a special foil container prepared for gas grills. If your hardware store doesn't carry these gas grill chips, you can prepare your own. Soak wood chips in water to cover for at least 30 minutes, then drain. Wrap the chips in heavy-duty aluminum foil. Poke holes all over the foil. Place the foil directly on the heating unit or lava rocks of the gas grill. The chips will heat through the foil and smoke away.

Buy a stiff wire brush at the hardware store to clean your grill after every use. (That burned-on crud doesn't add flavor to the foods, only germs.) Also oil the grill lightly with a paper towel dipped in oil (or use a long-handled grilling brush). This will keep the food from sticking during cooking.

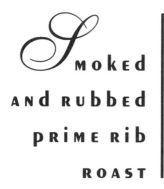

Smoked and Rubbed Prime Rib Roast

National Cowboy Hall of Fame, Oklahoma City

Makes 8 to 10 servings

This is a rip-roarin' way to cook beef, with a smoky, spicy flavor that will have everyone hollering for more.

Cookie's Dry Rub

   2 tablespoons sweet Hungarian paprika

   1 tablespoon garlic salt

   1 teaspoon freshly ground pepper

   1 teaspoon dried oregano

   1 teaspoon ground cumin

   ½ teaspoon onion powder

   ¼ teaspoon ground hot red (cayenne) pepper

   1 (6-pound) boneless rib roast

   3 cups mesquite chips, soaked in water for at least 30 minutes and drained

1   Make the dry rub: In a small bowl, combine all the ingredients. Makes about ¼ cup.

2   Using a sharp knife, cut off the fat "cap" from the roast in one piece. Cut just where the fat is attached to the meat, trimming off as little meat as possible. Reserve the fat cap. Rub the roast all over with 2 tablespoons of the dry rub (reserve the remaining dry rub for another use). Replace the fat cap and tie it back onto the roast with kitchen twine. (The roast can be prepared up to 6 hours ahead, covered, and refrigerated.)

3   Place a heatproof pan, approximately the same length and width as the roast (disposable aluminum foil pans work well), on one side of the bottom of a charcoal grill. Fill the pan with 1 inch of water. Bank charcoal on the empty side and make a hot fire according to the instructions on page 167.

4 Place the roast, fat side up, on a lightly oiled grill over the pan. Sprinkle the coals with a handful of drained mesquite chips and cover the grill immediately. Cook until a meat thermometer inserted in the thickest part of the roast reads 125°F for medium-rare meat, 2 to 2½ hours, allowing approximately 20 minutes per pound. (Allow about 25 minutes for medium meat, and about 30 minutes for well-done.) About every 45 minutes, add more hot coals and wood chips as needed to maintain an even grill temperature.

5 Let the roast stand for 10 minutes before removing the string and fat. Carve and serve immediately.

N O T E : To make the roast in a gas grill, place a disposable aluminum foil pan on one side of the grill and fill the pan with ½ inch of water. Turn the opposite side of the grill on and heat to medium. (Do not ignite the side of the grill with the pan.) Wrap handfuls of the soaked chips in heavy-duty aluminum foil and pierce the foil all over. Place the roast over the pan and place a foil packet of chips directly onto the heating unit or lava rocks. Cook the roast until a meat thermometer reads 125°F for medium-rare meat, 2 to 2½ hours, allowing about 20 minutes per pound. About every 30 minutes, replace the foil packet with a fresh one to maintain a smoky interior.

Grilled beef tenderloin

Clyde Nelson,
The Home Ranch, Clark, Colorado

Makes 8 to 10 servings

Beef tenderloin is a very pricey cut of beef, so save this for when you get your income tax refund or have struck oil or some similar time when you're feeling flush.

Clyde's Herb Rub

2 tablespoons chopped fresh parsley, squeezed dry in a towel

1½ teaspoons coarse (kosher) salt

1½ teaspoons coarsely ground black pepper

3 cloves garlic, crushed through a press

1 teaspoon sweet Hungarian paprika

2 bay leaves, pulverized in a spice grinder

½ teaspoon dry mustard

¼ teaspoon ground hot red (cayenne) pepper

1 (4-pound) trimmed beef tenderloin

Clyde's Moppin' Sauce

1 cup beef stock, preferably homemade, or canned low-sodium broth

¼ cup dry red wine

¼ cup Worcestershire sauce

3 tablespoons prepared barbecue sauce

2 tablespoons vegetable oil

1 fresh hot chile pepper (such as jalapeño), minced, seeds removed if desired
   for a milder sauce

2 garlic cloves, crushed

Chuckwagon Tomato Sauce, optional (see page 269)

1 Make the dry rub: In a small bowl, combine all the ingredients. Rub the tenderloin with the dry rub. Tie the tenderloin crosswise and lengthwise with kitchen twine. (The roast can be prepared up to 6 hours ahead, covered and refrigerated.)

2 Make the BBQ moppin' sauce: In a medium bowl, combine all the ingredients. (The sauce can be prepared up to 1 day ahead, covered, and refrigerated.)

3 Place a 13-by-9-inch disposable aluminum foil pan on one side of the bottom of a charcoal grill. Pour 1 inch of water into the pan. Bank charcoal briquets on the empty side of the grill, and make a hot charcoal fire according to the instructions on page 167.

4 Cook the tenderloin on a lightly oiled grill over the coals, turning and brushing with the moppin' sauce about every 5 minutes, until all sides are seared, about 15 minutes total. (Sear each section of the tenderloin before brushing with the sauce—moisture inhibits searing.) Move the tenderloin over the pan and brush well with the sauce. Cover the grill and cook until a meat thermometer reads 125°F for medium-rare meat, about 20 more minutes. (Check the meat's temperature frequently to avoid overcooking.)

5 Let the tenderloin stand for 10 minutes before removing the kitchen twine. Carve crosswise into ½-inch-thick slices and serve with the tomato sauce, if desired.

Beer-basted barbecued brisket

Makes 8 to 10 servings

Order a whole beef brisket from your butcher, still surrounded by its thick layer of fat. Supply yourself with a few long-neck beers, and get ready to make one of the finest meals on the planet.

1 (9-pound) untrimmed whole beef brisket
Cookie's Dry Rub (page 168), substituting 1 teaspoon garlic powder for
    the garlic salt

Beer Moppin' Sauce
    ¼ cup vegetable oil
    1 medium onion, finely chopped
    2 cloves garlic, minced
    1 (12-ounce) bottle beer
    ⅓ cup honey
    ⅓ cup cider vinegar
    2 tablespoons Worcestershire sauce
    2 tablespoons prepared brown mustard

4 cups mesquite chips, soaked in water for at least 30 minutes and drained
Cowboy Barbecue Sauce (page 267)
Salt to taste

1   Cut the brisket in half crosswise. Rub all over with the dry rub. Wrap in plastic wrap and refrigerate for at least 1 hour or overnight. If chilled, let the brisket come to room temperature before smoking.

2   Make the beer moppin' sauce: In a medium saucepan, heat the oil over medium heat. Add the onion and garlic and cook until the onion is softened, about 4 minutes. Stir in the beer, honey, vinegar, Worcestershire sauce, and mustard. Bring to a simmer, reduce the heat to low, and simmer for 10 minutes.

3 Build a medium fire (using about 20 briquets) on the bottom of one side of a charcoal grill. Place a large disposable aluminum foil pan on the other side. Fill the pan with 1 inch of water.

4 Place the brisket over the pan and immediately cover the grill. Sprinkle a handful of mesquite chips over the coals. Smoke the brisket until very tender, about 6 to 7 hours. About every 40 minutes, baste well with the beer sauce, and add more hot coals and chips to maintain a temperature of 190° to 220°F. (Some grills have thermostats on their lids. You may also place an oven thermometer next to the brisket to get a reading.)

5 Let the brisket stand 10 minutes, then carve the beef thinly across the grain. Serve with the barbecue sauce passed on the side. Allow guests to salt their own portions. (Many barbecue experts feel that salting brisket before smoking releases too many juices.)

N O T E : Brisket can be smoked in a gas grill, but be sure the grate is large enough to hold both brisket halves. With smaller grills, you will have to smoke one brisket half at a time. Place a disposable aluminum foil pan on one side of the grill and fill the pan with 1 inch of water. Turn the opposite side of the grill on and heat to low. (Do not ignite the side of the grill with the pan.) Wrap handfuls of the soaked and drained mesquite chips in heavy-duty aluminum foil and pierce the foil all over. Place the brisket over the pan and place a foil packet of chips directly onto the heating unit or lava rocks. Smoke the brisket until very tender, about 7 hours. Every 40 minutes, baste well with the beer sauce and replace the foil packet with a fresh one to maintain a smoky interior.

T-bone steaks with perini's steak rub

Tom Perini,
Perini's Steak House, Buffalo Gap, Texas

Makes 6 servings

Every steak house has its secret ingredient, and we are lucky indeed to have Perini's Steak House share theirs: a heady mix of herbs and spices rubbed onto the meat before it is grilled over mesquite coals. Basting the steaks with melted butter helps create the crisp, blackened crust Perini's customers prefer. If you like your steak less blackened, sear the steaks for only 2 minutes on each side. Move the steaks to the cooler edges of the grill, cover, and continue cooking until done to your liking. Be sure to use mesquite-scented briquets or mesquite charcoal to give these steaks authentic Texas flavor.

1 tablespoon coarsely ground pepper

2 teaspoons all-purpose flour

2 teaspoons salt

1 teaspoon garlic powder

1 teaspoon onion powder

1 teaspoon sweet Hungarian paprika

1 teaspoon granulated beef stock base or 1 beef bouillon cube, crushed well

½ teaspoon dried oregano

½ teaspoon lemon pepper

6 (14-ounce) T-bone steaks, about 1 inch thick

¼ cup (½ stick) unsalted butter, melted

1 Make the steak rub: In a small bowl, combine all the ingredients except the steaks and butter. Rub the mixture all over the steaks. Let stand at room temperature while building the fire.

2 Build a hot charcoal fire according to the instructions on page 167.

3 Cook the steaks on a lightly oiled grill, basting occasionally with the melted butter, until the undersides are well browned, about 4 minutes. Turn and continue cooking and basting for about 4 more minutes for rare meat. (One way to tell the doneness of steak is to press it—the softer the steak feels, the rarer it is. Medium steak will give slightly, and well-done meat is firm.)

N O T E : The steaks can be cooked over high heat on a gas grill.

Sourdough chicken-fried steak with cream gravy

Robert L. ''Buck'' Reams,
Fort Worth, Texas

Makes 4 to 6 servings

Dusted with dry rub, dipped in sourdough starter, and fried until golden brown, this is chicken-fried steak for the gods. Ask your butcher to run the steaks through the tenderizing (or "Swissing") machine that is used on cube steaks. Round steak is delicious but tougher than an old pair of boots. One more hint—properly pounded chicken-fried steak is too big for frying more than one steak at a time in a big skillet. If you have two large skillets, you can fry two at once, but don't crowd two big steaks in one pan.

*2 pounds round steaks, about ½ inch thick, cut into 4
    portions and tenderized by the butcher*

1 cup Sourdough Starter (page 147)

1 cup plus 2 tablespoons all-purpose flour

1 tablespoon Cookie's Dry Rub (page 168)

½ cup lard, bacon grease, or vegetable oil

1½ cups milk

¼ teaspoon salt

¼ teaspoon hot red pepper sauce

1 Using a meat pounder, pound the round steaks to a ¼-inch thickness. This could take some time, so take a sip of your favorite beverage to fortify yourself.

2 Place the sourdough starter in a medium bowl. Place 1 cup of the flour on a plate. Season both sides of the steak with the dry rub. Dip a steak in the starter and then coat with the flour, shaking off the excess.

3 Preheat the oven to 200°F. In a large skillet, heat the lard over medium-high heat. Add the steak and cook, turning occasionally, until golden brown on both sides, about 10 minutes. Transfer to paper towels to drain briefly. Then place on a baking sheet and keep warm in the oven while repeating the procedure with the remaining steak.

4 Pour off all but 2 tablespoons of the fat in the skillet. Reduce the heat to low and whisk in the remaining 2 tablespoons flour. Let bubble without browning for 2 minutes. Whisk in the milk, bring to a simmer, and cook until slightly thickened, about 2 minutes. Stir in the salt and red pepper sauce.

5 Serve the steaks immediately with the cream gravy.

Cecil's smothered steak

Cecil R. Gerloff,
X-G Ranch, Belen, New Mexico

Makes 4 servings

This cowboy version of Swiss steak makes plenty of sauce for spooning over mashed potatoes or noodles.

8 slices bacon

2 pounds round steak, about 1 inch thick, cut into 4 pieces

1 large onion, cut into ½-inch-thick half moons

1 small green bell pepper, cut into ½-inch-wide strips

1 fresh hot green chile pepper (such as jalapeño), seeded and minced (optional)

1 (8-ounce) can tomato sauce

½ cup water

½ teaspoon salt

½ teaspoon freshly ground pepper

1 In a large skillet, cook the bacon over medium heat, turning once, until crisp, about 5 minutes. Transfer with tongs to paper towels to drain, leaving the fat in the skillet. Crumble the bacon and set aside.

2 In the same skillet, in 2 batches, cook the steaks over medium–high heat, turning once, until browned on both sides, about 6 minutes. Transfer to a plate and set aside.

3 Pour out all but 2 tablespoons of the fat from the skillet. Add the onion and bell and chile peppers. Reduce the heat to medium and cook, stirring occasionally, until softened, about 5 minutes. Stir in the tomato sauce and water and bring to a simmer, scraping up the browned bits on the bottom of the skillet with a wooden spoon. Return the steaks to the skillet and reduce the heat to low. Cover and simmer, turning the meat occasionally, until very tender, about 1½ hours. During the last 10 minutes of cooking, add the bacon.

4 Skim any fat from the surface of the sauce. Season the sauce with salt and pepper, and serve immediately.

Garlic-stuffed pot roast

Robert L. ''Buck'' Reams,
Fort Worth, Texas

Makes 8 to 10 servings

Don't be alarmed at the amount of garlic in this pot roast. Long cooking makes it more docile, although you will know it's there. For something so easy, this sure is good.

2 tablespoons finely chopped garlic

1 teaspoon ground hot red (cayenne) pepper

1 teaspoon salt

1 (4-pound) boneless bottom round roast

3 tablespoons vegetable oil

3 cups beef stock, preferably homemade, or canned low-sodium stock

1 In a small bowl, combine the garlic, red pepper, and salt. Using the tip of a sharp knife, cut 1-inch-wide pockets, about 2 inches deep, all over the surface of the meat. Stuff the pockets with the garlic mixture. Scrape away any of the garlic mixture on the outside of the roast, or it will burn during browning.

2 In a large flameproof casserole, heat the oil over medium–high heat. Add the roast and cook, turning often, until browned on all sides, about 10 minutes. Transfer the roast to a plate.

3 Pour off the excess fat. Add the stock to the casserole and bring to a boil over high heat, scraping up the browned bits on the bottom of the casserole with a wooden spoon. Return the roast to the casserole and reduce the heat to low. Cover and simmer, turning the roast occasionally, until tender, about 2 hours.

4 Let stand for 10 minutes before carving. Serve the roast with the juices poured over.

N O T E : The roast can also be prepared outside in a 12-inch Dutch oven, according to the directions on page 203.

 **aked**

short ribs

Hearst Ranches, San Simeon, California

Makes 6 servings

Short ribs take their sweet time to simmer until tender, but the wait is worth it.

5 pounds beef short ribs, cut by the butcher into 3-inch lengths

¾ teaspoon salt

¼ teaspoon freshly ground pepper

½ cup all-purpose flour

2 tablespoons vegetable oil, plus more as needed

2 small onions, sliced

¾ cup ketchup

¾ cup water

¼ cup sugar

¼ cup Japanese soy sauce

3 tablespoons Worcestershire sauce

2 tablespoons cider vinegar

⅛ teaspoon ground hot red (cayenne) pepper

1   Preheat the oven to 325°F. Season the short ribs with salt and pepper. Coat the short ribs with the flour, shaking off the excess.

2   In a large skillet, heat the oil over medium-high heat. Working in batches and using additional oil as needed, add the short ribs and cook, turning occasionally, until browned on all sides, about 8 minutes. Place the short ribs and onions in a deep casserole.

3   In a medium bowl, stir the ketchup, water, sugar, soy sauce, Worcestershire sauce, vinegar, and ground hot pepper until combined. Pour over the short ribs.

4   Cover and bake until the short ribs are very tender, about 2½ hours. Transfer the short ribs to a deep serving platter. Skim any fat off the surface of the sauce, pour the sauce over the short ribs, and serve immediately.

N O T E :   The short ribs can be prepared outside in a 14-inch Dutch oven according to the directions on page 203. It is not necessary to brown the floured short ribs if it is not convenient. Stir occasionally to avoid scorching. You may also use 4 pounds pork spareribs, cut apart into individual ribs, cooking for 1½ to 2 hours.

Home-
made beef
jerky

M. K. Borchard,
Borchard Feedyard, Brawley, California

Makes about 1 pound

Making your own jerky may seem like a lot of fiddlin' around, but the actual working time is short; most of the time is spent sitting around waiting for the beef to dehydrate. And you'll end up with excellent preservative- and chemical-free jerky, a very decent reward.

2 pounds trimmed flank steak (lean venison or elk flank can also be used)

½ cup Worcestershire sauce

¼ cup soy sauce

2 tablespoons liquid smoke flavoring

1½ teaspoons seasoned salt

1½ teaspoons onion salt

½ teaspoon garlic powder

½ teaspoon freshly ground pepper

Nonstick vegetable cooking spray

1 Freeze the flank steak until partially frozen, about 1 hour. Using a sharp knife, cut diagonally across the grain into ¼-inch-thick strips. (For chewier jerky, cut with the grain, but this is only recommended for card-carrying cowboys.)

2 In a large plastic bag (preferably the self-sealing kind), mix the remaining ingredients except the cooking spray. Add the sliced beef and mix well. Seal the bag and refrigerate for at least 8 hours or up to 24 hours, turning the bag occasionally so the beef strips are evenly marinated.

3 Remove an oven rack from the oven and lightly spray the rack with nonstick vegetable spray. Remove the strips from the marinade, shaking off excess marinade. Pat the strips dry with paper towels. Arrange the strips, close together but not touching, on the rack. Line the bottom of the oven with aluminum foil (to catch drips).

4 Preheat the oven to 150°F. Place the oven rack with the jerky in the oven. Bake until a cool piece of jerky (remove from the oven and let cool 5 minutes) breaks when bent, about 5 hours. Blot any surface fat with paper towels. Cool completely. Store in an airtight container for up to 1 month at cool room temperature, 3 months in the refrigerator, or 6 months in the freezer.

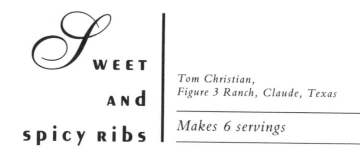

Sweet and spicy ribs

Tom Christian,
Figure 3 Ranch, Claude, Texas

Makes 6 servings

These ribs prove that cooking doesn't have to be complicated to be good. If you wish, brush the ribs with your favorite barbecue sauce during the last 15 minutes of cooking.

⅓ cup chili powder
⅓ cup packed brown sugar
1 teaspoon salt
5 pounds pork spareribs, cut into 3 or 4 slabs
1 cup mesquite chips, soaked in water for at least 30 minutes and drained

1 In a small bowl, combine the chili powder, brown sugar, and salt. Rub the ribs all over with the mixture and wrap each slab in a double thickness of aluminum foil. Let stand at room temperature for 1 hour or refrigerate for up to 1 day.

2 Make a medium-hot fire according to the instructions on page 167.

3 Place the foil packets on a lightly oiled grill. Cover and cook, turning often with kitchen tongs (don't pierce the foil), until the ribs are just tender, about 1 hour. Carefully unwrap the ribs, discarding the liquid in the foil. Add more hot coals to the grill and sprinkle with the mesquite chips. Cover the grill and cook the ribs, turning often, until they are browned, about 10 minutes. Cut the ribs between the bones and serve immediately.

N O T E : To cook the ribs on a gas grill, preheat the grill, then turn to low. Cook the ribs in foil for 1 hour, then unwrap. Wrap the soaked chips in heavy-duty aluminum foil and pierce the foil all over. Place the packet directly onto the heating unit or lava rocks. Cover and cook the ribs until tender, about 15 additional minutes.

FAR EAST smoked pork chops

Clyde Nelson,
The Home Ranch, Clark, Colorado

Makes 8 servings

Rubbing meats with a combination of spices and herbs is a time-honored cowboy cooking secret. This one is more exotic than most, and a great match for pork chops. Clyde always serves these with his Peach and Citrus Chutney.

Far Eastern Rub

- 1 tablespoon dry mustard
- 1½ teaspoons ground cumin
- 1½ teaspoons Madras-style curry powder
- 1½ teaspoons sweet Hungarian paprika
- ¾ teaspoon salt
- ¼ teaspoon ground hot red (cayenne) pepper
- ⅛ teaspoon ground allspice
- ⅛ teaspoon ground cloves

- 8 center-cut pork chops, ¾ inch thick
- 2 cups wood chips, preferably applewood, soaked in water for at least 30 minutes and drained

Peach and Citrus Chutney (page 273)

1 Make the dry rub: In a small bowl, combine all the ingredients. Rub all over the pork chops. Cover and refrigerate for at least 30 minutes or up to 2 hours.

2 Make a charcoal fire according to the instructions on page 167.

3 Toss half of the chips on the coals. Place the chops on a lightly oiled grill and cover immediately. Cook, turning once, until seared on both sides, about 6 minutes. Move the pork chops to the cooler edges of the grill and add the remaining chips to the coals. Cover the grill and cook until the meat shows no sign of pink when cut at the bone, about 20 minutes.

4 Serve the pork chops immediately with the peach chutney.

VENISON POT ROAST

National Cowboy Hall of Fame, Oklahoma City

Makes 6 to 8 servings

Every now and then, cowboys were lucky enough to bag a deer. Now some of the best venison in the country is farm-raised in Texas. Whether you hunt your own or buy the venison from a specialty butcher, you'll like this pot roast.

8 slices bacon, chopped

⅓ cup plus 2 tablespoons chopped fresh parsley

4 cloves garlic, minced

1 (3-pound) venison roast, preferably chuck or round

2 tablespoons vegetable oil, plus more if needed

1 medium onion, chopped

3 large carrots, sliced ½ inch thick

2 stalks celery, sliced ½ inch thick

2 cups beef broth, preferably homemade

1 (12-ounce) bottle ale or amber beer

2 tablespoons light brown sugar

1 teaspoon dried thyme

1 bay leaf

½ teaspoon salt

¼ teaspoon freshly ground pepper

¼ cup (½ stick) unsalted butter, softened

¼ cup all-purpose flour

1 In a small bowl, combine the bacon, ⅓ cup of the parsley, and 2 minced garlic cloves. Using the handle of a wooden spoon, poke 6 holes lengthwise through the roast. Use the handle to force the bacon mixture into the holes.

2 In a large flameproof casserole, heat the oil over medium-high heat. Add the venison and cook, turning occasionally, until browned. Transfer to a plate and set aside.

3 Add more oil to the casserole if needed. Add the onion, carrots, celery, and remaining garlic and reduce the heat to medium. Cook, stirring often, until the onion is softened, about 5 minutes. Stir in the beef broth, beer, and brown sugar, scraping up the browned bits on the bottom of the casserole. Return the venison to the casserole and bring the liquid to a simmer, skimming off any foam that rises to the surface. Add the remaining parsley and the thyme, bay leaf, salt, and pepper. Reduce the heat to low, cover, and simmer until the venison is tender, about 2 hours.

4 Using a slotted spoon, transfer the venison and vegetables to a serving platter and cover with aluminum foil to keep warm. Remove the casserole from the heat, let stand 5 minutes, and skim any fat that rises to the surface.

5 In a small bowl, work the butter and flour into a paste. Return the casserole to the stove and bring to a simmer over medium heat. Gradually whisk in the flour mixture and cook until the sauce is thickened, about 5 minutes.

6 Carve the venison crosswise into thick slices. Pour the sauce over the venison and vegetables and serve immediately.

N O T E : The venison can also be prepared outside in a 12-inch Dutch oven according to the directions on page 203.

Poultry and fish

$\mathcal{P}$rairie chickens, geese, ducks, quail, and wild turkey made delicious eating and were especially sought after for Thanksgiving and Christmas feasts. Western waters also produced a bounty of fresh fish, although the finned creatures did not figure significantly in the menu of open-range cowboys.

Asian-grilled chicken breasts

Hearst Ranches, San Simeon, California

Ann Hirschy,
Jack Hirschy Livestock Inc., Jackson, Montana

Makes 6 to 8 servings

Chinese laborers were brought to the West to build the railroads and were left stranded afterward to fend for themselves. Some of them found their way to become ranch cooks, bringing Asian seasonings to the cowboy menu. The tradition lives on in these succulent grilled chicken breasts served with grilled pineapple wedges.

Marinade

1 cup Japanese soy sauce

⅔ cup packed brown sugar

¼ cup dry sherry, scotch, or apple juice

2 cloves garlic, crushed

2 tablespoons grated fresh ginger or 2 teaspoons ground ginger

½ teaspoon freshly ground pepper

8 (8-ounce) chicken breast halves, bone in, skin on

1 ripe pineapple, peeled, cored, and cut lengthwise into 8 wedges

1 In a large nonreactive bowl, combine all the marinade ingredients. Pour one third of the marinade into a small bowl, cover, and refrigerate. Add the chicken to the large bowl, mix well, cover, and refrigerate, stirring occasionally, for at least 4 hours or overnight.

2 Make a hot charcoal fire in the bottom of a charcoal grill according to the instructions on page 167.

3 Remove the chicken, discarding the marinade it was in. Arrange the chicken around the cooler, outside edges of a lightly oiled grill. Cover the grill and cook, basting occasionally with the reserved marinade (not used to marinate the chicken), until the juices run clear yellow when pierced with the tip of a sharp knife, 40 to 50 minutes. During the last 10 minutes of cooking, place the pineapple wedges in the center of the grill and cook along with the chicken breasts, turning and basting occasionally with the reserved marinade, until lightly browned. Serve immediately.

NOTE: The chicken and pineapple can also be prepared over medium heat in a gas grill.

Barbecued chicken

Few foods are sadder than barbecued chicken burned black on the outside but still raw inside. This chicken gets soaked in a flavorful lemon marinade that won't scorch while it cooks and is finally glazed with the tomato-based sauce cowboys love.

Marinade

½ cup lemon juice

¼ cup vegetable oil

1 tablespoon Worcestershire sauce

1 tablespoon chili powder

2 cloves garlic, crushed through a press

½ teaspoon salt

2 (3⅓-pound) whole chickens, each cut into 8 pieces

2 cups California-Style Barbecue Sauce or Cowboy Barbecue Sauce (page 268 or 267)

1 In a large nonreactive bowl, combine all the marinade ingredients. Add the chicken and rub in the marinade. Cover and refrigerate for at least 2 hours or up to 6 hours.

2 Make a hot charcoal fire in the bottom of a charcoal grill according to the instructions on page 167.

3 Remove the chicken from the marinade and arrange around the cooler, outside edges of a lightly oiled grill. Cover the grill and cook, turning once, for 35 minutes. Baste the chicken with the barbecue sauce. Cover the grill and continue cooking, turning and basting occasionally, until the juices run clear yellow when pierced with the tip of a sharp knife, 15 to 20 more minutes. Serve immediately.

PECAN chicken bREASTS wiTh hONEY SAUCE

Clyde Nelson,
The Home Ranch, Clark, Colorado

Makes 6 servings

Here's another recipe that demonstrates the new wave in ranch cooking. The rich sauce can be prepared ahead of time and reheated before serving.

Honey Bourbon Sauce

 2 tablespoons unsalted butter

 1 tablespoon minced shallots or scallions

 1 cup freshly squeezed orange juice

 ¼ cup bourbon or apple juice

 1 cup heavy (whipping) cream

 2 tablespoons honey

 1 tablespoon cider vinegar

 ¼ teaspoon salt

 ¼ teaspoon freshly ground white pepper

 ¾ cup all-purpose flour

 ¾ cup pecans

 1 teaspoon dried thyme

 ½ teaspoon salt

 ¼ teaspoon freshly ground black pepper

 6 (6-ounce) boneless, skinless chicken breast halves

 ⅓ cup milk

 2 tablespoons vegetable oil

 2 tablespoons unsalted butter

1 Make the sauce: In a medium saucepan, melt the butter over low heat. Add the shallots and stir until wilted, about 2 minutes. Add the orange juice and bourbon, increase the heat to high, and boil until reduced to about ½ cup, about 10 minutes. Stir in the cream and reduce the heat to medium. Cook, being careful not to let the cream boil over, until slightly thickened, about 5 minutes. Stir in the honey, vinegar, salt, and pepper; cook until rethickened, about 2 minutes. Keep the sauce warm.

2 In a blender or a food processor fitted with the metal blade, pulse the flour, pecans, thyme, salt, and pepper until the pecans are finely chopped. Place on a plate.

3 One at a time, dip the chicken breasts in milk, then coat with the pecan mixture, patting to help it adhere.

4 In a large skillet, heat the oil and butter over medium heat. Add the chicken and cook, turning once, until golden brown on both sides and the juices run clear when the meat is pierced with the tip of a sharp knife, about 10 minutes. Transfer to a plate and cover loosely with foil to keep warm.

5 Divide the sauce evenly between 6 warm dinner plates. Place the chicken breasts on top of the sauce and serve immediately.

Chicken with Lemon and Wine

Jean True,
True Ranch, Casper, Wyoming

Makes 4 servings

This chicken dish makes a savory sauce to be served over hot rice or noodles.

2 tablespoons lemon juice

1 clove garlic, crushed through a press

1 (3½-pound) chicken, cut into 8 pieces

½ teaspoon ground ginger

½ teaspoon dry mustard

½ teaspoon dried thyme

½ teaspoon crushed sage

¼ teaspoon salt

⅛ teaspoon freshly ground pepper

1 tablespoon vegetable oil

½ cup dry white wine or dry vermouth

2 cups (7 ounces) sliced fresh mushrooms

1 scallion, finely chopped

Hot cooked rice

1 In a medium bowl, combine the lemon juice and garlic. Add the chicken and toss well. In a small bowl, combine the ginger, mustard, thyme, sage, salt, and pepper. Sprinkle over the chicken and toss again.

2 In a large skillet, heat the oil over medium-high heat. In two batches, add the chicken and cook, turning occasionally, until lightly browned, about 8 minutes. Transfer to a plate. Pour off any fat.

3 Return the chicken to the skillet with the wine and mushrooms. Bring to a simmer and reduce the heat to low. Cover tightly and simmer until the juices run clear yellow when the chicken is pierced with the tip of a sharp knife, about 35 minutes.

4 Using a slotted spoon, transfer the chicken to a platter and cover with foil to keep warm. Pour the cooking juices into a glass measuring cup and let stand for 3 minutes. Skim off the fat that rises to the surface. Pour the juices over the chicken. Sprinkle with the scallion and serve immediately with the rice, spooning the juices over all.

Wide open spaces turkey

Makes 8 to 12 servings

Once you've tried turkey cooked outside on a grill, you may never go back to roasting it in an oven. Don't try this with birds larger than 12 pounds—they simply won't fit on the grill. It's best to call the butcher ahead of time to order the right size bird.

1 (10- to 12-pound) turkey, giblets removed, rinsed, and patted dry

3 tablespoons olive oil

¼ cup chili powder

1 tablespoon garlic salt

1 large onion, chopped

6 cups mesquite chips, soaked in water for at least 30 minutes and drained

Cowboy Barbecue Sauce (page 267)

1 If the turkey has a pop-up thermometer, remove it. Brush the turkey all over with the olive oil. In a small bowl, mix the chili powder and garlic salt, then rub the mixture all over the turkey, inside and out. Place the chopped onion in the body cavity. Tie the turkey wings to its side with kitchen twine, and tie the drumsticks together. Refrigerate, uncovered, for at least 1 hour or up to 24 hours. Remove the turkey from the refrigerator 1 hour before smoking.

2 Place a large disposable aluminum foil pan on one side of the bottom of a charcoal grill and fill halfway with water. Bank charcoal briquets on the other side of the grill and make a hot fire according to the directions on page 167. Sprinkle a handful of drained chips over the coals, place the turkey on the pan, and immediately cover the grill.

3 Smoke the turkey until a meat thermometer inserted in the thickest part of the thigh, not touching the bone, reads 180°F, about 6 hours, allowing 30 minutes per pound. Maintain an even interior grill temperature by adding more hot coals and wood chips about every 45 minutes.

4 Let the turkey stand for 20 minutes before carving. Serve hot or warm with barbecue sauce passed on the side.

ROAST duck with sweet and sour grapes

Donna Harcourt,
Las Tablas Creek Ranch, Paso Robles, California

Makes 2 servings

Donna has access to lots of wild duck and likes to roast a feast of six ducks or more in her industrial-sized oven. Most cooks will find that they can fit only one duck comfortably in their regular-sized oven, but if you have more room, feel free to multiply the recipe. If you use wild ducks, remember that they are leaner than the supermarket variety and you need to cover their breasts with bacon strips, baste often, and don't overcook—they are most tender when served slightly rare. Serve the ducks with your favorite wild rice recipe and green peas.

1 (5- to 6-pound) duck
¼ teaspoon salt
¼ teaspoon freshly ground pepper
1 tart green apple, such as Granny Smith, halved
1 scallion, chopped
½ cup orange juice
1 clove garlic, crushed through a press

Sweet and Sour Grapes
2 cups seedless red grapes
2 tablespoons red currant jelly
2 tablespoons Dijon mustard

Sauce
¼ cup chicken stock, preferably homemade, or canned low-sodium broth
1 tablespoon cornstarch

1 Preheat the oven to 425°F. Using the upturned tines of a carving fork, pierce the duck skin all over, especially near the tail area (don't pierce the flesh). Season the duck inside and out with the salt and pepper. Stuff the body cavity with the apple and scallion. Place the duck on a large roasting rack in a large roasting pan.

2 Roast for 30 minutes. Pour the fat out of the pan and discard. Reduce the heat to 350°F.

3 In a small bowl, combine the orange juice and garlic. Baste the duck with the orange juice mixture. Continue roasting, basting occasionally, first with the orange juice mixture and then with the drippings in the pan, until the juices run clear yellow when a thigh is pierced with a knife, about 1½ hours. Transfer the duck to a large platter and set aside. Pour the pan drippings and juices from the body cavity into a glass measuring cup. Let stand 5 minutes, then skim off the clear fat on the surface.

4 Meanwhile, make the sweet and sour grapes: In a medium saucepan, combine the grapes, jelly, and mustard. Bring to a simmer over medium-low heat, stirring often, until the sauce is simmering and the grapes are heated through, about 5 minutes. Keep warm.

5 Make the sauce: In a small bowl, gradually whisk the degreased drippings and chicken stock into the cornstarch until dissolved. Pour into the roasting pan and place over a stove burner. Bring to a simmer over medium heat, scraping up the browned bits on the bottom of the pan with a wooden spoon. Cook until the sauce is thickened, about 1 minute. Season with additional salt and pepper to taste. Pour the sauce into a warmed sauceboat.

6 Using poultry shears or a very sharp knife, cut the duck in half lengthwise along one side of the backbone, discarding the stuffing vegetables. Serve with the sauce and grapes passed on the side.

Grilled quail with jalapeño glaze

National Cowboy Hall of Fame, Oklahoma City

Makes 8 servings

Folks on the ranch have a fondness for game birds, especially hot off the grill. This couldn't be easier to make—it's getting the quails that takes the effort. If you're not bagging your own, order them from the best butcher in town.

⅔ cup lime juice

Grated zest from 2 limes

¼ cup olive oil

1 fresh hot chile pepper (such as jalapeño), seeded and minced

1 clove garlic, crushed through a press

1 teaspoon salt

½ teaspoon freshly ground pepper

12 quail, split lengthwise, breast bones removed

¾ cup jalapeño jelly, melted

1 In a large nonreactive bowl, whisk the lime juice, lime zest, olive oil, chile pepper, garlic, salt, and pepper. Add the quail and toss gently to combine. Cover and refrigerate for at least 2 hours or up to 6 hours.

2 Make a moderately hot fire in the bottom of a charcoal grill according to the directions on page 167.

3 Remove the quail from the marinade and place on a lightly oiled grill. Cover and cook the quail, turning occasionally, until the meat is barely pink when pierced at the thigh bone, about 15 minutes. During the last 5 minutes of cooking, baste the quail with the melted jelly to glaze. Serve immediately.

Citrus-marinated grilled swordfish

Clyde Nelson,
The Home Ranch, Clark, Colorado

Makes 8 servings

Fresh fish used to be difficult to find in cow country, but supermarkets have filled the void. This citrus-flavored marinade is a great way to dress up familiar swordfish. Don't overmarinate the fish, or the citrus acids will "cook" it.

½ *cup orange juice*

¼ *cup lime juice*

¼ *cup rice vinegar*

3 tablespoons peanut or vegetable oil

2 tablespoons grated fresh ginger

1 tablespoon dark Asian sesame oil

2 scallions, thinly sliced

3 cloves garlic, thinly sliced

2 tablespoons chopped fresh cilantro (coriander)

8 (6-ounce) swordfish steaks, about ¾ inch thick

¼ *teaspoon salt*

¼ *teaspoon freshly ground pepper*

Tropical Pineapple Salsa (page 272)

1 In a large glass baking dish, whisk the orange and lime juices, rice vinegar, peanut oil, ginger, and sesame oil until combined. Stir in the scallions, garlic, and cilantro. Add the swordfish steaks and turn to coat with the orange marinade. Cover and refrigerate, basting occasionally, for 1 hour, no longer.

2 Make a moderately hot fire in the bottom of a charcoal grill according to the directions on page 167.

3 Remove the fish from the marinade and season with salt and pepper. Cook on a lightly oiled grill, turning once, until the fish is cooked to your liking, about 6 minutes for medium-rare fish. Serve immediately with the salsa.

PAN-FRIED TROUT WITH LEMON-MINT DRIZZLE

National Cowboy Hall of Fame, Oklahoma City

Makes 4 servings

Every now and then, cowboys would come across a mountain stream filled with trout, and there would be a fish fry in the blink of an eye. If your skillet isn't big enough to fit all the fish, cook them in batches and keep warm in a 200°F oven until they're all cooked.

4 slices bacon

⅓ cup milk

½ cup yellow cornmeal

½ cup all-purpose flour

¼ teaspoon salt

¼ teaspoon freshly ground pepper

4 (10-ounce) rainbow or mountain trout, cleaned, with heads and tails
    left on

3 tablespoons unsalted butter

2 tablespoons lemon juice

1 scallion, finely chopped

1 tablespoon finely chopped fresh mint or 1 teaspoon dried mint

1 In a very large skillet, cook the bacon until crisp, about 5 minutes. Transfer the bacon to paper towels to drain, leaving the fat in the skillet.

2 Place the milk in a shallow pie plate. In a plate, combine the cornmeal, flour, salt, and pepper. Dip the trout in the milk, then coat with the cornmeal mixture, shaking off the excess.

3 Place the trout in the skillet and cook over medium heat, turning once, until the coating is golden brown and the fish is opaque when flaked with a fork, about 4 minutes per side. Transfer the trout to a serving platter and cover with foil to keep warm.

4 Discard any fat in the skillet. Add the butter and melt over medium heat. Remove from the heat, add the lemon juice, scallion, and mint, and drizzle over the trout. Crumble the bacon, sprinkle over the fish, and serve immediately.

Seviche san juan

Nancy L. Jackson,
Silver Creek Ranch, Tuscarora, Nevada

Makes 6 servings

Seviche is most popular with ranchers in the south of Texas, who can get their hands on very fresh redfish from the Gulf. Red snapper is a good substitute. Seviche is often served as a first course but makes a tasty light lunch too.

1 pound very fresh red snapper fillets, skinned and cut into ½-inch pieces
1 cup freshly squeezed lime juice
4 ripe plum tomatoes, seeded and cut into ½-inch pieces
1¼ cups spicy tomato juice (such as Snappy Tom)
½ cup finely chopped onion, preferably white onion
20 pitted green olives, chopped
1 fresh hot chile pepper (such as jalapeño), seeded and minced
1 tablespoon extra-virgin olive oil
1 tablespoon chopped fresh cilantro (coriander)
½ teaspoon dried oregano
1 clove garlic, minced
6 large red leaf lettuce leaves, for garnish

1 In a medium nonreactive bowl, combine the red snapper and lime juice. Cover and refrigerate for at least 8 hours or up to 24 hours.

2 In another medium nonreactive bowl, combine the tomatoes, tomato juice, onion, olives, chile pepper, olive oil, cilantro, oregano, and garlic.

3 Drain the fish well and combine with the tomato mixture. Cover and refrigerate for at least 2 hours. To serve, spoon the chilled seviche onto lettuce leaves and serve immediately.

199

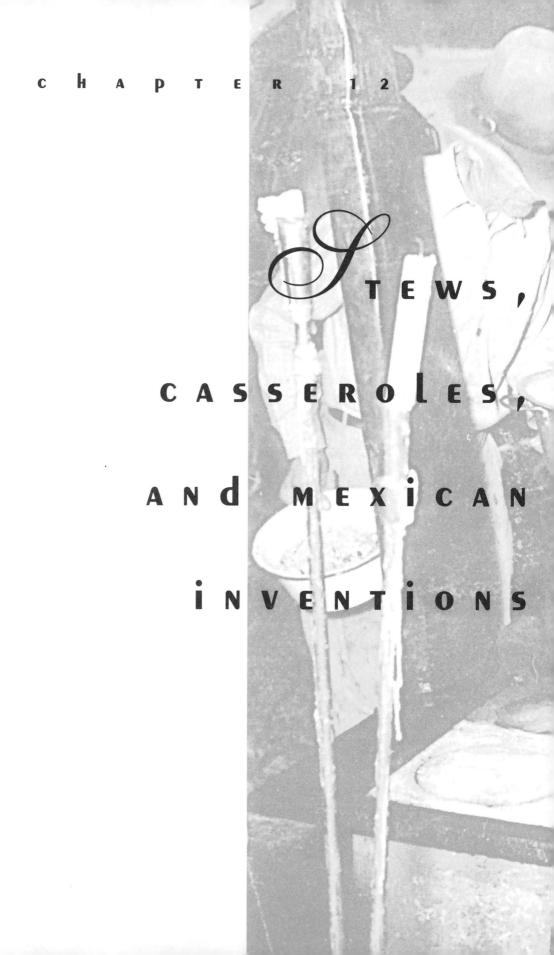

Stews,
Casseroles,
and Mexican
inventions

When Lewis and Clark traveled west, they listed the Dutch oven as one of their most valuable pieces of equipment.

dutch oven:

a chuck cook's best pal

*I*n colonial days Dutch peddlers sold a heavy cast-iron footed pot. The pot had a heavy indented lid, which allowed coals from the fire to be placed on top and apply extra heat to the food, cooking it quicker. When Lewis and Clark traveled west, they listed the Dutch oven as one of their most valuable pieces of equipment.

Cowboys were quick to utilize the Dutch oven and still use it outdoors on the campfire to prepare everything from stews to desserts and beans. Although we give conventional cooking instructions for all but a few recipes, we have also noted that many of them can be adapted to Dutch oven cookery.

Dutch ovens come in five diameters: 8, 10, 12, 14, and 16 inches. Most cooks don't have a wide selection and choose one pot that fits the amount of eaters they usually cook for. You can double (or even halve) the recipes as necessary to fit your particular Dutch oven. The suggested recipes are not complicated and won't be affected by adjustments.

Build your fire on top of a large piece of foil, which will reflect some of the heat and reduce any problems with damp earth. (Or if you are a backyard cook, use your grill. Square, brazier-type grills work better for Dutch oven cooking than kettle grills because the oven must sit flat.) Choose a site that is protected from the wind; you may need to build a wind guard of some type.

To slow-bake or simmer foods, use only moderate heat. To estimate how many charcoal briquets you'll need, multiply the diameter of your Dutch oven by 2. Place that number of ignited coals in a circle that is the same size as the diameter of your oven. For example, a 12-inch oven would use 24 coals in a 12-inch circle. The oven will sit over the circle of coals, but don't put any coals in the center. For higher heat to brown or boil foods, multiply the amount of coals by 3. Arrange one third of the coals in a circle, and place the remainder on the lid (use a small spade or long-handled tongs). These instructions are for charcoal briquets, but you can also use coals from a wood campfire if you are an old cowhand. If a dish needs to be cooked more than 45 minutes, you will have to add hot coals. Light them in a hibachi or charcoal chimney starter, or make another campfire nearby. You will only need half again as many coals to maintain the heat level.

Dutch oven cooking can be fun, but be prepared to cut yourself some slack if the elements don't come together in textbook perfection. The heat of the coals, the outside temperature, wind—all are factors that affect exact timing.

Dutch ovens can be purchased by mail order from Twin-K Enterprises, P.O. Box 4023, Logan, Utah 84321, (801) 752-1477 or 752-4254.

BRISKET CHUCKWAGON STEW

Tom Perini,
Perini's Steak House, Buffalo Gap, Texas

Makes 6 to 8 servings

No respectable "cookie" would be caught without his can of bacon drippings to use for browning stew meat. Tom states that bacon grease is the secret to his stew's success, so it's worth it to fry up a few slices to render some if you don't happen to have it on hand.

2 tablespoons bacon grease or vegetable oil

3 pounds beef brisket, trimmed of excess fat and cut into 1½-inch cubes

¾ teaspoon salt

½ teaspoon freshly ground pepper

1 large onion, chopped

2 cloves garlic, minced

4 cups beef stock, preferably homemade, or canned low-sodium broth

2 (4-ounce) cans chopped mild green chiles, drained

2 pounds red-skinned potatoes, scrubbed well and cut into 1-inch pieces

2 cups fresh or thawed frozen corn kernels

¼ cup chopped fresh cilantro (coriander) or parsley

⅓ cup all-purpose flour

1 In a large flameproof casserole, heat the bacon grease over medium heat. Season the beef brisket with the salt and pepper. Working in batches to avoid crowding, add the brisket and cook, turning occasionally, until browned on all sides, about 8 minutes. Transfer to a plate.

2 Add the onion and garlic to the casserole and cook, stirring often, until the onion is softened, about 4 minutes. Stir in the beef stock. Return the brisket to the skillet and add the chiles. Bring to a simmer over high heat, skimming off any foam that forms on the surface. Reduce the heat to low, cover, and simmer until the brisket is tender, about 2½ hours. During the last 30 minutes, stir in the potatoes, corn, and cilantro. Remove from the heat and let stand 5 minutes. Skim any fat from the top of the stew. (It is easier to remove the fat if the stew is cooled to room temperature, covered, and refrigerated overnight. Remove and discard any hardened fat from the surface. Reheat gently over low heat before proceeding.) Return the stew to a simmer over low heat.

3 In a small bowl, whisk 1 cup of the cooking liquid with the flour until smooth. Stir into the stew and simmer until the sauce is thickened, about 3 minutes. Season the stew with additional salt and pepper and serve hot.

N O T E : The stew can be prepared outside in a 12-inch Dutch oven according to the directions on page 203.

Old-Fashioned Oxtail Stew

Bette Ramsey,
Amarillo, Texas

Makes 4 to 6 servings

Oxtails make a fine stew because the bones add extra flavor to the sauce and the meat is particularly succulent. Instead of a flour thickening, the vegetables are mashed into the broth to form a gravy.

2 tablespoons vegetable oil, plus more as needed

3 pounds oxtails, cut into 1½-inch lengths

¾ teaspoon salt

¼ teaspoon freshly ground pepper

½ cup all-purpose flour

1 large onion, chopped

3 cloves garlic, minced

2 cups beef broth

2 cups water

1 (28-ounce) can peeled tomatoes, drained and chopped

2 tablespoons chopped fresh parsley

½ teaspoon dried thyme

½ teaspoon dried basil

½ teaspoon dried oregano

1½ pounds boiling potatoes, peeled and cut into 1-inch pieces

4 medium carrots, sliced ½ inch thick

1 In a large flameproof casserole, heat the oil over medium–high heat. Season the oxtails with salt and pepper and coat with the flour, shaking off the excess. Working in batches if necessary, add to the casserole and cook, turning often, until browned on all sides, about 8 minutes. Transfer to a plate.

2 Add more oil to the casserole if needed. Add the onion and garlic, reduce the heat to medium, and cook, stirring often, until the onion is softened, about 4 minutes. Return the oxtails to the casserole and stir in the beef broth, water, and tomatoes. Bring to a simmer over high heat, skimming any foam that forms on the surface. Stir in the parsley, thyme, basil, and oregano and reduce the heat to low. Cover and simmer until the oxtails are almost tender, about 2½ hours.

3 Add the potatoes and carrots. Cover and continue cooking until the oxtails and vegetables are tender, about 30 minutes. Skim any fat from the surface. Using a potato masher or large slotted spoon, mash enough vegetables in the pot to thicken the sauce to the desired consistency. Season the stew with additional salt and pepper and serve hot.

GREEN CHILE STEW

Dark green poblano chiles (sometimes called ancho chiles) give this chunky stew its special character. If they are unavailable, you can use Italian frying peppers, but the flavor won't be authentic. Some cooks add potato cubes during the last 30 minutes or stir in a can of hominy just at the end of cooking. Try the stew as a stuffing for burritos.

> 4 tablespoons olive oil, plus more as needed
> 3 pounds pork shoulder, trimmed of excess fat and cut into 1-inch pieces
> ¾ teaspoon salt
> ½ teaspoon freshly ground pepper
> ⅓ cup all-purpose flour
> 1 large onion, chopped
> 3 cloves garlic, minced
> 12 poblano chile peppers, roasted, peeled, seeded, and chopped (page 129)
> 2 cups chicken stock, preferably homemade, or canned low-sodium broth
> ½ teaspoon ground cumin
> ½ teaspoon dried oregano
> ¼ cup chopped fresh cilantro (coriander), optional

1 In a large flameproof casserole, heat 2 tablespoons of the oil over medium-high heat. Season the pork with salt and pepper and coat with the flour, shaking off the excess. Working in batches to avoid crowding, and adding more oil as needed, cook the pork, turning occasionally, until browned on all sides, about 8 minutes. Transfer to a plate.

2 Heat the remaining 2 tablespoons of oil in the casserole over medium heat. Add the onion and garlic and cook, stirring often, until the onion is softened, about 4 minutes. Stir in the chiles. Transfer half of the vegetables to a blender. Add 1 cup of the chicken stock and process until smooth.

3 Return the green sauce and the pork cubes to the casserole. Stir in the remaining 1 cup of chicken stock, the cumin, and oregano. Bring to a simmer over medium heat. Reduce the heat to low and cover. Simmer, stirring occasionally and adding water if the sauce thickens too much, until the pork is tender, about 1½ hours. During the last 10 minutes, stir in the cilantro if desired. Serve hot.

New Mexican Red Chili

Eva M. Holleyman,
Corona, New Mexico

Makes 8 to 10 servings

Every ranch cook has a closely guarded recipe for chili. The New Mexican version uses the state's famous dried chiles, which have been previously transformed into Sauce Caribe, courtesy of Eva's excellent recipe.

4 tablespoons vegetable oil, plus more as needed
5 pounds beef chuck, cut into ½-inch cubes
2 teaspoons salt
2 medium onions, chopped
4 cups Sauce Caribe (page 265)
1 cup chile-soaking liquid from Sauce Caribe
¼ cup yellow cornmeal

1 In a large flameproof casserole, heat 2 tablespoons of the oil over medium-high heat. Season the beef with the salt. Working in batches to avoid crowding, cook the beef, turning occasionally, until browned, about 5 minutes. Transfer with a slotted spoon to a platter.

2 Add the remaining 2 tablespoons of oil to the casserole and heat over medium heat. Add the onions and cook, stirring often, until they are softened, about 5 minutes. Return the beef to the casserole and stir in the sauce and chile-soaking liquid. Bring to a simmer, stirring often. Reduce the heat to low, cover, and simmer, stirring occasionally, until the beef is tender, about 2 hours.

3 In a small bowl, combine the cornmeal with ½ cup water. Stir into the chili and cook until the sauce is thickened, about 5 minutes.

Chicken and Hominy chili

With an eye to reducing fat intake, some ranch cooks are cooking with poultry more often than their predecessors at the stove (or the campfire). This recipe uses meaty-flavored chicken thighs, which work well as a substitute for beef.

Nonstick vegetable spray

2 pounds boneless, skinless chicken thighs, cut into 1-inch pieces

1 medium onion, chopped

1 medium red bell pepper, seeded and chopped

1 fresh hot chile pepper (such as jalapeño), seeded and minced

2 cloves garlic, chopped

¼ cup chili powder

1 (16-ounce) can peeled tomatoes, drained and chopped

1 (8-ounce) can tomato sauce

1 cup chicken stock, preferably homemade, or canned low-sodium broth

¼ teaspoon salt

3 tablespoons yellow cornmeal

1 (16-ounce) can hominy, drained

Nonfat sour cream substitute

1 Spray a large nonstick skillet with cooking spray and place over medium-high heat. Working in batches, add the chicken and cook, turning occasionally, until lightly browned on all sides, about 5 minutes. Transfer to a large saucepan.

2 Spray the skillet again with cooking spray. Add the onion, bell pepper, chile pepper, and garlic. Cover and cook over medium heat, stirring often, until the onion is softened, about 5 minutes. Add the chili powder and cook, stirring, for 1 minute. Stir into the saucepan along with the tomatoes, tomato sauce, chicken stock, and salt.

3 Bring to a simmer and reduce the heat to low. Cover and simmer until the chicken is tender, about 45 minutes.

4 In a small bowl, whisk the cornmeal into ¼ cup of water until smooth. Stir into the chili along with the hominy. Simmer until the sauce is thickened, about 5 minutes. Serve in soup bowls, topped with a dollop of the sour cream substitute.

Herbed beef stew with corn dumplings

Clyde A. "C.A." Wheeler, Jr.,
and Barbara Dodd Wheeler,
Clear Creek Ranch, Laverne, Oklahoma

Makes 8 servings

Because it is a little more "gourmet" than most ranch stews, you may want to save this recipe for a special Sunday supper. If you really want to put on the dog, substitute 1 cup red wine for 1 cup of the beef broth.

2 tablespoons vegetable oil, plus more as needed

2 pounds stew beef, cut into 1-inch pieces

1 teaspoon salt

¼ teaspoon freshly ground pepper

⅓ cup all-purpose flour

3 cups beef stock, preferably homemade, or canned low-sodium broth

2 (8-ounce) cans tomato sauce

1 tablespoon chopped fresh parsley

½ teaspoon dried marjoram

½ teaspoon dried thyme

½ teaspoon dried rosemary

2 bay leaves

4 medium carrots, cut into 1-inch lengths

12 small boiling onions (9 ounces), peeled

¾ cup water

1 tablespoon unsalted butter

1 teaspoon sugar

Corn Dumplings

1¾ cups all-purpose flour

⅓ cup yellow cornmeal

1 tablespoon baking powder

½ teaspoon salt

1 cup milk

3 tablespoons unsalted butter, melted

2 tablespoons chopped fresh parsley

1 In a large flameproof casserole, heat the oil over medium heat. Season the beef with the salt and pepper and coat in the flour, shaking off excess flour. Working in batches, add the beef and cook, turning occasionally, until browned on all sides, about 8 minutes; add more oil as needed. Transfer to a plate. Drain any excess oil from the casserole.

2 Return the beef to the casserole. Stir in the stock, tomato sauce, parsley, marjoram, thyme, rosemary, and bay leaves. Bring to a simmer and reduce the heat to low. Cover and simmer for 1 hour.

3 Meanwhile, in a large skillet, combine the carrots, onions, water, butter, and sugar. Bring to a boil over medium heat. Cover and cook for 2 minutes. Uncover and cook until the liquid is evaporated, about 10 minutes. Continue cooking, stirring often, until the vegetables are tender and glazed, about 3 more minutes. Stir the glazed vegetables into the stew. Cook until the beef is just tender, about 15 minutes.

4 Make the dumplings: In a medium bowl, whisk the flour, cornmeal, baking powder, and salt to combine. Make a well in the center and pour in the milk and melted butter. Stir just to combine, then stir in the parsley.

5 Drop the dumpling batter by tablespoons on top of the simmering stew. Cover and cook until the dumplings are cooked through, about 20 minutes.

Taco salad casserole

Hearst Ranches, San Simeon, California

Makes 8 to 10 servings

Here's a one-dish meal with its tomato, lettuce, cheese, and olive garnish that looks great on a supper or buffet table, and it will round up compliments for taste, too.

1 tablespoon olive oil

2 pounds ground round

1 medium onion, chopped

2 cloves garlic, minced

2 tablespoons chili powder

1 tablespoon sweet Hungarian paprika

1 teaspoon salt

1 teaspoon dried oregano

½ teaspoon ground cumin

⅛ teaspoon ground hot (cayenne) pepper

2 (16-ounce) cans stewed tomatoes, undrained

1 (4-ounce) can chopped green chile peppers, drained

2 cups small-curd cottage cheese

1 cup (4 ounces) shredded Monterey Jack cheese

1 large egg

12 corn tortillas

2 cups shredded iceberg lettuce

4 ripe plum tomatoes, seeded and chopped

1 cup (4 ounces) shredded sharp Cheddar cheese

½ cup sliced ripe black olives

2 scallions, chopped

1   In a large skillet, heat the oil over medium-high heat. Add the ground round, onion, and garlic. Cook, stirring to break up the meat with a wooden spoon, until the meat loses its pink color, about 6 minutes. Tilt the pan to drain off the excess fat. Add the chili powder, paprika, salt, oregano, cumin, and hot pepper. Stir for 1 minute.

2 Stir in the stewed tomatoes with their juices and the chiles. Bring to a simmer and reduce the heat to low. Simmer, uncovered, until the excess liquid is evaporated, about 30 minutes.

3 Preheat the oven to 350°F. Lightly oil a 9-by-13-inch baking dish. In a medium bowl, combine the cottage cheese, Monterey Jack, and egg.

4 Place an overlapping layer of half the tortillas in the baking dish. Spread with the meat mixture. Top with the remaining tortillas, then spread with the cheese mixture.

5 Bake until the topping is firm in the center, about 30 minutes. Let the casserole stand for 5 minutes.

6 Top the casserole with a layer of lettuce, then sprinkle with the tomatoes, Cheddar cheese, olives and scallions. Cut into rectangles and serve immediately.

Tamale Casserole

Cecil R. Gerloff,
X-G Ranch, Belen, New Mexico

Makes 6 servings

Cornmeal and beef make a particularly robust pair, and this casserole will satisfy the hungriest rustler.

1 pound ground round

1 medium onion, chopped

1 clove garlic, minced

1 tablespoon chili powder

½ teaspoon ground cumin

1 teaspoon salt

1 teaspoon freshly ground pepper

1 (16-ounce) can peeled tomatoes, drained and chopped

1 (8-ounce) can tomato sauce

1 cup water

1 cup fresh or thawed frozen corn kernels

½ cup chopped ripe black olives

½ cup yellow cornmeal

2 large eggs, at room temperature

1 cup (4 ounces) shredded sharp Cheddar cheese

1 Preheat the oven to 300°F. Lightly butter a 12-by-7-inch glass baking dish.

2 In a large nonstick skillet, cook the ground round, onion, and garlic over medium-high heat, stirring often with a spoon to break up the meat, until the meat is cooked through, about 8 minutes. Tilt the skillet to drain off the excess fat. Add the chili powder, cumin, salt, and pepper, and cook, stirring constantly, for 1 minute.

3 Stir in the tomatoes, tomato sauce, water, corn, and olives. Bring to a boil and gradually stir in the cornmeal. Remove from the heat.

4 In a small bowl, beat the eggs. Gradually stir about 1 cup of the meat mixture into the eggs. Stir the egg mixture into the skillet, along with ½ cup of the cheese. Spread evenly in the prepared baking dish.

5 Bake until the casserole is firm in the center, about 45 minutes. During the last 15 minutes of baking, sprinkle with the remaining ½ cup cheese.

Huevos Rancheros

While huevos rancheros are *muy buenos* by themselves, they are even better when served with fried chorizo sausages. The secret to fine huevos rancheros is the sauce, and there's a great one used in this recipe.

½ cup vegetable oil

6 corn tortillas

1½ cups Guacamole (page 266), removed from the refrigerator 1 hour
     before serving

6 large eggs

Salt and freshly ground pepper to taste

2 cups Ranchero Sauce (page 270), heated

Chopped fresh cilantro (coriander), for garnish

1 In a large skillet, heat the oil over medium heat until very hot but not smoking. One at a time, fry the tortillas, turning once, until crisp and golden brown, about 2 minutes. Transfer the tortillas to paper towels to drain and cool. Spread each tortilla evenly with about ¼ cup guacamole and set aside.

2 In the same skillet carefully break the eggs into the oil remaining in the skillet. Fry, spooning the oil over the tops of the eggs, until the whites are set, about 3 minutes. Season the eggs with salt and pepper to taste. (Huevos rancheros are usually served sunny side up, but you may turn the eggs and cook to your desired doneness.)

3 Place each tortilla on a warmed dinner plate and top with a fried egg. Spoon about ⅓ cup of ranchero sauce in a ring around each egg, sprinkle with the cilantro, and serve immediately.

Mexican "Lasagne"

Mitzi Riley,
Riley Ranch, Aledo, Texas

Makes 8 servings

Bow-tie pasta stands in for lasagne noodles to make an unfussy version of a much-requested ranch dinner.

1 tablespoon olive oil

2 pounds ground round

2 medium onions, chopped

3 stalks celery, chopped

8 ounces fresh mushrooms, sliced

1 medium green bell pepper, seeded and chopped

1 fresh hot chile pepper (such as jalapeño), seeded and minced

2 cloves garlic, minced

3 tablespoons chili powder

1 tablespoon dried oregano

$\frac{1}{2}$ teaspoon ground cumin

1 teaspoon salt

$\frac{1}{4}$ teaspoon freshly ground pepper

2 (28-ounce) cans peeled tomatoes, undrained

1 (16-ounce) can tomato sauce

1 pound bow-tie pasta

2 cups (8 ounces) shredded sharp Cheddar cheese

$\frac{1}{2}$ cup freshly grated imported Parmesan cheese

1 In a large saucepan, heat the oil over medium heat. Add the ground round, onions, celery, mushrooms, bell pepper, chile pepper, and garlic. Cook, stirring to break up the meat with a wooden spoon, until the meat loses its pink color, about 10 minutes. Stir in the chili powder, oregano, cumin, salt, and pepper and cook for 1 minute.

2 Stir in the tomatoes with their juices and the tomato sauce, breaking up the tomatoes with the side of a large spoon, and bring to a simmer. Reduce the heat to medium-low and simmer, stirring often, until the sauce is thickened, about 2 hours. Remove from the heat and skim the fat from the surface of the sauce.

3 Meanwhile, in a large pot of boiling salted water, cook the pasta over high heat until just tender, about 9 minutes. Drain well.

4 Preheat the oven to 350°F. Lightly oil a 13-by-9-inch baking dish. In the dish, layer half of the noodles, half the Cheddar cheese, and half the sauce. Repeat with the remaining noodles, Cheddar cheese, and sauce. Sprinkle with the Parmesan cheese.

5 Bake until bubbling throughout, about 35 minutes. Let the casserole stand for 5 minutes before serving.

Hearty beef pie

Guy and Pipp Gillette,
Gillette Ranch, Lovelady, Texas

Makes 8 servings

Beefy meat pies are just the ticket to fill a hungry cowhand's belly after a hard-riding day on the range.

4 slices bacon, cut into 1-inch pieces

3 pounds stew beef, cut into 1½-inch cubes

¾ teaspoon salt

½ teaspoon freshly ground pepper

1 large onion, chopped

4 medium carrots, cut into 1-inch lengths

3 stalks celery, cut into 1-inch lengths

4 ounces fresh mushrooms, halved crosswise

1¾ cups beef stock, preferably homemade, or canned low-sodium broth

3 tablespoons all-purpose flour

1 (12-ounce) bottle dark beer

1 tablespoon Worcestershire sauce

1 teaspoon dried thyme

Pie Crust (page 256)

1 cup fresh or thawed frozen peas

1 large egg yolk mixed with 2 teaspoons milk, for glaze

⅓ cup freshly grated imported Parmesan cheese

1 Preheat the oven to 350°F. In a large skillet over medium heat, cook the bacon until crisp, about 5 minutes. Transfer the bacon to paper towels to drain, leaving the fat in the casserole.

2 Season the beef with salt and pepper. Working in batches to avoid crowding, add the beef cubes to the skillet and cook, turning occasionally, until browned, about 8 minutes. Transfer to a 13-by-9-inch baking dish. Add the bacon to the baking dish.

3 Add the onion, carrots, celery, and mushrooms to the skillet. Cook, stirring often, until the onion is softened, about 4 minutes.

4 In a small bowl, gradually whisk about ½ cup of the beef stock into the flour to make a thin paste. Stir into the skillet with the remaining beef stock and the beer, Worcestershire sauce, and thyme. Bring to a simmer and pour into the baking dish.

5 Cover and bake until the meat is tender, about 1½ hours.

6 Meanwhile, on a lightly floured surface, roll out the pie crust into a rectangle about ⅛ inch thick. Using a pastry wheel or a sharp knife, cut the pastry into ½-inch-wide strips.

7 Remove the baking dish from the oven. Stir in the peas, then arrange the pastry strips in a tight lattice pattern on top of the stew, trimming the strips as needed. Brush lightly with some of the egg glaze, then sprinkle with the cheese.

8 Bake, uncovered, until the lattice is golden brown, about 25 minutes. Serve the beef pie immediately.

N O T E : The beef pie can also be prepared outside in a 14-inch Dutch oven, according to the directions on page 203.

Beans, vegetables, and potatoes

Buck's

peppery

beans

Robert L. "Buck" Reams,
Fort Worth, Texas

Makes 4 to 6 servings

These beans pack a peppery punch and are best served next to simple grilled meats or poultry. They get an extra fillip from a handful of cilantro stirred in at the end. If you aren't a cilantro fan, substitute fresh oregano or parsley.

1 pound dried pinto beans, rinsed, drained, and picked over

4 strips bacon, cut into 1-inch pieces

1 small onion, chopped

1 clove garlic, minced

1 tablespoon plus 1 teaspoon chili powder

1 teaspoon freshly ground black pepper

¼ teaspoon ground hot red (cayenne) pepper, or more to taste

1½ teaspoons salt

⅓ cup chopped fresh cilantro (coriander)

1 In a large pot, combine the beans and enough cold water to cover by 2 inches. Bring to a boil over high heat and boil for 2 minutes. Remove from the heat, cover the pot, and let stand for 1 hour; drain well. (The beans can also be soaked overnight in a large bowl with enough cold water to cover by 2 inches, then drained.)

2 Rinse out the pot and dry it. Return to the stove and add the bacon. Cook over medium–high heat until wilted and beginning to crisp, about 4 minutes. Add the onion and garlic. Cook, stirring often, until the onion is softened, about 5 minutes. Stir in the chili powder, black pepper, and hot red pepper.

3 Return the beans to the pot. Add enough fresh water to barely cover. Bring to a boil over high heat. Reduce the heat to low and simmer, uncovered, adding more hot water if needed to keep the beans barely covered, until the beans are almost tender, about 20 minutes. (The exact cooking time will depend on the age and dryness of the beans.) Add the salt and cook until the beans are fully tender, about 20 minutes.

4 Stir in the cilantro. Using a potato masher or large spoon, mash enough of the beans in the pot to thicken the cooking liquid to the desired thickness. Serve the beans hot.

BUCKAROO
SAUCY BEANS

Cleo Rude,
Enid, Oklahoma

Makes 4 to 6 servings

Tomato puree adds tang and a bright red color to these beans. Don't be tempted to stir in the tomato puree before the beans are tender, as the acid in the tomatoes will inhibit the beans from softening if added too early.

1 pound dried pinto beans, rinsed, drained, and picked over

2 strips bacon, chopped

2 medium onions, chopped

1 small green bell pepper, seeded and chopped

2 cloves garlic, minced

1 bay leaf

1 teaspoon salt

1½ cups tomato puree

1 tablespoon chili powder

1 tablespoon brown sugar

1 teaspoon dry mustard

1 teaspoon dried oregano

1 In a large pot, combine the beans and enough cold water to cover by 2 inches. Bring to a boil over high heat and boil for 2 minutes. Remove from the heat, cover the pot, and let stand for 1 hour; drain well. (The beans can also be soaked overnight in a large bowl with enough cold water to cover by 2 inches, then drained.)

2 Return the beans to the pot and stir in the bacon, onions, bell pepper, garlic, and bay leaf. Add enough fresh water to barely cover. Bring to a boil over high heat. Reduce the heat to low and simmer, uncovered, adding more hot water if needed to keep the beans barely covered, until the beans are almost tender, about 20 minutes. (The exact cooking time will depend on the age and dryness of the beans.) Stir in the salt and continue cooking until the beans are barely tender, about 10 more minutes.

3 Stir in the tomato puree, chili powder, brown sugar, mustard, and oregano. Bring to a simmer over medium heat, reduce the heat to low, and simmer until the beans are fully tender and the sauce is thickened, about 10 minutes. Remove the bay leaf and serve the beans hot.

$\mathcal{P}$orky
piNTO bEANS

Lionel Bevan 3,
Fort Worth, Texas

Makes 4 to 6 servings

Plenty of pork (both salt pork and a ham hock) makes for an extra-hearty pot of beans.

1 pound dried pinto beans, rinsed, drained, and picked over

4 ounces salt pork, rind removed, rinsed well, and cut into ½-inch cubes

1 (9-ounce) smoked ham hock, rind scored in a diamond pattern with a sharp knife

2 medium onions, chopped

1 fresh hot chile pepper (such as jalapeño), seeded and minced

2 cloves garlic, minced

1 tablespoon chili powder

1 tablespoon lemon juice

1 teaspoon dried oregano

1 bay leaf

1 teaspoon salt

1 In a large pot, combine the beans and enough cold water to cover by 2 inches. Bring to a boil over high heat and boil for 2 minutes. Remove from the heat, cover the pot, and let stand for 1 hour; drain well. (The beans can also be soaked overnight in a large bowl with enough cold water to cover by 2 inches, then drained.)

2 Return the drained beans to the pot and stir in the salt pork cubes and ham hock. Add enough fresh water to barely cover the beans. Bring to a simmer over high heat, skimming any foam that rises to the surface. Add the onions, chile pepper, garlic, chili powder, lemon juice, oregano, and bay leaf. Reduce the heat to low and simmer, adding more hot water if needed to barely cover the beans, until the beans are almost tender, about 20 minutes. (The exact cooking time depends on the age and dryness of the beans.)

3 Stir in the salt and continue simmering until the beans are barely tender, about 20 more minutes. Remove the ham hock and set aside. Increase the heat to high and boil the beans until the cooking liquid is about 1 inch below the surface of the beans, about 10 minutes.

4 Chop the meat from the ham hock, discarding the rind and bones, and stir back into the beans. Remove the bay leaf, and serve the beans hot.

SWEET AND TANGY BEANS

Clyde Nelson,
The Home Ranch, Clark, Colorado

Makes 4 to 6 servings

Not every good bean recipe starts with dried beans. In this one, canned pintos get dressed up with barbecue sauce, apples, and raisins. They make a perfect pairing with baked ham.

3 strips bacon

1 medium apple, peeled, cored, and cut into
  ½-inch pieces

1 medium onion, finely chopped

1 cup golden raisins

1 cup prepared barbecue sauce

¾ cup packed light brown sugar

3 (16-ounce) cans pinto beans, drained

1 Preheat the oven to 350°F. Rub the inside of a 2-quart round flameproof casserole with one of the bacon strips to lightly grease, and place the bacon strip in the bottom of the casserole. Cut the remaining 2 bacon strips into 1-inch pieces.

2 In a large bowl, stir the apple, onion, raisins, barbecue sauce, and sugar until well combined. Stir in the beans. Transfer to the prepared casserole. Top with the bacon pieces.

3 Cover and bake for 30 minutes. Uncover and continue baking until bubbling throughout and the bacon is browned, about 30 more minutes. Serve the beans hot.

$\mathscr{B}$eefy

beans

Nancy R. Jackson,
Silver Creek Ranch, Tuscarora, Nevada

Makes 4 to 6 servings

These beans are thick and meaty enough to be a main course.

1 pound dried pink or pinto beans, rinsed, drained, and picked over

4 strips bacon, cut into 1-inch pieces

8 ounces ground round

1 medium onion, chopped

2 cloves garlic, minced

3 tablespoons chili powder

1 teaspoon ground cumin

1 teaspoon salt

½ teaspoon dried oregano

¼ teaspoon ground hot red (cayenne) pepper, or more to taste

¾ cup tomato-vegetable juice blend (such as V-8)

1 In a large pot, combine the beans and enough cold water to cover by 2 inches. Bring to a boil over high heat and boil for 2 minutes. Remove from the heat, cover the pot, and let stand for 1 hour; drain well. (The beans can also be soaked overnight in a large bowl with enough cold water to cover by 2 inches, then drained.)

2 Return the beans to the pot and add enough fresh water to barely cover. Bring to a simmer over high heat. Reduce the heat to low and simmer, uncovered, adding hot water as needed to barely cover the beans, until the beans are almost tender, about 20 minutes. (The exact cooking time depends on the age and dryness of the beans.)

3 Meanwhile, in a large skillet, cook the bacon over medium–high heat until beginning to crisp, about 4 minutes. Add the ground round, onion, and garlic. Cook, stirring to break up the meat with a wooden spoon, until the meat loses its pink color, about 5 minutes. Tilt the pan to drain off the excess fat. Add the chili powder, cumin, salt, oregano, and hot red pepper and stir for 1 minute. Stir in the tomato juice and bring to a simmer.

4 Stir the beef mixture into the beans. Simmer until the beans are tender, about 20 more minutes. Serve the beans hot.

Cowboy potato and vegetable bake

Nell Shaw,
Stonewall, Oklahoma

Makes 6 to 8 servings

The best way to get cowboys to eat their vegetables is to mix them with plenty of potatoes. No one at the dinner table will turn up their noses at this casserole.

½ cup (1 stick) unsalted butter, melted

4 medium baking potatoes (about 2½ pounds), peeled and sliced ⅛ inch thick

3 medium carrots, sliced ¼ inch thick

2 medium zucchini, scrubbed and sliced ½ inch thick

4 ounces fresh mushrooms, sliced ¼ inch thick

1 medium onion, chopped

1 medium green bell pepper, seeded and chopped into ½-inch pieces

1 teaspoon salt

¼ teaspoon freshly ground pepper

½ cup (4 ounces) shredded sharp Cheddar cheese

1 Preheat the oven to 400°F. Brush the inside of a 13-by-9-inch baking dish with some of the melted butter.

2 Add the vegetables, drizzle with the remaining melted butter, sprinkle with the salt and pepper, and toss well.

3 Bake, stirring occasionally, until the potatoes are tender, about 1 hour. During the last 15 minutes, sprinkle with the cheese.

CATTLEMEN'S club TWICE-baked POTATOES

Christine L. Francis,
Francis Hat Creek Ranch, Lusk, Wyoming

Makes 8 servings

Few cowboys fret about their fat intake because they get plenty of exercise to work off any extra calories. These spuds will be an indulgence for regular folks—just round up a few steers to help you burn off the fat.

4 large baking potatoes, scrubbed well

3 strips bacon

5 tablespoons unsalted butter, softened

1 cup (3 ounces) thinly sliced fresh mushrooms

1 clove garlic, crushed through a press

⅓ cup half-and-half

⅓ cup sour cream

1 cup (4 ounces) shredded sharp Cheddar cheese

1 large egg, beaten

1 scallion, finely chopped

1 tablespoon chopped fresh parsley

½ teaspoon salt

¼ teaspoon freshly ground pepper

1 Preheat the oven to 350°F. Place the potatoes on a baking sheet and bake until tender when pierced with a sharp knife, about 1 hour.

2 Meanwhile, in a medium skillet, cook the bacon over medium heat until crisp, about 5 minutes. Transfer to paper towels, leaving the fat in the skillet. Cool the bacon, crumble, and set aside.

3 In the same skillet, add 1 tablespoon of the butter and heat over medium heat. Add the mushrooms and cook, stirring often, until they begin to brown, about 5 minutes. Add the garlic and stir for 1 minute. Set the mushrooms aside.

4 When the potatoes are cooked, cool slightly, then cut in half lengthwise. With a spoon, carefully scoop out the potato pulp into a medium bowl, leaving ¼-inch-thick shells. Add the half-and-half, sour cream, and remaining butter. Mash with a potato masher or a hand-held electric mixer set at low. (The mixture should be softer than regular mashed potatoes.) Stir in the cooked mushrooms, crumbled bacon, ½ cup of the Cheddar cheese, egg, scallion, parsley, salt, and pepper.

5 Mound the mixture into the potato shells and arrange on a lightly buttered baking sheet. Sprinkle the tops with the remaining ½ cup Cheddar cheese. Return the potatoes to the oven. Bake until the cheese is melted and the potatoes are heated through, about 20 minutes.

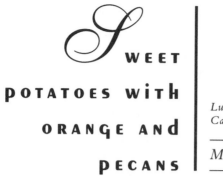

SWEET POTATOES WITH ORANGE AND PECANS

Lucy Angie Guercio,
Caribou Ranch, Nederland, Colorado

Makes 8 to 12 servings

These candied yams have a pecan topping that takes them out of the ordinary. They're a special treat with Wide Open Spaces Turkey (page 193).

8 medium sweet potatoes (about 4½ pounds)

2 cups (8 ounces) coarsely chopped pecans

1 cup packed light brown sugar

¾ cup (1½ sticks) unsalted butter, melted

1 teaspoon vanilla extract

Grated zest of 1 large orange

⅛ teaspoon salt

1 Preheat the oven to 375°F. Lightly butter a 13-by-9-inch baking dish.

2 Place the sweet potatoes on a baking sheet and bake until tender when pierced with the tip of a sharp knife, about 1 hour. Cool until easy to handle, then peel and slice into ½-inch-thick rounds. Arrange in overlapping rows in the baking dish.

3 In a medium saucepan, bring the pecans, brown sugar, and butter to a simmer over medium heat, stirring constantly to dissolve the sugar. Reduce the heat to low and cook for 2 minutes. Stir in the vanilla, orange zest, and salt. Pour the syrup over the sweet potatoes.

4 Bake until bubbling, about 10 minutes. Serve hot.

Jalapeño corn pudding

Kent Moore,
Diamond K Ranch, Lindsay, Oklahoma

Makes 4 to 6 servings

Some corn puddings are wimpy, tenderfoot food, but not this one. If you can find them, Kent suggests adding 1 cup drained canned cactus (*nopales*) pieces.

2 (16-ounce) cans cream-style corn

2 cups (8 ounces) shredded sharp Cheddar cheese

½ cup yellow cornmeal

½ cup vegetable oil

2 large eggs, beaten

2 tablespoons canned chopped green chiles, drained

2 cloves garlic, minced

½ teaspoon salt

1 Preheat the oven to 350°F. Lightly butter a 12-by-7-inch baking dish.

2 In a medium bowl, whisk the corn, 1 cup of the cheese, the cornmeal, oil, eggs, chiles, garlic, and salt. Spread the batter in the baking dish, then sprinkle with the remaining 1 cup cheese.

3 Bake until the center feels set when pressed gently with a finger, about 1 hour. Let stand 5 minutes before serving.

Chuckwagon scalloped CORN

Jimbo Humphreys,
Double X Wagon, Dickens, Texas

Makes 4 to 6 servings

This is a sure-fire side dish. Leave the chiles out if you wish.

4 tablespoons unsalted butter

1 medium onion, chopped

3 cups fresh or thawed frozen corn kernels

1 (8-ounce) package cream cheese, cut into 1-inch cubes

2 tablespoons canned chopped green chiles, drained

1 cup fresh bread crumbs

1 Preheat the oven to 350°F. Lightly butter a 9-inch square baking dish.

2 In a large skillet, melt 3 tablespoons of the butter over medium heat. Add the onion and cook, stirring often, until softened, about 5 minutes. Add the corn, cream cheese, and chiles. Reduce the heat to low and stir until the cheese is melted. Transfer the mixture to the baking dish and sprinkle with the bread crumbs. Cut the remaining 1 tablespoon butter into small pieces and dot over the bread crumbs.

3 Bake until the dish is bubbling and the crumbs are browned, about 20 minutes. Serve hot.

New Mexican Zucchini and Corn

Eva M. Holleyman,
Corona, New Mexico

Makes 8 servings

Spanish-speaking cowhands know this classic Mexican squash and cheese casserole as *calabasitas* ("little squashes," named after the size of the chopped vegetables.)

3 tablespoons olive oil

3 medium zucchini, scrubbed and cut into ½-inch cubes

3 medium yellow squash, scrubbed and cut into ½-inch cubes

1 large onion, chopped

2 hot fresh chile peppers (such as jalapeños), seeded and minced

2 cloves garlic, minced

2 cups fresh or thawed frozen corn kernels

½ teaspoon salt

¼ teaspoon freshly ground pepper

2 cups (8 ounces) shredded Monterey Jack cheese

1 Preheat the oven to 400°F. Lightly butter the inside of a 13-by-9-inch baking dish.

2 In a large skillet, heat the oil over medium heat. Add the zucchini, yellow squash, onion, chiles, and garlic. Cook, stirring often, until the squash is lightly browned, about 8 minutes. Stir in the corn, salt, and pepper. Transfer the mixture to the prepared casserole and sprinkle with the cheese.

3 Bake until the cheese is melted, about 20 minutes. Serve hot.

Grilled VEGETABLES with Herb MARINADE

Clyde Nelson,
The Home Ranch, Clark, Colorado

Makes 6 to 8 servings

Grilled vegetables are best to make in the summer when the herb garden is ready to bolt and the vegetables are especially tasty. If you plan to serve this dish with grilled meats, cook the vegetables first and serve them at room temperature—the vegetables will take up all the room on the grill, and you probably won't have space to cook meat at the same time.

Herb Marinade

- *1 cup packed fresh basil leaves*
- *2 tablespoons chopped fresh sage or 2 teaspoons crushed dried sage*
- *2 tablespoons chopped fresh parsley*
- *2 tablespoons lemon juice*
- *2 tablespoons pine nuts*
- *2 tablespoons freshly grated imported Parmesan cheese*
- *1 shallot, chopped*
- *2 cloves garlic, crushed*
- *1 teaspoon salt*
- *¼ teaspoon freshly ground pepper*
- *½ cup olive oil*

- *2 small Japanese eggplants, halved lengthwise*
- *2 small zucchini, scrubbed and halved lengthwise*
- *2 small yellow squash, scrubbed and halved lengthwise*
- *2 yellow bell peppers, seeded and cut into 6 wedges*
- *2 red bell peppers, seeded and cut into 6 wedges*
- *Smoky Tomato Vinaigrette (page 271), optional*

1 Make the marinade: In a food processor fitted with the metal blade, pulse all of the ingredients but the olive oil until finely chopped. With the machine running, gradually add the oil and process until smooth.

2 Place the vegetables in large plastic bags (preferably self-sealing). Pour the marinade over the vegetables and mix well. Let stand at room temperature, turning occasionally so that the vegetables are evenly marinated, for at least 2 hours.

3 Make a medium-hot charcoal fire in the bottom of a grill according to the directions on page 167.

4 Cook the vegetables on a lightly oiled grill, turning occasionally, until just tender, about 6 minutes. Serve the vegetables hot, warm, or at room temperature. Pass the vinaigrette if desired.

$\mathcal{D}$ESSERTS

Baking

ON TOP OF OLD

smoky

$\mathcal{C}$huck cooks often found themselves high above sea level, where the atmospheric pressure wreaked havoc with their baked goods. These recipes were tested at sea level. If you live in a high-altitude area (above 3,500 feet), you are probably aware of the adjustments you have to make in leavening proportions.

There are no hard and fast rules, but these guidelines will help. At 3,500 feet, decrease the amount of baking powder or baking soda by one third. At 5,000 feet, decrease by one half, and above 5,000, by two thirds. Oven temperatures should be increased by 25 degrees. Eggs make batters rise too, so don't beat them as much as you would at sea level. Beating incorporates air into the batter, and too much air could cause overrising, resulting in a dry, crumbly cake.

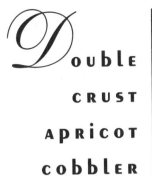

Double

CRUST

APRICOT

COBBLER

Garnet and Helen Brooks,
—B (Bar B) Brand, El Reno, Oklahoma

Makes 6 servings

Cowboys showed skill at making delicious desserts from dried fruits when the fresh variety wasn't available. Here dried apricots are plumped to make a sweet, slightly tangy filling for a tender crust. This dessert is for pie crust fans.

Crust

    2 cups all-purpose flour

    1 teaspoon salt

    ⅔ cup chilled vegetable shortening

    ½ cup (approximately) ice water

Filling

    4 cups (9 ounces) dried apricots, rinsed

    1 cup water

    1 cup plus 1 tablespoon sugar

    1 tablespoon all-purpose flour

    1 tablespoon lemon juice

    1 tablespoon unsalted butter

    ½ teaspoon ground cinnamon

    ¼ teaspoon ground nutmeg

    1 tablespoon heavy (whipping) cream, for glaze

1 Make the crust: In a medium bowl, combine the flour and salt. Using a pastry blender, cut the shortening into the flour until the mixture resembles coarse meal. Tossing with a fork, sprinkle on the water, mixing until the dough holds together when pinched between your thumb and forefinger. (You may have to add more or less water.) Gather the dough up into a thick rectangle, wrap in waxed paper, and refrigerate for at least 1 hour.

(continued)

2   Make the filling: In a medium saucepan, combine the apricots and water. Partially cover and simmer over medium-low heat, stirring occasionally, until the apricots are tender and the liquid is absorbed, about 20 minutes. Stir in 1 cup of the sugar and the flour, lemon juice, butter, cinnamon, and nutmeg. Cool completely.

3   Preheat the oven to 350°F. Lightly butter the inside of a 12-by-7-inch glass baking dish.

4   On a lightly floured work surface, roll out two thirds of the dough into a 13-by-9-inch rectangle about ⅛ inch thick. Place the dough in the bottom of the prepared pan. Pour the filling evenly into the pan. Roll out the remaining dough into an 11-by-7-inch rectangle. Place over the filling and pinch the edges of the crust together to enclose the filling. Cut a 2-inch slash in the top crust. Brush with the heavy cream and sprinkle with the remaining 1 tablespoon sugar.

5   Bake until the top is golden brown, 35 to 45 minutes. Serve the cobbler warm.

PEACH AND bOURbON cObblER

Bill Cauble,
Lambshead Ranch, Albany, Texas

Makes 8 servings

This cobbler is topped with a buttermilk biscuit crust. You can delete the bourbon if you wish.

Biscuit Crust

  2 cups all-purpose flour

  2 tablespoons sugar

  1 tablespoon baking powder

  ½ teaspoon baking soda

  ½ teaspoon salt

  ⅓ cup chilled vegetable shortening

  1 cup buttermilk

        ★   ★   ★

6 tablespoons (¾ stick) unsalted butter

¾ cup packed light brown sugar

¾ cup granulated sugar

1 cup heavy (whipping) cream

¼ cup bourbon

½ teaspoon ground cinnamon

½ teaspoon ground nutmeg

8 ripe peaches, peeled, pitted, and cut into
  ½-inch-thick slices (about 6 cups)

1 Make the biscuit crust: Sift the flour, sugar, baking powder, baking soda, and salt into a medium bowl. Using a pastry blender, cut the vegetable shortening into the flour until the mixture resembles coarse meal. Add the buttermilk and stir just to make a soft dough.

2 Preheat the oven to 350°F. Place the butter in a 13-by-9-inch baking pan and bake until melted, about 5 minutes. Remove from the oven and stir in the sugars, cream, bourbon, cinnamon, and nutmeg. Add the peaches and toss well.

3 Drop the biscuit dough by tablespoons on top of the peaches. Return to the oven and bake until the top is golden brown, about 25 minutes. Serve the cobbler warm.

NOTE: The cobbler can also be prepared outside in a 12-inch Dutch oven according to the directions on page 203.

Apple buttermilk campfire cake

Robert L. ''Buck'' Reams,
Forth Worth, Texas

Red Steagall,
Azle, Texas

Makes 8 to 10 servings

We give instructions for baking in a conventional oven, but cowboys prefer this cooked outside in their trusty Dutch oven. Both Buck and Red contributed similar recipes, and this is a combination of both. Red sometimes cooks his a tad less, and spoons it up as a pudding.

> 2 cups all-purpose flour
> 2 cups sugar
> 1 tablespoon baking powder
> 1 teaspoon ground cinnamon
> 1 teaspoon ground nutmeg
> ½ teaspoon baking soda
> 2 cups buttermilk
> 1 teaspoon vanilla extract
> 1 cup (2 sticks) unsalted butter, melted
> 8 cups sliced ripe fruit (apples, peaches, plums, pears, apricots—whatever's
> on the closest tree), peeled and cored or pitted as necessary

1 Preheat the oven to 350°F. Lightly butter the inside of a 13-by-9-inch baking pan. Place the pan in the oven and bake until very hot, about 3 minutes.

2 In a large bowl, combine the flour, sugar, baking powder, cinnamon, nutmeg, and baking soda. Make a well in the center; pour in the buttermilk and vanilla. Stir just until combined.

3 Remove the baking dish from the oven. Pour in the batter and spread evenly. Pour the melted butter over the batter, but do not mix in. Top with the sliced fruit.

4 Bake until a toothpick inserted in the center of the cake comes out clean, about 40 minutes. Serve warm.

N O T E : The cake can also be made in a 14-inch Dutch oven according to the directions on page 203.

Aunt bett's butter cake

Decie Goodspeed,
Wetumpka, Oklahoma

Makes 10 to 12 servings

Nope—the long baking time and low oven temperature aren't a mistake. They contribute to this excellent cake's chewy, almost candylike texture. Around the holidays, some cooks substitute candied fruit for part of the raisins to make a cow country fruit cake.

5 cups all-purpose flour

1 teaspoon baking soda

1 teaspoon salt

2 cups (4 sticks) unsalted butter, at room temperature

2 cups granulated sugar

6 large eggs, separated, at room temperature

1 teaspoon lemon extract

4 cups (1 pound) coarsely chopped pecans

3 cups raisins

1 Preheat the oven to 250°F. Lightly butter and flour a 10-inch tube pan (preferably nonstick) with a removable insert, shaking out the excess flour.

2 Sift the flour, baking soda, and salt together into a medium bowl.

3 In a large bowl, using a hand-held electric mixer on high speed, beat the butter and sugar until light in color and texture, about 2 minutes. One at a time, beat in the egg yolks, then the lemon extract. Gradually beat in the flour mixture to make a stiff dough. Stir in the pecans and raisins.

4 In a medium bowl, using a hand-held mixer with clean beaters at high speed, beat the egg whites until stiff. Stir about one fourth of the whites into the batter, then fold in the remaining whites. The batter will be stiff and the egg whites will deflate, but don't be alarmed. Transfer to the tube pan and smooth the top.

5 Bake until a long broom straw or bamboo skewer inserted in the center of the cake comes out clean, about 3 hours. Cool the cake in the pan on a wire rack for 10 minutes. Run a sharp knife around the inside of the pan to release the cake from the sides, then lift up and remove the sides of the pan. Cool the cake completely before removing the tube section.

Apple crumble

Bill Cauble,
Lambshead Ranch, Albany, Texas

Makes 8 servings

Fruit crisps were popular with cowboys because they could be made without eggs (even if a cow did have to be milked in order to get the butter for the topping). Use apples that will hold their shape after cooking, such as Golden Delicious or Granny Smith.

5 pounds cooking apples, peeled, cored, and cut into ½-inch-thick wedges

1 cup plus 2 tablespoons all-purpose flour

1 cup granulated sugar

1 tablespoon ground cinnamon

2 teaspoons ground nutmeg

⅛ teaspoon salt

½ cup (1 stick) unsalted butter, at room temperature

1 cup packed light brown sugar

1 Preheat the oven to 350°F. In a 13-by-9-inch baking dish, toss the apples, 2 tablespoons of the flour, the granulated sugar, cinnamon, nutmeg, and salt.

2 In a large bowl, using the tips of your fingers, combine the butter, remaining 1 cup flour, and brown sugar until crumbly. Sprinkle over the apples.

3 Bake until the apples are tender and the topping is browned, 30 to 40 minutes. Serve warm.

NOTE: The apple crisp can also be prepared in a 14-inch Dutch oven according to the directions on page 203.

Raisin

long cake

Jean True,
True Ranch, Casper, Wyoming

Makes 12 servings

Here's another cake that fits all of a chuck cook's criteria for a successful dessert: It is easy to make (no creaming of butter or whipping of egg whites or any of that other French cookin' stuff), makes plenty of servings, keeps well (if there are any leftovers, which is doubtful), and is frugal (it doesn't have any eggs, but you'd never know).

2 cups raisins

2 cups water

2 cups granulated sugar

½ cup (1 stick) unsalted butter, cut into pieces

1 teaspoon ground cinnamon

½ teaspoon ground nutmeg

¼ teaspoon ground cloves

3 cups all-purpose flour

2 teaspoons baking soda

½ teaspoon baking powder

½ teaspoon salt

Confectioner's sugar, for garnish

1 Preheat the oven to 350°F. Butter and flour a 13-by-9-inch baking pan, shaking out the excess flour.

2 In a large saucepan, bring the raisins, water, sugar, butter, cinnamon, nutmeg, and cloves to a boil over high heat. Reduce the heat to medium and boil, uncovered, for 5 minutes. Transfer to a large bowl and cool completely.

3 Sift the flour, baking soda, baking powder, and salt into the raisin mixture and stir until smooth. Transfer to the baking pan.

4 Bake until a toothpick inserted in the center of the cake comes out clean, 35 to 45 minutes. Cool the cake completely in the pan on a wire rack. Sift the confectioner's sugar over the top of the cake before serving.

Spiced
PRUNE CAKE

Cliff Teinert,
Long X Ranch, Kent, Texas

Makes 12 servings

Cooks in cow country always appreciated recipes that used dried fruits, since fresh fruits couldn't always be found. This is a winner, especially good with a big dollop of whipped cream.

1 cup (8 ounces) coarsely chopped pitted prunes

1 cup (4 ounces) coarsely chopped walnuts

2 cups plus 2 tablespoons all-purpose flour

1 teaspoon baking soda

½ teaspoon ground cinnamon

½ teaspoon ground cloves

½ teaspoon ground nutmeg

½ teaspoon salt

2 cups granulated sugar

1 cup vegetable oil

2 large eggs, at room temperature

1 cup buttermilk

Confectioner's sugar, for garnish

Sweetened whipped cream, for serving

1 Preheat the oven to 350°F. Butter and flour a 13-by-9-inch baking pan, shaking out the excess flour.

2 In a small bowl, soak the prunes in enough boiling water to cover until plump, about 15 minutes. Drain well, then pat dry with paper towels. In a small bowl, toss the prunes with the walnuts and 2 tablespoons of the flour.

3 Sift the remaining 2 cups flour and the baking soda, cinnamon, cloves, nutmeg, and salt together onto a piece of waxed paper.

4 In a medium bowl, using a hand-held electric mixer on high speed, beat the granulated sugar and oil until well combined. Add the eggs and continue beating until thick and light in color, about 2 minutes. Adding one third at a time, with the mixer on low speed, alternately beat in the flour mixture and buttermilk. Stir in the prune mixture. Spread evenly in the baking pan.

5 Bake until the cake springs back when gently pressed in the center with your finger, 50 minutes to 1 hour. Cool completely in the pan on a wire cake rack. Sift confectioner's sugar over the top before serving. Top each serving with a dollop of whipped cream.

Applesauce-Pecan Cake

Mitzi Riley,
Riley Ranch, Aledo, Texas

Makes 12 servings

Many chuck cooks put up applesauce every fall, and one of the benefits of their labor is this extra-moist and spicy cake.

2½ cups all-purpose flour
1 tablespoon ground cinnamon
1 teaspoon baking powder
½ teaspoon baking soda
½ teaspoon ground allspice
½ teaspoon ground cloves
½ teaspoon salt
1 cup (4 ounces) chopped pecans
1 cup raisins
2 cups granulated sugar
½ cup (1 stick) unsalted butter, at room temperature
2 large eggs, at room temperature
1 cup applesauce
½ cup warm water
Confectioner's sugar, for garnish

1   Make the cake: Preheat the oven to 350°F. Butter and flour a 13-by-9-inch baking pan, shaking out the excess flour.

2   Sift 2 cups of the flour and the cinnamon, baking powder, baking soda, allspice, cloves, and salt onto a piece of waxed paper. In a small bowl, toss the remaining ½ cup flour with the pecans and raisins.

3   In a medium bowl, using a hand-held electric mixer on high speed, beat the granulated sugar and butter until well combined, about 2 minutes. One at a time, beat in the eggs. Add the flour mixture, applesauce, and water and beat on low speed until smooth. Stir in the raisin-pecan mixture. Transfer to the baking pan and spread evenly.

4   Bake until a toothpick inserted in the center comes out clean, about 40 minutes. Cool completely in the pan on a wire cake rack. Sift confectioner's sugar over the top of the cake before serving.

Apple spice cake

Liz McKee,
Tailgate Ranch, Tonganoxie, Kansas

Makes 10 to 12 servings

Choose a not-too-juicy variety of apple (such as Golden Delicious or Granny Smith) for the best results in this delicious cake that is as fine as a breakfast treat as it is an after-dinner dessert.

2 cups all-purpose flour

1 teaspoon ground cinnamon

1 teaspoon baking soda

½ teaspoon salt

¼ teaspoon ground nutmeg

3 large eggs, at room temperature

2 cups granulated sugar

1 cup vegetable oil

1 teaspoon vanilla extract

4 Golden Delicious apples, peeled, cored, and cut into ½-inch cubes (about 5 cups)

1 cup (4 ounces) chopped pecans

1 Preheat the oven to 350°F. Butter and flour a 10-inch fluted tube pan, shaking out the excess flour.

2 Sift the flour, cinnamon, baking soda, salt, and nutmeg onto a piece of waxed paper.

3 In a large bowl, using a hand-held electric mixer on high speed, beat the eggs and sugar until combined. Add the oil and vanilla and beat until thick and light colored, about 2 minutes. Reduce the speed to medium and beat in the flour mixture just until smooth. The batter will be very thick. Stir in the apples and pecans. Transfer to the tube pan.

4 Bake until a toothpick inserted in the center comes out clean, about 1 hour. Cool in the pan for 10 minutes. Invert onto a wire cake rack, remove the pan, and cool completely.

Mocha Pecan Layer Cake

Lucy Angie Guercio,
Caribou Ranch, Nederland, Colorado

Makes 8 servings

When a ranch cook makes a fancy layer cake, it has to be hassle-free in order to fit into the kitchen's busy schedule. Not only is this one of the simplest layer cakes around—it is one of the best.

Cake

2 cups all-purpose flour

2 cups granulated sugar

½ cup cocoa powder (use a non-alkalized brand like Hershey's)

2 teaspoons baking soda

¼ teaspoon salt

1 cup vegetable oil

1 cup buttermilk

2 large eggs, at room temperature

1 cup hot, strong brewed coffee

Frosting

2 (3-ounce) packages cream cheese, at room temperature

2 tablespoons unsalted butter, softened

4 cups confectioner's sugar

½ cup cocoa powder

1 tablespoon instant coffee dissolved in 2 tablespoons boiling water

1 cup (4 ounces) finely chopped pecans

1 Make the cake: Preheat the oven to 350°F. Butter 2 (9-inch) round cake pans. Line the bottoms of the pans with rounds of waxed paper, and dust the insides of the pans with flour, shaking out the excess flour.

2 In a large bowl, whisk flour, sugar, cocoa powder, baking soda, and salt until combined. Make a well in the center and add the oil and buttermilk to the well. Stir gently to combine. One at a time, add the eggs, beating well after each addition. Beat in the coffee. The batter will be thin. Pour into the cake pans.

3   Bake until the tops of the cakes spring back when pressed gently in the center with a finger, 25 to 35 minutes. Cool on wire racks for 10 minutes. Invert and unmold the cakes onto wire cake racks, remove the waxed paper rounds, and cool completely.

4   Meanwhile, make the frosting: In a medium bowl, using a hand-held electric mixer on low speed, beat the cream cheese and butter until smooth. Sift the confectioner's sugar and cocoa powder together and gradually beat into the cream cheese mixture. Gradually beat in enough of the coffee mixture until the frosting is smooth and spreadable. (You may not need all of the coffee mixture.)

5   Place one layer of cake upside down on a serving platter. Spread the layer with about ½ cup of the frosting, then top with the second layer, right side up. Frost the top and sides of the cake with the remaining frosting. Press the chopped pecans around the sides of the cake.

TEXAS CHOCOLATE SHEET CAKE

Hearst Ranches, San Simeon, California

Makes 12 to 16 servings

This cake is highly unusual for its sugarless batter, which is balanced by the sweet frosting. It's one of the most popular desserts to be found at a Texas barbecue.

Cake

    1 cup water

    1 cup (2 sticks) unsalted butter, cut into pieces

    ⅓ cup cocoa powder (use a non-alkalized brand such as Hershey's)

    2 cups all-purpose flour

    ½ cup sour cream

    2 large eggs, at room temperature

    1 teaspoon baking soda

Frosting

    ½ cup (1 stick) unsalted butter, cut into pieces

    ¼ cup plus 2 tablespoons milk

    4 cups (1 pound) confectioner's sugar

    1 teaspoon vanilla extract

    1 cup finely chopped walnuts

1 Make the cake: Preheat the oven to 350°F. Lightly butter and flour a 17-by-11-inch jelly roll pan, shaking out the excess flour.

2 In a large saucepan, bring the water, butter, and cocoa powder to a boil over medium-high heat, whisking often to dissolve the cocoa. Remove from the heat.

3 One ingredient at a time, in the following order, add the flour, sour cream, eggs, and baking soda, beating well after each addition. Transfer to the jelly roll pan and spread evenly.

4 Bake until the cake springs back when gently pressed in the center with a fingertip, 10 to 15 minutes.

5 Meanwhile, make the frosting: In a medium saucepan, bring the butter and milk just to a simmer over medium-low heat, stirring often to melt the butter and avoid boiling over. Remove from the heat and stir in the confectioner's sugar and vanilla until smooth. Stir in the nuts. Keep warm.

6 As soon as the cake is removed from the oven, pour the warm frosting over the cake and spread gently and evenly. Cool the cake completely in the pan on a wire rack.

PANHANDLE PECAN PIE

Betty Price,
Lubbock, Texas

Makes 6 to 8 servings

Cowboys use whatever they have on hand to fix their vittles. Because pecans grow in profusion in Oklahoma and Texas, pecan pie shows up as dessert with regularity. This is the most popular recipe, but it gets a special touch with a dash of nutmeg.

Crust

1½ cups all-purpose flour

½ teaspoon salt

½ cup chilled lard or vegetable shortening

5 tablespoons (approximately) ice water

Filling

1 cup coarsely chopped pecans

1 cup granulated sugar

1 cup light corn syrup

3 tablespoons unsalted butter, cut into ½-inch pieces

3 large eggs

1 teaspoon vanilla extract

¼ teaspoon ground nutmeg

1. Make the crust: In a medium bowl, combine the flour and salt. Using a pastry blender, cut the lard into the flour until the mixture resembles coarse meal. Tossing with a fork, sprinkle on the water, mixing until the dough holds together when pinched between your thumb and forefinger. (You may have to add more or less water.) Gather the dough up into a thick rectangle, wrap in waxed paper, and refrigerate for at least 1 hour.

2 Preheat the oven to 350°F. On a lightly floured work surface, roll out the dough to a 12-inch circle about ⅛ inch thick. Transfer the dough to a deep 9-inch pie plate. Trim the excess dough to a 1-inch border. Fold up the edge of the dough into a double thickness, then flute the edge. Place the crust in the freezer while making the filling.

3 Make the filling: In a medium bowl, whisk all the ingredients until combined. Pour into the prepared pie shell.

4 Bake until the filling is puffed and browned (the center will jiggle slightly when shaken), about 1 hour. Cool completely on a wire rack.

Mexican wedding cookies

Eva M. Holleyman,
Corona, New Mexico

Makes about 3 dozen cookies

These melt-in-your-mouth morsels traveled over the border to become beloved Christmas cookies. Of course, they're excellent any time of year.

2 cups confectioner's sugar

1 cup (2 sticks) unsalted butter, at room temperature

1 teaspoon vanilla extract

2 cups all-purpose flour

⅛ teaspoon salt

1 cup (4 ounces) finely chopped pecans

1 Preheat the oven to 325°F.

2 In a medium bowl, using a hand-held electric mixer on high speed, beat 1 cup of the sugar with the butter and vanilla until combined, about 1 minute. Using a wooden spoon, gradually work in the flour and salt, then the pecans.

3 Using a level tablespoon for each, roll the dough into 36 balls. Place 1 inch apart on ungreased baking sheets.

4 Bake, switching the position of the sheets from top to bottom halfway through baking, until lightly browned, about 15 minutes. Do not overbake the cookies. Place the remaining 1 cup confectioner's sugar on a plate. Roll the warm cookies in the sugar to coat well. Place the cookies on wire racks to cool completely.

LONE STAR GINGERBREAD COOKIES

Betty Price,
Lubbock, Texas

Makes about 4 dozen 3-inch cookies

Betty never makes less than a few dozen cookies, so this recipe is for a big batch. You can use any shape cookie cutter you want, of course. You can also make the dough ahead and refrigerate it for up to 3 days.

5 cups all-purpose flour, or more as needed

1 teaspoon baking soda

1 teaspoon salt

1 cup vegetable shortening

1 cup packed light brown sugar

½ cup granulated sugar

1½ cups unsulphured molasses

2 large eggs

Grated zest of 1 lemon

2 teaspoons hot water

1 teaspoon cider vinegar

1 teaspoon ground cinnamon

1 teaspoon ground ginger

1 Sift the flour, baking soda, and salt together into a large bowl.

2 In a large bowl, using a hand-held electric mixer on high speed, beat the shortening with the brown and granulated sugars until light in color and texture, about 2 minutes. Beat in the molasses, then the eggs, lemon zest, water, vinegar, cinnamon, and ginger.

3 Gradually beat in the flour mixture. (You may have to change to a wooden spoon to beat in the last additions of flour unless you have a heavy-duty mixer. Also add more flour as needed to make a stiff dough.) Cover tightly with plastic wrap and refrigerate for at least 12 hours or up to 3 days.

4 Preheat the oven to 350°F. Lightly butter 2 baking sheets.

5 On a lightly floured work surface, roll out the dough to a ¼-inch thickness. (This thickness will make plump, chewy cookies; roll the dough ⅛ inch thick for thin, crisp cookies.) Using a 3-inch star cookie cutter, cut out cookies and transfer to the baking sheets.

6 Bake, switching the sheets from top to bottom halfway through baking, until the cookies are lightly browned, 10 to 12 minutes. Cool for 2 minutes, then transfer to wire racks to cool completely. Cool the baking sheets completely before baking more batches.

Biscuit bread pudding with Lemon Sauce

Jimbo Humphreys,
Double X Wagon, Dickens, Texas

Makes 6 servings

It's rare that biscuits stay around in a ranch kitchen long enough to go stale, but when it happens, they are often turned into a pudding like this one.

Pudding

    1 (12-ounce) can evaporated milk

    1½ cups granulated sugar

    3 large eggs, well beaten

    6 tablespoons (¾ stick) unsalted butter, melted

    1½ teaspoons vanilla extract

    ½ teaspoon ground cinnamon

    8 stale biscuits

Lemon Sauce

    1 cup granulated sugar

    2 large eggs, well beaten

    ¼ cup water

    3 tablespoons lemon juice

    ½ cup (1 stick) unsalted butter, cut into pieces

1   Preheat the oven to 325°F. Lightly butter a 12-by-8-inch baking dish.

2   Make the pudding: In a large bowl, whisk together the milk, sugar, eggs, melted butter, vanilla, and cinnamon. Crumble the biscuits into the bowl and stir gently. Let stand 30 minutes, stirring occasionally, until the biscuits have absorbed some of the milk mixture. Transfer to the baking dish.

3   Place the baking dish in a larger pan and place in the oven. Fill the pan with enough hot water to come ½ inch up the sides of the dish. Bake until a knife inserted in the center comes out clean, about 45 minutes.

4 Meanwhile, make the sauce: In a medium saucepan, whisk the sugar, eggs, water, and lemon juice. Add the butter. Cook over low heat, stirring constantly, until the butter is melted and the sauce is thickened, about 5 minutes. Do not boil. Strain into a warm sauceboat and cover to keep warm.

5 Serve the pudding hot, topping each serving with some of the warm lemon sauce.

Spotted pup rice pudding

Guy and Pipp Gillette,
Gillette Ranch, Lovelady, Texas

Makes 8 servings

A cowboy favorite and a great way to use up leftover rice.

> 1½ cups milk
> ½ cup heavy (whipping) cream
> 5 large eggs, beaten
> 6 tablespoons granulated sugar
> 1 teaspoon vanilla extract
> ⅛ teaspoon salt
> 1½ cups cooked rice
> 1 cup raisins

1 Preheat the oven to 300°F. Lightly butter a 9-inch square glass baking dish.

2 In a large bowl, whisk the milk, cream, eggs, sugar, vanilla, and salt. Stir in the rice and raisins. Transfer to the baking dish.

3 Bake until a knife inserted in the center comes out clean, about 1 hour. Serve the pudding warm, chilled, or at room temperature.

N O T E : The pudding can also be prepared in a 10-inch Dutch oven according to the directions on page 203. In this case, mix the pudding directly in the buttered Dutch oven. Use a few less coals than usual to keep the heat moderately low, or the eggs may curdle.

Sauces, salsas, and beverages

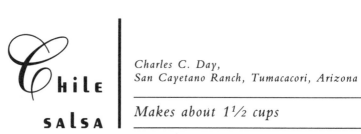

Chile salsa

Charles C. Day,
San Cayetano Ranch, Tumacacori, Arizona

Makes about 1½ cups

Salsa is at its best served with tortilla chips but also makes a mighty fine condiment for grilled salmon, swordfish steaks, or chicken.

> 5 ripe plum tomatoes, seeded and chopped
> ¼ cup chopped white onion
> 1 fresh hot chile pepper (such as jalapeño), seeded and minced, or
>   1 (4-ounce) can chopped mild chiles, drained
> 1 clove garlic, minced
> 1 tablespoon red wine vinegar
> 1 tablespoon lime juice
> 1 tablespoon olive oil
> 1 teaspoon dried oregano
> ¼ teaspoon salt

1 In a medium bowl, combine all the ingredients. Cover and refrigerate until ready to serve, no longer than 1 day.

Sauce Caribe

Eva M. Holleyman,
Corona, New Mexico

Makes about 2 cups

Chili sauce is as spicy as the chiles you use. Be sure that you buy only mildly hot chile peppers because New Mexican chiles come in a full range of heat intensities. If you are using this sauce to make New Mexican Red Chili (page 209), reserve the chile-soaking liquid.

> 7 dried mild to medium-hot New Mexican chile peppers
> 2 cups boiling water
> 1 (16-ounce) can peeled tomatoes in juice, drained
> 2 cloves garlic, minced
> ½ teaspoon ground cumin
> ½ teaspoon dried oregano

1 Rinse the chile peppers, split them open, and remove and reserve the seeds. Remove and discard the stems. In a medium bowl, soak the chiles in the boiling water. Let stand until they are softened, about 20 minutes. Drain the chiles, reserving the soaking liquid.

2 In a blender, combine the soaked chiles with ¼ cup of the soaking liquid and the tomatoes, garlic, cumin, and oregano; process until smooth. (Taste the sauce; if you like it hotter, add some of the reserved chile pepper seeds. Also, if you feel the sauce could be a little thinner, add more of the reserved soaking liquid.) Cover and refrigerate for up to 1 week.

Guacamole

For the best guacamole, use Hass avocados with dark, pebbly skins. And never make guacamole in a blender—it should be chunky, not smooth.

3 ripe medium avocados, halved, pitted, and peeled

¼ cup finely chopped onion, preferably white onion

1 ripe plum tomato, seeded and finely chopped

1 clove garlic, crushed through a press

2 tablespoons lime juice

2 tablespoons chopped fresh cilantro (coriander), optional

1 hot fresh chile pepper (such as jalapeño), seeded and minced, or to taste

½ teaspoon salt

1 In a medium bowl, mash all of the ingredients together with a fork until well mixed but still chunky. Press a piece of plastic wrap directly on the surface and refrigerate until ready to serve, up to 2 days.

Cowboy barbecue sauce

Makes about 2 cups

You'll never use bottled barbecue sauce again after you try this.

2 tablespoons bacon grease or vegetable oil

1 large onion, finely chopped

2 cloves garlic, minced

1 cup tomato catsup

1 cup bottled chili sauce

½ cup packed light brown sugar

½ cup lemon juice

2 tablespoons Worcestershire sauce

Hot red pepper sauce to taste

1 In a large saucepan, heat the bacon grease over low heat. Add the onion and garlic and cook, stirring, until the onion is softened, about 5 minutes.

2 Stir in the catsup, chili sauce, sugar, lemon juice, and Worcestershire sauce. Bring to a simmer and cook, stirring often to prevent sticking, until slightly thickened, about 45 minutes. Season with hot sauce to taste. (The sauce can be made up to 5 days ahead, cooled, covered, and refrigerated.)

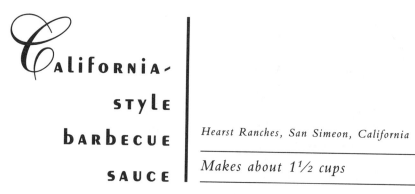

CALIFORNIA-STYLE BARBECUE SAUCE

Hearst Ranches, San Simeon, California

Makes about 1½ cups

The influence of Asian ranch cooks is found in this soy sauce– and sherry-spiked barbecue sauce.

¾ cup granulated sugar

½ cup Japanese soy sauce

½ cup tomato catsup

½ cup dry sherry

3 cloves garlic, crushed

1 teaspoon ground ginger

½ teaspoon freshly ground pepper

1 In a medium bowl, stir all ingredients until combined. Cover and refrigerate until ready to use. (The sauce can be prepared up to 3 days ahead, covered, and refrigerated.)

Chuckwagon

TOMATO SAUCE

Clyde Nelson,
The Home Ranch, Clark, Colorado

Makes about 3½ cups

This is a kissin' cousin to Ranchero Sauce, but its Italian seasonings make it a great pasta topping, as well as a condiment for meats. To peel plum tomatoes, cook them in boiling water for 1 minute, drain, and rinse under cold water. The skins will come right off with the help of a small sharp knife.

2 tablespoons vegetable oil

1 medium red onion, chopped

2 cloves garlic, minced

2 pounds ripe plum tomatoes, peeled, seeded, and chopped

1 poblano chile pepper, roasted, peeled, seeded, and chopped (page 129)

1 cup tomato sauce

1 tablespoon red wine vinegar

1 teaspoon dried basil

1 teaspoon dried oregano

¼ teaspoon salt

¼ teaspoon freshly ground pepper

2 tablespoons cold unsalted butter, cut into pieces

1　In a large saucepan, heat the oil over low heat. Add the onion and garlic and cook, stirring often, until the onion is softened, about 5 minutes.

2　Stir in the tomatoes, chile pepper, tomato sauce, vinegar, basil, and oregano. Bring to a simmer and cook until slightly thickened, about 10 minutes. Season with salt and pepper. Off heat, whisk in the butter. Serve the sauce hot. (The sauce can be prepared up to 3 days ahead, cooled, covered, and refrigerated. Reheat gently before serving.)

RANCHERO SAUCE

Greta and William L. Arrington,
Rocking Chair Ranch, Pampa, Texas

Makes about 4 cups

Ranchero sauce is an important ingredient in Huevos Rancheros (page 217), but also hits the bull's-eye when served with grilled steaks or pork chops. This recipe makes a large batch, and it freezes well.

¼ cup olive oil

1 medium onion, chopped

1 small stalk celery, chopped

1 medium green bell pepper, seeded and chopped

2 cloves garlic, minced

1 (28-ounce) can chopped tomatoes, undrained

1 (4-ounce) can chopped mild green chile peppers, drained

2 tablespoons Worcestershire sauce

2 tablespoons chopped fresh parsley

2 teaspoons sweet or hot Hungarian paprika

1 teaspoon dried oregano

¼ teaspoon freshly ground pepper

½ teaspoon hot red pepper sauce, or to taste

1 In a medium saucepan, heat the oil over medium heat. Add the onion, celery, bell pepper, and garlic and cook, covered, until the vegetables are lightly browned, about 10 minutes.

2 Add the tomatoes with their juices, green chiles, Worcestershire sauce, parsley, paprika, oregano, and pepper and bring to a simmer. Reduce the heat to low and simmer, uncovered, until slightly thickened and the tomato juices are almost evaporated, about 30 minutes. Stir in the hot sauce. Serve the sauce hot, warm, or at room temperature. (The sauce can be prepared up to 5 days ahead, cooled, covered, and refrigerated. Reheat gently before serving.)

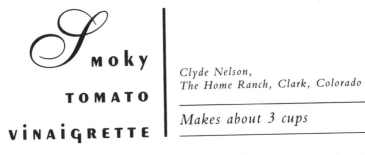

Smoky Tomato Vinaigrette

Clyde Nelson,
The Home Ranch, Clark, Colorado

Makes about 3 cups

This scarlet dressing was designed to go with grilled vegetables, but it can be served on greens too.

8 ripe plum tomatoes

½ cup lemon juice

½ cup chopped shallots or scallions

½ cup chopped mixed herbs (basil, tarragon, marjoram, fennel fronds, in any combination)

½ teaspoon salt

¼ teaspoon freshly ground pepper

2 cups extra-virgin olive oil

1 Make a hot charcoal fire according to the instructions on page 167.

2 Grill the tomatoes on a lightly oiled grill, turning often, just until the skins are charred and peeling on all sides, about 5 minutes. Remove from the grill and cool completely. Discard the skins and seeds. Finely chop the tomato flesh. Put the chopped tomatoes into a fine sieve placed over a large bowl and let stand and drain for 30 minutes. Discard the drained tomato juices.

3 In a medium bowl, combine the drained chopped tomatoes, lemon juice, shallots, herbs, salt, and pepper. Gradually whisk in the oil. Cover and refrigerate until ready to serve.

Tropical Pineapple Salsa

Clyde Nelson,
The Home Ranch, Clark, Colorado

Makes about 3 cups

Clyde adds chopped mango, yellow bell pepper, and jicama (a crisp, bland tuber found in Latin markets) to his salsa, but this streamlined version is great too. Serve with grilled pork, chicken, or swordfish.

1 ripe pineapple, finely chopped

⅔ cup finely chopped red bell pepper

1 tablespoon freshly grated ginger

2 fresh hot chile peppers (such as jalapeños), seeded and minced, or to taste

2 cloves garlic, minced

¼ cup fresh lime juice

1 tablespoon soy sauce

1 tablespoon rice wine vinegar

1 tablespoon dark Asian sesame oil

½ cup chopped fresh mint leaves

2 tablespoons chopped fresh cilantro (coriander)

1 In a large bowl, combine all the ingredients except the mint and cilantro. Cover with plastic wrap and refrigerate for 1 hour or up to 4 hours.

2 When ready to serve, stir in the mint and cilantro.

ℐEACH AND CITRUS CHUTNEY

Clyde Nelson,
The Home Ranch, Clark, Colorado

Makes about 3 cups

Peach chutney is just the thing to serve with pork chops, ham, or smoked turkey. It might even persuade a cowboy to eat lamb chops.

1 cup orange juice, preferably freshly squeezed

½ cup granulated sugar

½ cup raspberry or cider vinegar

3 large peaches, peeled, pitted, and coarsely chopped

1 medium red onion, finely chopped

1 medium red bell pepper, seeded and finely chopped

⅓ cup dried currants

⅓ cup golden raisins

2 tablespoons grated fresh ginger

Grated zest of 2 lemons

Grated zest of 1 large orange

1 teaspoon Madras-style curry powder

¼ teaspoon salt

1 In a large saucepan, bring the orange juice, sugar, and vinegar to a simmer over medium heat, stirring often to dissolve the sugar. Reduce the heat to low and cook for 5 minutes.

2 Stir in the remaining ingredients and bring to a simmer. Cook, stirring often, until thickened, about 20 minutes. Transfer to a medium bowl and cool completely. (The chutney can be prepared up to 1 week ahead, covered, and refrigerated.)

Cowboy

CAMP COFFEE

Garnet and Helen Brooks,
—B (Bar B) Brand, El Reno, Oklahoma

Makes 6 to 8 servings

Add a crumbled eggshell to the mixture if you want "gourmet" cowboy coffee.

1 quart plus ½ cup cold water
⅓ cup ground coffee

1 In a large coffeepot, bring 1 quart of the water and the coffee to a boil over a hot campfire. As soon as coffee boils, remove from the heat. Pour ½ cup cold water in the pot and let stand for 1 minute to allow the grounds to settle to the bottom of the pot. Carefully pour the coffee into the cups, trying not the disturb the grounds too much.

Old-Fashioned Egg Nog

Mitzi Riley,
Riley Ranch, Aledo, Texas

Makes 12 to 16 servings

Before refrigeration, egg nog was served in winter because that was the only time of year it could be stored without souring. Its keeping qualities were also aided by copious amounts of alcohol.

6 large eggs, separated, at room temperature
¾ cup granulated sugar
2 cups milk
2 cups bourbon
½ cup dark rum
2 cups heavy (whipping) cream, chilled
Ground nutmeg, for serving

1 In a large bowl, using a hand-held electric mixer on high speed, beat the egg whites just until soft peaks form. Gradually beat in half (6 tablespoons) of the sugar until stiff peaks form. Set aside.

2 In another large bowl, using the same mixer set on high speed, beat the egg yolks with the remaining 6 tablespoons sugar until light in color, about 2 minutes. Beat in the milk, bourbon, and rum. Add the whites and fold gently to barely combine.

3 In a chilled large bowl, beat the heavy cream until stiff. Add to the egg mixture and fold in until the egg nog is smooth, with just a few fluffs of egg whites. Cover and chill for at least 4 hours or overnight.

4 Pour the egg nog into a large punch bowl, dust the top with nutmeg, and serve chilled.

Mitzi Riley,
Riley Ranch, Aledo, Texas

ANGRIA

Makes 8 servings

Sangria was brought over the border by Mexican ranch hands, and anyone who has enjoyed a glass on a hot summer afternoon is glad they did so.

½ cup granulated sugar

½ cup water

1 lemon, thinly sliced

1 orange, thinly sliced

1 lime, thinly sliced

1 (750-ml) bottle dry red wine, such as Zinfandel, chilled

¼ cup brandy or Cognac

1½ cups club soda, chilled

1 The day before serving the sangria, in a small saucepan, stir the sugar and water over medium–high heat until the sugar dissolves and the syrup is boiling. Stop stirring and boil for 1 minute. Transfer the syrup to a medium bowl and cool completely.

2 Add the lemon, orange, and lime slices and mix well. Cover and refrigerate overnight, stirring occasionally.

3 In a large pitcher, stir the fruits with the syrup, wine, and brandy. Add about 2 handfuls of ice cubes, cover, and refrigerate for at least 20 minutes or up to 4 hours.

4 When ready to serve, add the club soda. Pour into large wine glasses, spooning some of the fruit into each glass.

$\mathscr{N}$OTES

CHAPTER 1.

COOKING ON THE RANGE AND TRAIL

1. Richard Dallam, "Diary of Richard Dallam, Cattle Drover over the Trail from Texas to California and in California and Oregon from December 5, 1852, to May 26, 1864," Western History Manuscript #131, Bienecke Library, Yale University, New Haven, Conn.

2. Mark J. Withers to J. Evetts Haley, typed interview, October 8, 1932, Lockhart, Tex. Biographical File, J. Evetts Haley Collection, Nita Stewart Haley Memorial Library, Midland, Tex. [NSHML].

3. Mark H. Brown and W. R. Felton, *Before Barbed Wire: L. A. Huffman, Photographer on Horseback* (New York: Bramhall House, 1956), p. 145.

4. Laura V. Hamner, "What Was Time to a Cowboy?" *The Cattleman* 33 (Dec. 1946), p. 124.

5. Brown and Felton, *Before Barbed Wire,* p. 145.

6. "W. B. Hester, Rotan, Texas," *The Cattleman* 12 (May 1927), p. 29.

7. James H. Cook, *Fifty Years on the Old Frontier, as Cowboy, Hunter, Guide, Scout and Ranchman* (New Haven, Conn.: Yale University Press, 1923), p. 39.

8. Quoted in Notes on Camp Cooks, J. Frank Dobie Collection, Harry Ransom Humanities Research Center, University of Texas, Austin [HRHRC].

9. *Ibid.*

10. Jo Rainbolt, *The Last Cowboy: Twilight Era of the Horseback Cowhand, 1900–1940* (Helena, Mont.: American and World Geographic Publishing, 1992), p. 59.

11. Gerry Burton, "Aging Cowboy Still Rides Matador Range," *Lubbock Avalanche-Journal,* July 4, 1982.

12. Quoted in Notes on Camp Cooks, J. Frank Dobie Collection, HRHRC.

13. J. Evetts Haley, *The XIT Ranch of Texas* (Chicago: Lakeside Press, 1929), p. 246.

14. J. Frank Dobie, *Cow People* (Boston: Little, Brown Co., 1964), p. 140.

15. Steve Kelton, *Renderbrook: A Century Under the Spade Brand* (Fort Worth: Texas Christian University Press, 1990), p. 81.

16. "The Cowboy as He Is," *Democratic Leader* (Cheyenne, Wyo.), Jan. 11, 1885.

17. Hamlin Garland, "Round-Up on the Range," *Rocky Mountain News* (Denver, Colo.), Aug. 18, 1895.

18. Joseph G. McCoy, *Historic Sketches of the Cattle Trade of the West and Southwest* (Kansas City: Ramsey, Millett, & Hudson, Printers, 1874), p. 137.

19. E. C. ("Teddy Blue") Abbott and Helena Huntington Smith, *We Pointed Them North: Recollections of a Cowpuncher* (New York: Farrar and Rinehart, 1939), p. 161.

20. "The Montana Cow Boy," *Kansas Cowboy,* July 25, 1885.

21. Estelle Tinkler, "History of the Rocking Chair Ranch," *Panhandle-Plains Historical Review* 15 (1942), p. 82.

22. Quoted in *Ibid.,* p. 84.

23. "Slade as a Cowboy," *Texas Live Stock Journal* (Fort Worth, Tex.), Sept. 23, 1882.

24. Haley, *The XIT Ranch*, p. 250.

25. William C. Holden, *Rollie Burns* (Dallas: Southwest Press, 1932), p. 154.

26. Frank X. Tolbert, "Luxuries Softening Cowboys, Chuck Wagon Cook Decides," *Dallas Morning News,* April 9, 1953.

27. Frank X. Tolbert, "Pitchfork Dares the Sourdoughs," *Dallas Morning News,* July 6, 1958.

CHAPTER 2.

"POT RASSLERS" AND "BELLY CHEATERS": COW CAMP COOKS

1. Anonymous, untitled typescript, Cooks File, Topical files, J. Evetts Haley Collection, NSHML.

2. "The Round-Up," *Las Animas Leader,* July 27, 1877.

3. "A Cowboy's Life," *Trinidad Daily Advertiser,* June 24, 1883.

4. J. Marvin Hunter, comp. & ed., *The Trail Drivers of Texas* (Nashville: Cokesbury Press, 1925), p. 364.

5. Anonymous, untitled typescript, NSHML.

6. Fred Gipson, *Cowhand* (New York: Harper & Brothers, 1953), p. 163.

7. Quoted in J. Evetts Haley, Memorandum, July 20, 1933, Cooks File, Topical files, J. Evetts Haley Collection, NSHML.

8. George F. Ellis, *Bell Ranch as I Knew It* (Kansas City: Lowell Press, 1973), p. 141.

9. Hervey E. Chesley, *Adventuring with the Old-Timers: Trails Traveled—Tales Told* (El Paso: Nita Stewart Haley Memorial Library, 1979), p. 25.

10. Evan G. Barnard, *A Rider of the Cherokee Strip* (Boston: Houghton Mifflin, 1936), p. 53.

11. V. H. Whitlock ("Ol' Waddy"), *Yellowhouse Canyon* (Beaumont, Tex.: Privately printed, 1939), p. 179.

12. C. W. (Charlie) Walker, W. W. (Walter) Walker, and W. D. (Bill) Walker to J. Evetts Haley, typed interview, Aug. 5, 1937, Dunlap, N. Mex., Biographical Files, J. Evetts Haley Collection, NSHML.

13. Cordia Sloan Duke and Joe B. Frantz, *6000 Miles of Fence: Life on the XIT Ranch of Texas* (Austin: University of Texas Press, 1961), p. 172.

14. Quoted in Notes on Camp Cooks, J. Frank Dobie Collection, HRHRC.

15. John Arnot, "The Wagon," manuscript, Bx. 2H472, Earl Vandale Collection, Center for American History, University of Texas, Austin.

16. Walter Day, "The Days of Their Glory," typescript, Notes on Camp Cooks, J. Frank Dobie Collection, HRHRC.

17. Con Price, "Camp Cook," typescript, Notes on Camp Cooks, J. Frank Dobie Collection, HRHRC.

18. J. Evetts Haley, "Sour Dough," typescript, Cooks File, Topical files, J. Evetts Haley Collection, NSHML.

19. Quoted in Notes on Camp Cooks, J. Frank Dobie Collection, HRHRC.

20. L. A. Huffman, "Last Busting at Bow-Gun," *Scribner's* 42 (July 1907), p. 75.

21. Cal Polk, Diary, manuscript copy, Historic Research Center, Panhandle Plains Historical Museum, Canyon, Tex. Polk's spelling and punctuation have been corrected to provide for easier reading.

22. Quoted in Notes on Camp Cooks, J. Frank Dobie Collection, HRHRC.

23. Holden, *Rollie Burns,* p. 42.

24. Frank Hastings to S. M. Swenson and Sons, June 2, 1915, SMS Ranch Papers, Center for American History, University of Texas, Austin.

CHAPTER 3.

"EVERYTHING BUT THE HIDE, HOOVES, AND BAWL": MEAT

1. Anonymous, untitled typescript, Cooks File, Tropical files, J. Evetts Haley Collection, NSHML.

2. Kelton, *Renderbrook*, p. 82.

3. Anonymous, untitled typescript, NSHML.

4. Haley, *The XIT Ranch*, p. 248.

5. "A Cowboy's Life," *Trinidad Daily Advertiser*, June 24, 1883.

6. Oliver Nelson, *The Cowman's Southwest, Being the Reminiscences of Oliver Nelson . . . 1878–1893*, ed. Angie Debo (Glendale, Calif.: Arthur H. Clark Co., 1953), p. 161.

7. Reba Pierce Cunningham, "Roundup Cook: King of the Range," *Persimmon Hill* 6 (Autumn 1976), p. 10.

8. Frank X. Tolbert, "On Stew Called 'Son-of-a-Blank,' " *Dallas Morning News*, Jan. 10, 1960.

9. Duke and Frantz, *6000 Miles of Fence*, p. 168.

10. Polk, Diary, p. 42.

11. Johnnye Montgomery, "Spence Jowell and Life on the JAL," in *Cowboys Who Rode Proudly*, ed. J. Evetts, Haley, Jr. (Midland, Tex.: Nita Stewart Haley Memorial Library, 1992), p. 42.

12. Z. T. Scott, *Robert Benjamin Masterson, Pioneer Ranchman of the Texas Panhandle* (Austin: Privately printed, 1930), p. 11.

CHAPTER 4.

STAPLES OF THE RANGE: FRESH, DRIED, AND CANNED

1. McCoy, *Historic Sketches of the Cattle Trade*, p. 137.

2. Montgomery, "Spence Jowell," p. 42.

3. William A. Baillie-Grohman, *Camps in the Rockies* (London: Sampson Low, Marston, Searle & Rivington, 1882), p. 190.

4. Burr G. Duval, Diary 1879–1880, typed excerpt quoted in Notes on Camp Cooks, J. Frank Dobie Collection, HRHRC.

5. Ed Harrell to J. Evetts Haley and Hervey Chesley, typed interview, June 13, 1939, p. 21, Biographical Files, J. Evetts Haley Collection, NSHML.

6. Kelton, *Renderbrook*, p. 81.

7. *Ibid.*

8. Holden, *Rollie Burns*, pp. 94–95.

9. Polk, Diary, pp. 42–43.

10. Kelton, *Renderbrook*, p. 81.

11. William French, *Some Recollections of a Western Ranchman*, reprint ed. (New York: Argosy Antiquarian Ltd., 1965), p. 40.

12. *Ibid.*, p. 39.

13. Laura V. Hamner, *Short Grass and Longhorns* (Norman: University of Oklahoma Press, 1943), pp. 110–111.

CHAPTER 5.

"SINKERS" AND "SPLATTER DABS": BREAD

1. Duke and Frantz, *6000 Miles of Fence*, p. 171.

2. Haley, "Sour Dough."

3. Florence Fenley, "Sal Armstrong: Cattleman," *The Cattleman* 26 (Oct. 1939), p. 48.

4. Abbott and Smith, *We Pointed Them North*, p. 161.

5. Haley, "Sour Dough."

6. Tolbert, "Luxuries Softening Cowboys, Chuck Wagon Cook Decides," *Dallas Morning News*, April 9, 1953.

7. Nelson, *The Cowman's Southwest*, p. 101.

8. Mary J. Jaques, *Texan Ranch Life* (London: Horace Cox, 1894), pp. 63–64.

9. Dennis Collins, *The Indians' Last Fight; or, The Dull Knife Raid* (Girard, Kans.: Press of the Appeal to Reason, 1915), pp. 133–134.

10. Quoted in Notes on Camp Cooks, J. Frank Dobie Collection, HRHRC.

11. J. Frank Dobie, *A Vaquero of the Brush Country* (Dallas: Southwest Press, 1929), p. 13.

12. "Slade as a Cowboy," *Texas Live Stock Journal,* Sept. 23, 1882.

13. Quoted in Notes on Camp Cooks, J. Frank Dobie Collection, HRHRC.

14. Kelton, *Renderbrook,* p. 81.

15. Floyd C. Bard, *Horse Wrangler: Sixty Years in the Saddle in Wyoming and Montana* (Norman: University of Oklahoma Press, 1961), p. 56.

CHAPTER 6.

"SPOTTED PUP" AND "SHIVERIN' LIZ": DESSERTS

1. "A Great Cow Country," *New York Times,* May 8, 1881.

2. Quoted in B.C.D. Bynum, "Out of the Files," undated clipping, Cooks File, Topical files, J. Evetts Haley Collection, NSHML.

3. Kelton, *Renderbrook,* p. 81.

4. Cunningham, "Roundup Cook," p. 9; Brown and Felton, *Before Barbed Wire,* p. 146.

5. "The Round-Up," *Las Animas Leader,* July 27, 1877.

6. Rainbolt, *The Last Cowboy,* pp. 67–68.

7. Kelton, *Renderbrook,* p. 81.

8. James Emmit McCauley, *A Stove-Up Cowboy's Story* (Dallas: Texas Folklore Society, 1943), p. 39.

9. O. S. Clark, *Clay Allison of the Washita* (Attica, Ind.: G. M. Williams, 1920), pp. 60–61.

10. Kelton, *Renderbrook,* p. 81.

CHAPTER 7.

"BELLY WASH": COFFEE AND TEA

1. James Cox, *My Native Land,* p. 127, as cited in Wesley L. Fankhauser, "Son-of-a-Gun to Pâté de Foie Gras: Chow on Early Great Plains Ranches," *Journal of the West* 16 (Jan. 1977), p. 30.

2. George Pattullo, "Glimpses of Cowboy Life in Texas," *Photo-Era* 20 (June 1908), p. 292.

3. Jaques, *Texan Ranch Life,* p. 81.

ℬibliography

Abernathy, John R. ("Jack"). *In Camp with Theodore Roosevelt*. Oklahoma City: Times-Journal Publishing Co., 1933.

Abbott, E. C. ("Teddy Blue"). "Cooking Under Difficulties." Misc. newspaper clipping titled "Tall Tales." Cooks File, Topical files, J. Evetts Haley Collection, Nita Stewart Haley Memorial Library, Midland, Tex.

———, and Helena Huntington Smith. *We Pointed Them North: Recollections of a Cowpuncher*. New York: Farrar and Rinehart, 1939.

Adams, Ramon F. *Come An' Get It*. Norman: University of Oklahoma Press, 1952.

———. *The Old-Time Cowhand*. New York: The Macmillan Company, 1961.

Alexander, G. M. "Tip" to J. Evetts Haley. Typed interview, Oct. 8, 1926, Cuero, Texas. Interview Files, Historic Research Center, Panhandle-Plains Historical Museum, Canyon, Tex.

"Ancestry and Early Life of Colonel C. C. Slaughter." Typescript. Federal Writer's Program, Castro Co. Notes, Bx. 2H486, Earl Vandale Collection, Center for American History, University of Texas, Austin.

Arnot, John. "The Wagon." Manuscript. Bx. 2H472, Earl Vandale Collection, Center for American History, University of Texas, Austin.

———. "The Wagon Cook." Manuscript. Bx. 2H472, Earl Vandale Collection, Center for American History, University of Texas, Austin.

Baillie-Grohman, William A. *Camps in the Rockies*. London: Sampson Low, Marston, Searle & Rivington, 1882.

Bard, Floyd C. *Horse Wrangler: Sixty Years in the Saddle in Wyoming and Montana*. Norman: University of Oklahoma Press, 1961.

Barker, Robert M. "Economics of Cattle-Ranching in the Southwest." *The American Monthly Review of Reviews* 24 (Sept. 1901), pp. 305–313.

Barnard, Evan G. *A Rider of the Cherokee Strip*. Boston: Houghton Mifflin, 1936.

Barnes, Will C. "Cowpunching Forty Years Ago." Arizona Cattle Growers' Association, *Weekly Market Report and News Letter* 8 (March 10, 1931), pp. 1–4.

———. "On the Old Western Cattle Range." *The Cattleman* 17 (Dec. 1930), pp. 38–39.

———. *Tales from the X-Bar Horse Camp*. Chicago: Breeder's Gazette, 1920.

Benedict, Carl Peters. *A Tenderfoot Kid on Gyp Water*. Dallas: Texas Folklore Society, 1943.

Billings, John D. *Hardtack and Coffee*. Chicago: People's Publishing Co., 1887.

"Biscuits, Not Bullets, Won West, Ex-Cowboy Thinks." *Fort Worth Star-Telegram*, Sept. 17, 1939.

Blasingame, Ike. *Dakota Cowboy: My Life in the Old Days*. New York: G. P. Putnam's Sons, 1958.

Blasingame, Tom, as told to Richard Chamberlain. "Eight Decades a Cowboy." *The Quarter Horse Journal* 36 (Oct. 1983), pp. 162–172.

Bolt, Richard. *Forty Years Behind the Lid*. n.p.: Privately printed, 1973.

Boyd, George Washington, to Eunice M. Mayer. Typed interview, April 16, 1937, Mangum, Okla. Indian-Pioneer History Collection, Vol. 1, pp. 279–280, Oklahoma Historical Society, Oklahoma City.

Branch, E. Douglas. *The Cowboy and His Interpreters*. New York: D. Appleton & Co., 1926.

Bratt, John. *Trails of Yesterday*. Lincoln, Nebr.: University Publishing Co., 1921.

Brittin, Helen C., and Cheryl E. Nossaman. "Iron Content of Food Cooked in Iron Utensils." *Journal of the American Dietetic Association* 86 (1986), pp. 897–901.

Brown, Mark H., and W. R. Felton. *Before Barbed Wire: L. A. Huffman, Photographer on Horseback*. New York: Bramhall House, 1956.

Burns, Mamie S. *This I Can Leave You*. College Station: Texas A&M University Press, 1986.

Burns, Rollie C. "A One-Man Cattle Outfit." *The Cattleman* 17 (July 1931), p. 31.

Burton, Gerry. "Aging Cowboy Still Rides Matador Range." *Lubbock Avalanche-Journal*, July 4, 1982.

Burton, Harley T. *A History of the JA Ranch*. Austin: Von Boeckmann-Jones Press, 1928.

Bush, T. L. *A Cowboy's Cookbook*. Austin: Texas Monthly Press, [1985].

Cambern, Lois Marsh. *They Came to Stay*. Quanah, Tex.: Nortex Offset Publications, 1974.

Carlson, Verne. *Cowboy Cookbook*. Los Angeles: Sonica Press, 1981.

Casement, Dan. *Random Recollections*. Kansas City: Walker Publications, Inc., 1955.

Chesley, Hervey E. *Adventuring with the Old-Timers: Trails Traveled—Tales Told*. Ed. B. Byron Price. El Paso: Nita Stewart Haley Memorial Library, 1979.

Clark, O. S. *Clay Allison of the Washita*. Attica, Ind.: G. M. Williams, 1920.

Coe, Wilbur. *Ranch on the Ruidoso: The Story of a Pioneer Family in New Mexico, 1881–1968*. New York: Alfred A. Knopf, 1968.

"Coffee Breaks Were Part of Cowboy Life." *Dallas Times Herald,* April 2, 1967.

Cohea, Mrs. C. M. "Mrs. J. R. (Poor Bob) Thompson." Typescript. Bx. 2H476, Earl Vandale Collection, Center for American History, University of Texas, Austin.

———. "Pioneer Women." Typescript. Bx. 2H476, Earl Vandale Collection, Center for American History, University of Texas, Austin.

Collins, Dennis. *The Indians' Last Fight; or The Dull Knife Raid*. Girard, Kans.: Press of the Appeal to Reason, 1915.

Collinson, Frank. *Life in the Saddle*. Ed. Mary Whatley Clarke. Norman: University of Oklahoma Press, 1963.

Colville, Ida, to Zaidee B. Bland. Typed interview, April 27, 1937, Elmer, Okla. Indian-Pioneer History Collection, Vol. 79, pp. 251–258, Oklahoma Historical Society, Oklahoma City.

Cook, James H. *Fifty Years on the Old Frontier, as Cowboy, Hunter, Guide, Scout and Ranchman*. New Haven, Conn.: Yale University Press, 1923.

Coolidge, Dane. *Texas Cowboys*. New York: E. P. Dutton & Co., 1937.

Cross, F. M. *A Short Sketch-History from Personal Reminiscences of Early Days in Central Texas*. Brownwood, Tex.: Greenwood Printing Co., 1912.

Crudgington, C. A. "Panhandle Ranches." Typescript. Bx. 2H466, Earl Vandale Collection, Center for American History, University of Texas, Austin.

Cunningham, Reba Pierce. "Roundup Cook: King of the Range." *Persimmon Hill* 6 (Autumn 1976), pp. 6–11.

Dale, Edward Everett. *Cow Country*. Norman: University of Oklahoma Press, 1942.

———. *Frontier Ways*. Austin: University of Texas Press, 1959.

Dallam, Richard. "Diary of Richard Dallam, Cattle Drover over the Trail from Texas to California and in California and Oregon from December 5, 1852, to May 26, 1864." Western History Manuscript #131, Bienecke Library, Yale University, New Haven, Conn.

David, Robert B. *Malcolm Campbell, Sheriff*. Casper: Wyomingana, 1932.

Delo, David Michael. *Peddlers and Post Traders: The Army Sutler on the Frontier*. Salt Lake City: University of Utah Press, 1992.

Dobie, J. Frank. *Cow People*. Boston: Little, Brown Co., 1964.

———. *The Flavor of Texas*. Dallas: Dealey and Lowe, 1936.

———. *A Vaquero of the Brush Country*. Dallas: Southwest Press, 1929.

Doshier, Inez C. "Camp Life of a Cowpuncher." Typescript. Bx. 2H488, Earl Vandale Collection, Center for American History, University of Texas, Austin.

———. "George Richard Doshier." Typescript. Bx. 2H464, Earl Vandale Collection, Center for American History, University of Texas, Austin.

Duke, Cordia Sloan, and Joe B. Frantz. *6000 Miles of Fence: Life on the XIT Ranch of Texas*. Austin: University of Texas Press, 1961.

Eggen, John E. "*The West That Was*." West Chester, Pa.: Schiffer Publishing, Ltd., 1991.

Ellis, George F. *Bell Ranch as I Knew It*. Kansas City: Lowell Press, 1973.

Ellis, Mattie, and Mark Wood. *Bell Ranch Wagon Work*. Amarillo, Tex.: Ellis Book Co., 1984.

Evans, Joe M. *A Corral Full of Stories*. El Paso: McMath Co., 1939.

Evans, Manda S., to Ethel Mae Yates. Typed interview, June 25, 1937, Elk City, Okla., Indian-Pioneer History Collection, Vol. 79, pp. 480–492, Oklahoma Historical Society, Oklahoma City.

Fankhauser, Wesley L. "Son-of-a-Gun to Pâté de Foie Gras: Chow on Early Great Plains Ranches." *Journal of the West* 16 (Jan. 1977), pp. 29–35.

Fenley, Florence. *Oldtimers: Their Own Stories*. Uvalde, Tex.: Hornsby Press, 1939.

———. "Sal Armstrong: Cattleman." *The Cattleman* 26 (Oct. 1939), pp. 45, 48–49, 51.

"Former Cook of XIT Recalls Her First Glimpse of Ranch." *Dalhart Texan,* August 7, 1937.

Franklin, Linda C. *From Hearth to Cookstove*. Florence, Ala.: House of Collectibles, Inc., 1978.

Fudge, Bob. "An Old Cattleman's Story." Typescript. Bx. 2H463, Earl Vandale Collection, Center for American History, University of Texas, Austin.

Fugate, Francis L. "Arbuckles': The Coffee That Won the West." *The American West* 21 (Jan.–Feb. 1984), pp. 61–68.

Gay, Beatrice G. "*Into the Setting Sun.*" n.p.: Privately printed, 1936.

Gipson, Fred. *Cowhand*. New York: Harper & Brothers, 1953.

Goodnight, Charles. "Notes by, Book II." Typescript. Bx. 2H465, Earl Vandale Collection, Center for American History, University of Texas, Austin.

———, to J. Evetts Haley. Typed interview, Dec. 14, 1928. Goodnight Interview File, J. Evetts Haley Collection, Nita Stewart Haley Memorial Library, Midland, Tex.

Goodwyn, Frank. *Life on the King Ranch*. New York: Thomas Y. Crowell Company, 1951.

Gowan, Hugh, and Judy Gowan. *Blue and Grey Cookery: Authentic Recipes from the Civil War Years*. Martinsburg, Pa.: Daisy Publishing, 1980.

Graham, E. V., to Laura V. Hamner. Typed interview, Nov. 17, 1936, Odessa, Tex. Bx. 2H478, Earl Vandale Collection, Center for American History, University of Texas, Austin.

Hale, Winnie Davis. "Blazing Roads on the LX." Typescript. Bx. 2H476, Earl Vandale Collection, Center for American History, University of Texas, Austin.

Haley, J. Evetts. *Charles Goodnight: Cowman and Plainsman*. Boston: Houghton Mifflin, 1936.

———. *George Littlefield, Texan*. Norman: University of Oklahoma Press, 1943.

———. *Life on the Texas Range*. Austin: University of Texas Press, 1952.

———. "A Log of the Montana Trail as Kept by Ealy Moore." *Panhandle-Plains Historical Review* 5 (1932), pp. 44–56.

———. "Sour Dough." Typescript. Cooks File, Topical files, J. Evetts Haley Collection, Nita Stewart Haley Memorial Library, Midland, Tex.

———. *The XIT Ranch of Texas and the Early Days of the Llano Estacado*. Chicago: The Lakeside Press, 1929.

Haley, J. Evetts, Jr., ed. *Cowboys Who Rode Proudly*. Midland, Tex.: Nita Stewart Haley Memorial Library, 1992.

Haley, R. A. ("Bob"), to J. Evetts Haley. Typed interview, June 8, 1935. Biographical File, J. Evetts Haley Collection, Nita Stewart Haley Memorial Library, Midland, Tex.

Hall, Sharlot M. *Cactus and Pine*. Phoenix: Arizona Republican Print Shop, 1924.

Hamner, Laura V. *Short Grass and Longhorns*. Norman: University of Oklahoma Press, 1943.

———. "What Was Time to a Cowboy?" *The Cattleman* 33 (Dec. 1946), pp. 122–124.

Harrell, Ed, to J. Evetts Haley and Hervey Chesley. Typed interview, June 13, 1939. Biographical Files, Nita Stewart Haley Memorial Library, Midland, Tex.

Hendrix, John. "Beans." *The Cattleman* 31 (May 1944), p. 18.

Holden, William C. *The Espuela Land and Cattle Company: A Study of a Foreign-Owned Ranch in Texas*. Austin: Texas State Historical Association, 1970.

———. *Rollie Burns*. Dallas: Southwest Press, 1932.

———. *The Spur Ranch*. Boston: Christopher Publishing House, 1934.

Horsbrugh, Mrs. Fred, as told to Laura V. Hamner. "When You Could See Farther Than You Could Go in a Day Related by Amarillo Woman." *Amarillo Daily News,* May 17, 1937.

Huffman, L. A. "Last Busting at Bow-Gun." *Scribner's* 42 (July 1907), pp. 75–86.

Hughes, Stella. "The Art of Dutch Oven Cooking." *The Western Horseman* n.v. (Aug. 1985), pp. 90–92, 94, 96.

———. *Bacon and Beans*. Colorado Springs: Western Horseman, Inc., 1990.

———. *Chuck Wagon Cookin'*. Tucson: University of Arizona Press, 1974.

———. "Gusto Grub at the National Cowboy Hall of Fame." *Western Horseman* n.v. (Nov. 1992), pp. 108–112.

[Hunter, J. Marvin], comp. *Cooking Recipes of the Pioneers*. Bandera, Tex.: Frontier Times, [ca. 1936].

———, comp. & ed. *The Trail Drivers of Texas*. Nashville: Cokesbury Press, 1925.

Ingerton, Harry, to J. Evetts Haley. Typed interview, June 19, 1937. Biographical Files, J. Evetts Haley Collection, Nita Stewart Haley Memorial Library, Midland, Tex.

Irwin, Mr. and Mrs. Hunter, to Laura V. Hamner. Typed interview, Nov. 18, 1936. Bx. 2H478, Earl Vandale Collection, Center for American History, University of Texas, Austin.

"Issuing Rations to Families of Ranch Workers Old Custom." *Corpus Christi Caller-Times,* July 12, 1953.

Jaques, Mary J. *Texan Ranch Life*. London: Horace Cox, 1894.

J. Evetts Haley Collection. Nita Stewart Haley Memorial Library, Midland, Tex.

J. Frank Dobie Collection. Harry Ransom Humanities Research Center, University of Texas, Austin.

Kelton, Steve. *Renderbrook: A Century Under the Spade Brand*. Fort Worth: Texas Christian University Press, 1990.

Kenny, A. M., to Robert W. Small. Typed interview, Nov. 17, 1937, Blackwell, Okla. Indian-Pioneer History Collection, Vol. 62, pp. 488–499, Oklahoma Historical Society, Oklahoma City.

King, Frank M. *Longhorn Trail Drivers*. Burbank, Calif.: Privately printed, 1940.

———. *Wranglin' the Past*. Pasadena, Calif.: Trail's End Publishing Co., Inc., 1946.

Lang, Lincoln A. *Ranching with Roosevelt*. Philadelphia: J. B. Lippincott & Co., 1926.

Lanning, Jim, and Judy Lanning. *Texas Cowboys: Memories of the Early Days*. College Station: Texas A&M University Press, 1984.

Lard, J. Dave, to J. Evetts Haley. Typed interview, June 26, 1937. Biographical Files, Hot Springs, N.M., J. Evetts Haley Collection, Nita Stewart Haley Memorial Library, Midland, Tex.

Lauderdale, R. J. ("Bob"), and John M. Doak. *Life on the Range and on the Trail*. Ed. Lela Neal Pirtle. San Antonio: Naylor Company, 1936.

Lindsey, Matthew C. *The Trail of Years in Dawson County, Texas*. Fort Worth: John Wallace, Inc., 1960.

Lord, Francis A. *Civil War Collector's Encyclopedia*. Secaucus, N.J.: Castle Books, 1965.

Lovell, Louva. "A Day at the JA Chuck Wagon in 1936." *Panhandle-Plains Historical Review* 55 (1982), pp. 37–47.

Lozier, Roy, and Doris Platts. *Cowboys on the Green River Circa 1918*. Wilson, Wyo.: Sunshine Ranch and Friends, 1982.

Lucey, Donna M. *Photographing Montana 1894–1928: The Life and Work of Evelyn Cameron*. New York: Alfred A. Knopf, 1990.

McAfee, W. R. *The Cattlemen*. Alvin, Tex.: Davis Mountain Press, 1989.

McAvoy, Mack. "Death, Dream and Cold." *The Cattleman* 14 (June 1927), pp. 21–22.

McCarty, John. *Some Experiences of Boss Neff in the Texas and Oklahoma Panhandle*. Amarillo: Globe-News Publishing Co., 1941.

McCauley, James Emmit. *A Stove-Up Cowboy's Story*. Dallas: Texas Folklore Society, 1943.

McCormick, Dave R., to J. Evetts Haley. Typed interview, March 2, 1935. San Antonio, Texas. Biographical Files, J. Evetts Haley Collection, Nita Stewart Haley Memorial Library, Midland, Tex.

McCoy, Joseph G. *Historic Sketches of the Cattle Trade of the West and Southwest*. Kansas City: Ramsey, Millett, & Hudson, Printers, 1874.

MacIntosh, P. J. R. "The Texas Cowboy Today." *The Texas Monthly* 4 (Aug. 1929), pp. 11–27.

McNeill, J. C. ("Cap"), III. *The McNeill's S.R. Ranch*. College Station: Texas A&M University Press, 1988.

Matador Ranch. Records. Southwest Collection, Texas Tech University, Lubbock.

Mitchell, H. Frank, to J. Evetts Haley. Typed interview, June 10, 1935, Amarillo, Texas. Biographical Files, J. Evetts Haley Collection, Nita Stewart Haley Memorial Library, Midland, Tex.

Mitchell, Patricia B. *Confederate Camp Cooking*. Rev. ed. Chatham, Va.: Privately printed, 1992.

———. *Union Army Camp Cooking 1861–1865*. Rev. ed. Chatham, Va.: Privately printed, 1993.

Mooar, J. Wright, to J. Evetts Haley. Typed interview, July 28, 1937, Snyder, Tex. Biographical Files, J. Evetts Haley Collection, Nita Stewart Haley Memorial Library, Midland, Tex.

Moore, Dan. *Shoot Me a Biscuit: Stories of Yesteryear's Roundup Cooks*. Tucson: University of Arizona Press, 1974.

Moore, J. Ealy. Explanatory note, Nov. 28, 1922. Typescript. Bx. 2H474, Earl Vandale Collection, Center for American History, University of Texas, Austin.

Mora, Jo. *Trail Dust and Saddle Leather*. New York: Scribners, 1946.

Murrah, David J. *The Pitchfork Land and Cattle Company: The First Century*. Lubbock: Texas Tech University Press, 1983.

Neff, Boss. "Boss" Neff's Diary, 1939. Typescript. Bx. 2H474, Earl Vandale Collection, Center for American History, University of Texas, Austin.

Nelson, Oliver. *The Cowman's Southwest, Being the Reminiscences of Oliver Nelson . . . 1878–1893*. Ed. Angie Debo. Glendale, Calif.: Arthur H. Clark Co., 1953.

"1938 Texas Cowboy Reunion." *The Cattleman* 25 (June 1938), p. 31.

Nordyke, Lewis. "The Cowboy's Brand of Coffee." *Ranch Romances* n.v. (May 1946), pp. 45–49.

O'Connor, Louise S. *Cryin' for Daylight: A Ranching Culture in the Texas Coastal Bend*. Austin: Wexford Publishing, 1989.

"Odessa Cowman Recalls Early Ranch Roundup." Typescript. Bx. 2H487, Earl Vandale Collection, Center for American History, University of Texas, Austin.

"The Old Time Cowboy." *Field and Farm* n.v. (January 1, 1898), p. 17.

Oliver, Herman. *Gold and Cattle Country*. Portland, Ore.: Binfords and Mort Publishers, 1961.

Osgood, Ernest. *The Day of the Cattleman*. Minneapolis: University of Minnesota Press, 1929.

Parker, Harry. "My Autobiography," 1937. Typescript. Bx. 2H479, Earl Vandale Collection, Center for American History, University of Texas, Austin.

Pattullo, George. "Glimpses of Cowboy Life in Texas." *Photo-Era* 20 (June 1908), pp. 288–295.

Paul, Rodman W. *The Far West and the Great Plains in Transition 1859–1900*. New York: Harper & Row, 1988.

Paxton, Wheeler, to Eunice M. Mayer. Typed interview, Sept. 10, 1937, n.p. Indian-Pioneer History Collection, Vol. 39, pp. 234–238, Oklahoma Historical Society, Oklahoma City.

Peake, Ora B. *The Colorado Range Cattle Industry.* Glendale, Calif.: Arthur H. Clark Co., 1937.

Polk, Cal. Diary. Manuscript copy. Historic Research Center, Panhandle Plains Historical Museum, Canyon, Tex.

Propps, Pat, to Billy W. Hunt. Typed interview, March 12, 1980, Electra, Tex. Interview File, Historic Research Center, Panhandle Plains Historical Museum, Canyon, Tex.

Ragsdale, John G. *Dutch Ovens Chronicled: Their Use in the United States.* Fayetteville, Ark.: University of Arkansas Press, 1991.

Rainbolt, Jo. *The Last Cowboy: Twilight Era of the Horseback Cowhand 1900–1940.* Helena, Mont.: American and World Geographic Publishing, 1992.

Raine, William MacCleod, and Will C. Barnes. *Cattle.* New York: Doubleday, Doran & Co., 1930.

"Ranch Life Kept by Mrs. R. L. Duke Diary." *Dalhart Texan,* Aug. 7, 1937.

Redondo, Margaret P. "Valley of Iron: One Family's History of Madera Canyon." *The Journal of Arizona History* 34 (Autumn 1993), pp. 233–274.

Reeves, Frank. "The Chuck Wagon." *The Cattleman* 30 (Oct. 1943), p. 5.

Remington, Frederic. "An Outpost of Civilization." *Frederic Remington's Own West.* New York: Dial Press, 1960, pp. 137–145.

Richardson, T. C. "Trail Driving to Shreveport and Jefferson and Other Early Day Experiences of Kossuth Barry, 86 Year Old Ranchman." *Farm and Ranch* 55 (July 1, 1936), p. 2.

Rockfellow, John A. *Log of an Arizona Trail Blazer.* Tucson: Acme Printing Co., 1933.

Rollins, Philip Ashton. *The Cowboy.* New York: Scribners, 1922.

Rollinson, John K. *Pony Trails in Wyoming.* Caldwell, Idaho: Caxton Printers, 1941.

Russell, Charles M. *Good Medicine.* New York: Doubleday, 1930.

———. *Trails Plowed Under.* New York: Doubleday, Page, 1927.

Sanders, William Perry. *Days That Are Gone.* Los Angeles: Grafton Publishing Corp., 1918.

Schlereth, Thomas J. *Victorian America: Transformations in Everyday Life.* New York: HarperCollins, 1991.

Scott, Z. T. *Robert Benjamin Masterson, Pioneer Ranchman of the Texas Panhandle.* Austin: Privately printed, 1930.

Sears, Roebuck and Co. *1897 Sears, Roebuck and Co. Catalog,* reprint ed. Ed. Fred L. Israel. New York: Chelsea House, 1968.

Shaw, James C. *North from Texas.* Ed. Herbert O. Brayer. Evanston, Ill.: Branding Iron Press, 1952.

"Slade as a Cowboy." *Texas Live Stock Journal,* Sept. 23, 1882, p. 2.

Slatta, Richard W. *Cowboys of the Americas.* New Haven, Conn.: Yale University Press, 1990.

Smith, Joe Heflin. "Lite An' Eat, Pardner." *The Cattleman* 34 (Oct. 1947), pp. 33, 44, 46.

Smithers, W. D. *Early Trail Drives in the Big Bend.* Southwestern Studies Monograph No. 55. El Paso: University of Texas, 1979.

SMS Ranch. Papers. Center for American History, University of Texas, Austin.

SMS Ranch [F. S. Hastings]. *The Story of the SMS Ranch.* n.p., 1919.

Spur Ranch. Records. Southwest Collection, Texas Tech University, Lubbock.

Stanbery, Lon R. *The Passing of the 3D Ranch.* Tulsa: George W. Henry Printing Co., [ca. 1930].

Steedman, Charles J. *Bucking the Sagebrush.* New York: G. P. Putnam's Sons, 1904.

Studebaker Trade Catalog Collection. Studebaker National Museum, South Bend, Indiana.

Terry, Jerry. "Civilization Built on Buffalo Chips." Typescript. Bx. 2H485, Earl Vandale Collection, Center for American History, University of Texas, Austin.

Thompson, Albert W. *They Were Open Range Days.* Denver: The World Press, 1946.

Tinkler, Estelle. "History of the Rocking Chair Ranch." *Panhandle-Plains Historical Review* 15 (1942), pp. 9–85.

Tinsley, Jim Bob. *The Hash Knife Brand.* Gainesville: University Press of Florida, 1993.

Tolbert, Frank X. "Big Ranch's Lonesome Acres Can Hide a Chuck Wagon Easy." *Dallas Morning News,* September 10, 1953.

———. "Good Cooks Scarce." *Dallas Morning News,* Sept. 29, 1968.

———. "Grains of Paradise Used in a Contest." *Dallas Morning News,* March 15, 1965.

———. "Is Zack the Last Range Hoodlum?" *Dallas Morning News,* March 24, 1955.

———. "Luxuries Softening Cowboys, Chuck Wagon Cook Decides." *Dallas Morning News,* April 9, 1953.

———. "McKittrick Canyon Isolated." *Dallas Morning News,* Sept. 29, 1968.

———. "Moving 3-D's Chuck Wagon on Ignorant Ridge in Rain." *Dallas Morning News,* Nov. 2, 1969.

———. "Peanut Brittle Fed by Ton to Catfish." *Dallas Morning News,* April 3, 1972.

———. "Pitchfork Dares the Sourdoughs." *Dallas Morning News,* July 6, 1958.

———. "Pitchfork Works Old Fashion Way." *Dallas Morning News,* July 7, 1958.

———. "A 'Romantic Roundup' on 3 D's 550,000 Acres." *Dallas Morning News,* March 28, 1972.

———. "Roundup Time on the Four 6's." *Dallas Morning News,* Sept. 19, 1964.

———. "Rowdy Recommends Mesquite Bean Jelly." *Dallas Morning News,* Sept. 30, 1968.

———. "On Stew Called 'Son-of-a-Blank.'" *Dallas Morning News,* Jan. 10, 1960.

———. "Thousands Request Recipe for 'Stew.'" *Dallas Morning News,* Feb. 3, 1964.

———. "Zack Built Many Branding Fires." *Dallas Morning News,* Aug. 7, 1958.

Trayer, James. *Foodbook.* New York: Grossman Publishers, 1970.

Vandiver, Mrs. W. M., to Virgil Coursey. Typed interview, June 18, 1937, Altus, Okla. Indian-Pioneer History Collection, Vol. 48, pp. 78–83, Oklahoma Historical Society, Oklahoma City.

Veale, Fannie Davis [Mrs. H. H. Beck]. "On the Texas Frontier, the Story of My Life." Typescript. Bx. 2H472, Earl Vandale Collection, Center for American History, University of Texas, Austin.

Vernam, Glenn R. *Man on Horseback.* New York: Harper & Row, 1964.

Villareal, Roberto M. "The Mexican-American Vaqueros of the Kenedy Ranch: A Social History." Master's thesis, Texas A&I University, 1972.

Vincent, C. F., to J. Evetts Haley. Interview notes, June 26, 1927. J. Evetts Haley Collection, Nita Stewart Haley Memorial Library, Midland, Tex.

Walker, C. W. (Charlie), W. W. (Walter) Walker, and W. D. (Bill) Walker to J. Evetts Haley. Typed interview, Aug. 5, 1937, Dunlap, N. Mex. Biographical File, J. Evetts Haley Collection, Nita Stewart Haley Memorial Library, Midland, Tex.

Ward, Fay E. *The Cowboy at Work,* reprint ed. Norman: University of Oklahoma Press, 1987.

"W. B. Hester, Rotan, Texas," *The Cattleman* 12 (May 1927), p. 29.

Westermeier, Clifford P. *Trailing the Cowboy: His Life and Lore as Told by Frontier Journalists.* Caldwell, Idaho: Caxton Printers, 1955.

White, Peter, and Mary Ann White. *"Along the Rio Grande:" Cowboy Jack Thorp's New Mexico.* Santa Fe: Ancient City Press, 1988.

Whitlock, V. H. ("Ol' Waddy"). *Cowboy Life on the Llano Estacado.* Norman: University of Oklahoma Press, 1970.

———. *Yellowhouse Canyon.* Beaumont, Tex.: Privately printed, 1939.

Wister, Owen. *The Virginian,* reprint ed. New York: New American Library, 1979.

Withers, Mark J., to J. Evetts Haley. Typed interview, Oct. 8, 1932, Lockhart, Tex. Biographical Files, J. Evetts Haley Collection, Nita Stewart Haley Memorial Library, Midland, Tex.

Works Progress Administration. "The History of Dickens County." Typescript. Bx. 2H487, Earl Vandale Collection, Center for American History, University of Texas, Austin.

Wunder, John R., ed. *At Home on the Range*. New York: Greenwood Press, 1985.

XIT Ranch. Papers. Historic Research Center, Panhandle-Plains Historical Museum, Canyon, Tex.

"XIT White House Still Stands." *Austin American-Statesman*, Nov. 18, 1962.

Youngblood, B., and A. B. Cox. *An Economic Study of a Typical Ranching Area on the Edwards Plateau of Texas*. Texas Agricultural Experiment Station, Bulletin No. 297. College Station, Tex.: July 1922.

Grateful acknowledgment is made to the following organizations and individuals for permission to reprint photographs:

PANHANDLE PLAINS HISTORICAL MUSEUM COLLECTION. Pages: 17, 19, 20 bottom, 21–23, 25, 27–28, 31, 33–35, 40, 42, 54, 57–58, 60 bottom, 62, 64–65, 72–73, 77, 80, 85–86, 104–105, 107, 110, 114–115, 144, 238, 263.

FRANK SHERMAN, COURTESY JOHN E. EGGEN COLLECTION. Pages: 14–15, 18, 29, 30 top, 49, 67, 79, 91, 93, 94, 95, 96, 117, 120.

TEXAS AND SOUTHWESTERN CATTLE RAISERS ASSOCIATION. Pages: 20 top, 36 top, 45 bottom, 46, 53 (Frank Reeves), 55 bottom, 59, 60 top (Frank Reeves), 61 (Frank Reeves), 71, 78 (Frank Reeves), 89 (Frank Reeves), 97 (Frank Reeves), 263.

NATIONAL COWBOY HALL OF FAME COLLECTION. Pages: 12–13, 22 (Barnes & Caplin), 30 bottom, 36 bottom (Wyatt Davis), 38, 39, 41, 43 top (L. A. Huffman), 43 bottom, 44 top (Reba Pierce Cunningham), 45 top (Wyatt Davis), 50–51 (Barnes & Caplin), 55 top (Barnes & Caplin), 56, 63 top (Barnes & Caplin), 63 bottom (Reba Pierce Cunningham), 66, 69 (Reba Pierce Cunningham), 75 (L. A. Huffman), 82 (Wyatt Davis), 99 (Reba Pierce Cunningham), 100–101 (S. A. Morton), 103 (S. A. Morton), 106 (S. A. Morton), 109 (S. A. Morton), 110–111, 116 (Wyatt Davis), 119 (Wyatt Davis), 124–125, 127 (L. A. Huffman), 145 (S. A. Morton), 164–165 (Wyatt Davis), 200–201 (Reba Pierce Cunningham), 239, 262 (Reba Pierce Cunningham).

ＩＮＤＥＸ

Page numbers in **boldface** refer to recipes.

Abbott, "Teddy Blue," 46, 47, 112

African-American cooks, 68

agate ware, 37

age, and cowboy careers, 67

air tights, 96

alcoholism, 66

Alford, Fat, 67

alkaline water, 34, 93, 97

Amburgey, Jeff, 24–25

antelope jerky, 83

aparatos (cooking tables), 29

appetizers:
  chile con queso, **132–133**
  cowboy beefy cheese dip, **134**
  quesadillas ricas, **130–131**
  spicy pecan pinwheels, **133**

apple(s):
  buttermilk campfire cake, **244–245**
  in cowboy diet, 92–93
  crumble, **246**
  spice cake, **251**
  sweet and tangy beans, **227**

applesauce-pecan cake, **250**

apricot:
  cobbler, double crust, **241–242**
  nut bread, **154**

Arbuckle Brothers Company, 119–121

Ariosa brand coffee, 120

Arkansas River, 24

army cots, 59

army vehicles, chuck wagons replaced by, 58

arnica salve, 66

Arnot, John, 70

Arrington, Greta and William L., 270

Asa, George, 107

Asian-grilled chicken breasts, **188**

Atarque Ranch, 68

Aunt Bett's butter cake, **245**

automobiles, wagons replaced by, 57–58

avocado(s):
  guacamole, **266**
  huevos rancheros, **217**
  and lime salad, **141**

bacon:
  beefy beans, **228**
  cattlemen's club twice-baked potatoes, **230–231**
  Cecil's smothered steak, **178**
  in cowboy diet, 80, 81
  as fuel, 37
  hearty beef pie, **220–221**
  layered salad, **137**
  pan-fried trout with lemon-mint drizzle, **198–199**
  and potato salad, German, **139**
  sweet and tangy beans, **227**
  venison pot roast, **184–185**

Baillie-Grohman, William A., 93

baking, slow, technique for, 203

baking powder, in bread baking, 103

Bar B Brand, 147, 241, 274

barbecue(d):
  brisket, beer-basted, **172–173**
  chicken, **189**
  sauce, California-style, **268**
  sauce, cowboy, **267**
  sweet and tangy beans, **227**
  wide open spaces turkey, **193**

barbecuing:
  for campsite cowboys, 84
  modern methods of, 166–167

barbed wire, 56–58, 67

Bard, Floyd, 53

Bard Ranch, 53

Barnard, Evan G., 71

beanmasters, 70

beans:
  beefy, **228**
  buckaroo saucy, **225**
  Buck's peppery, **224**
  in cowboy diet, 92–93
  pinto, porky, **226**
  sweet and tangy, **227**

bear sign, 115

Beaver River, 35

bedding, 41–42

Bedo, George, 42–43

bed tents, 59

bed wagons, 42

beef:
  beans, **228**
  beer-basted barbecued brisket, **172–173**
  brisket chuckwagon stew, **204–205**
  campsite cooking of, 84–86
  Cecil's smothered steak, **178**
  cheese dip, cowboy, **134**
  chuckwagon soup, **142**
  cowboy demand for, 22, 24
  curing of, 83–84
  as diet mainstay, 80
  garlic-stuffed pot roast, **179**
  jerky, homemade, **181**
  Mexican "lasagne," **218–219**
  New Mexican red chili, **209**
  pie, hearty, **220–221**
  smoked and rubbed prime rib roast, **168–169**
  sourdough chicken-fried steak with cream gravy, **176–177**
  steers slaughtered for, 81–83
  stew, herbed, with corn dumplings, **212–213**
  taco salad casserole, **214–215**
  tamale casserole, **216**
  T-bone steaks with Perini's steak rub, **174–175**
  tenderloin, grilled, **170–171**
beer-basted barbecued brisket, **172–173**
bell pepper(s):
  and cabbage slaw, **138**
  roasting of, 129
Bell Ranch:
  chuck wagons replaced by cars at, 58
  horses of, 67
Bellyache Charley Colic, 70
belly-cheaters, 70
berry oatmeal pancakes, **163**
beverages:
  cowboy camp coffee, **274**
  in cowboy diet, 118, 121–122
  old-fashioned egg nog, **275**
  sangria, **276**
Big Hank, 75
Big Horn Mountains, 42
Big Nose George, 70
biscuit(s):
  bread pudding with lemon sauce, **260–261**
  crust, **242–243**
  Dutch oven, **153**
  sourdough, **152**
biscuit shooters, 70
blackberry oatmeal pancakes, **163**
blacksmiths, 21–22

Blocker, Ab, 103, 121
Blocker, John, 103
Blue Hen brand tomato juice, 97
blue vitriol, 66
Bluff City Stove Works, 31
Bolt, Richard, 148
bone decalcification, 52
boot (storage compartment), 21
Borchard, M. K., 181
Borchard Feedyard, 181
bourbon:
  honey sauce, **190–191**
  old-fashioned egg nog, **275**
  and peach cobbler, **242–243**
bowleggedness, 52
Bracey, Perry, 65
bread:
  apricot nut, **145**
  buttermilk coffee cake, **158–159**
  buttermilk rolls, **160**
  cinnamon buckwheat, **155–156**
  in cowboy diet, 102–115
  cowboy's Dutch oven delight, **150**
  Dutch oven biscuits, **153**
  Mom's cloverleaf rolls, **159**
  overnight coffee cake, **156–157**
  pudding, biscuit, with lemon sauce, **260–261**
  sourdough, **148–149**
  sourdough biscuits, **152**
  sourdough orange-spice raisin rolls, **151**
  sourdough starter, **147**
  see also corn bread
breakfast, 25–26, 27, 39
breaking camp, 27–29, 42
Brewster, O. E., 24
brindle gravy, 84
briquets, 167, 203
brisket:
  beer-basted barbecued, **172–173**
  chuckwagon stew, **204–205**
Brooks, Garnet and Helen, 147, 152, 241, 274
brown gravy, 84
brushfires, 35
buckaroo saucy beans, **225**
Buck's peppery beans, **224**
buckwheat cinnamon bread, **155–156**
buffalo:
  chips, 34–35
  jerky, 83–84
bulk supplies, 48
bull shit coal, 34–35

Burnett, Burk, 67
Burns, Mamie, 99
Burns, Rollie, 76
Bushyhead "Tub-Handle" Ranch, 134, 136
business drawers, 19
butane-burning cook stoves, 58
butchering, of beef, 83
butter cake, Aunt Bett's, **245**
buttermilk:
  apple campfire cake, **244–245**
  coffee cake, **158–159**
  rolls, **160**
butter substitutes, 72

cabbage and pepper slaw, **138**
cabrito (kid), in cowboy diet, 87
cake:
  apple buttermilk campfire, **244–245**
  applesauce-pecan, **250**
  apple spice, **251**
  butter, Aunt Bett's, **245**
  buttermilk coffee, **158–159**
  chocolate sheet, Texas, **254–255**
  mocha pecan layer, **252–253**
  overnight coffee, **156–157**
  raisin long, **247**
  spiced prune, **248–249**
calcium deficiencies, 52
California-style barbecue sauce, **268**
  barbecued chicken, **189**
calomel, 66
campfire(s), 24, 203
  fuel for, 34–37
Canadian River, 24, 35
cane sugar, in cowboy cooking, 112
canned goods, 34
  and food processing industry, 48, 96–98
Capt., A. W., 65
Caribou Ranch, 232, 252
carne asada, carne seco (jerky), 83–84
carretas (carts), 17
cars, wagons replaced by, 57–58
casserole:
  taco salad, **214–215**
  tamale, **216**
cast-iron cookware, 31
castor oil, 66
cattle, on trail drives, 22, 23
cattlemen's club twice-baked potatoes, **230–231**
Cauble, Bill, 242, 246
cayenne peppers, 128

Cecil's smothered steak, **178**
cedar, as fuel, 34
charcoal:
    chimneys, 166–167
    cooking with, 35, 167, 203
Charley Taylor (butter
        substitute), 72
charqui (jerky), 83–84
charros a pie, charros a caballo
        (Mexican boiled and fried
        beans), 92
cheese:
    chile con queso, **132–133**
    chile corn bread, **161**
    dip, cowboy beefy, **134**
    Mexican "lasagne," **218–219**
    quesadillas ricas, **130–131**
    taco salad casserole, **214–215**
chicken:
    barbecued, **189**
    breasts, Asian-grilled, **188**
    in cowboy diet, 88
    and hominy chili, **210–211**
    with lemon and wine, **192**
    -pecan breasts with honey
        sauce, **190–191**
chicken-fried steak with cream
        gravy, sourdough, **176–
        177**
chicory, as coffee bean substitute,
        122
chile peppers, 128–129
    Cecil's smothered steak, **178**
    cheesy chile corn bread, **161**
    chuckwagon tomato sauce,
        269
    con queso, **132–133**
    cowboy beefy cheese dip, **134**
    grilled quail with jalapeño
        glaze, **196**
    guacamole, **266**
    heat level of, 128–129
    huevos rancheros, **217**
    jalapeño corn pudding, **233**
    Mexican "lasagne," **218–219**
    porky pinto beans, **226**
    quesadillas ricas, **130–131**
    ranchero sauce, **270**
    salsa, **264**
    sauce Caribe, **265**
    seviche San Juan, **199**
    spicy pecan pinwheels, **133**
    stew, green, **208–209**
    taco salad casserole, **214–215**
    tomato and rice soup, **143**
    tropical pineapple salsa, **272**
chili:
    chicken and hominy, **210–211**
    New Mexican red, **209**
chilipiquines (wild peppers), 86

chimney:
    charcoal, 166–167
    starters, 203
chip wagons, 35
Chiricahua Cattle Company, 76
Chisholm trail, 22
chocolate:
    mocha pecan layer cake, **252–
        253**
    sheet cake, Texas, **254–255**
chow call, 25–26
Christian, Tom, 151, 182
Christmas dinner, 56, 88
chuck boxes, 17–21
chuck lines, 24, 37
chuck wagons, 17
    construction of, 21–22
    and evolution of stock farms,
        56–57
    prototype for, 17
    storage in, 18–21
chuckwagon scalloped corn, **234**
chuckwagon soup, **142**
chuckwagon tomato sauce, **269**
chutney, peach and citrus, **273**
    Far East smoked pork chops
        with, **183**
cinnamon buckwheat bread,
        155–156
citrus:
    -marinated grilled swordfish,
        197
    and peach chutney, **273**
    see also fruit
Civil War, food processing in,
        96
Clark, William, 202
cleanliness, 76, 107
cleanup, 39
Clear Creek Ranch, 212
clothing, of ranch cooks, 73
Clyde's herb rub and moppin'
        sauce, **170**
coal, cooking with, 35, 167, 203
cobbler:
    double crust apricot, **241–242**
    peach and bourbon, **242–243**
codfish, in cowboy diet, 88
coffee:
    Arbuckle Brothers Company,
        119–121
    cowboy camp, **274**
    in cowboy diet, 24, 118, 122
    mocha pecan layer cake, **252–
        253**
    roasting of, 32, 119
coffee cake:
    buttermilk, **158–159**
    overnight, **156–157**
Cold Bread Phil, 107

coleslaw, cabbage and pepper,
        138
commercialization, of cowboys,
        60
commissaries, 48–52
compressed hay, 34–35
Cook, James, H., 26
cookies:
    lone star gingerbread, **258–
        259**
    Mexican wedding, **257**
Cookie's dry rub, **168**
    beer-basted barbecued brisket,
        172–173
    sourdough chicken-fried steak
        with cream gravy, **176–
        177**
cooks, campsite:
    age of, 67
    chores of, 66
    clothing of, 73
    disposition of, 70–71, 75
    domain of, 70
    ingenuity of, 92–93
    intellect of, 74
    nicknames for, 70
    qualifications of, 67–68
    recipes as used by, 72
    status of, 64, 67, 75
    wages of, 65, 67, 68
cook tents, 42–44
cookware, 31
    see also utensils
coonies (storage cradles), 21
Coonskin Sam, 70
Cooty Slim, 70
Corder, Mr. and Mrs. Bill, 77
corn:
    chuckwagon scalloped, **234**
    and corn bread, **162**
    dumplings, herbed beef stew
        with, **212–213**
    as fuel, 37
    pudding, jalapeño, **233**
    and tomatoes, ranch macaroni
        salad with, **140**
    and zucchini, New Mexican,
        235
corn bread:
    cheesy chile, **161**
    and corn, **162**
    in cowboy diet, 102
    salad, **136**
corn dodgers, 103
cornmeal, 102, 103
corn pone, 103
corporate ranches, 54, 65
cots, army, 59
"Cotton-Eyed Joe" (fiddle tune),
        74

coupons, in coffee marketing, 121
cowboy barbecue sauce, **267**
  barbecued chicken, **189**
  wide open spaces turkey, **193**
cowboy beefy cheesy dip, **134**
cowboy boxes, 19
cowboy camp coffee, **274**
cowboy potato and vegetable bake, **229**
cowboy's Dutch oven delight, **150**
cow chips, 34–35
Craig Ranch, irrigation on, 98
cream gravy, sourdough chicken-fried steak with, **176–177**
credit, in supply transactions, 48
critics, of chuck wagon cooking, 64–65
Cross L Ranch, cooking fuel of, 37
Crow Indians, 68
crust:
  biscuit, **242–243**
  double, for apricot cobbler, **241–242**
  for panhandle pecan pie, **256–257**
cunas (storage cradles), 21
curing, of meat, 83
Curley the Crow, 68
currants:
  in cowboy diet, 92–93
  peach and citrus chutney, **273**
Custer, George Armstrong, 68
cutlery, *see* utensils

dairy products, in cowboy diet, 112
Dallam, Richard, 17
Daugherty Ranch, goat meat cooked at, 87
Day, Charles C., 264
deer meat:
  jerky, 83
  venison pot roast, **184–185**
Depression, Great, 58
desserts:
  apple buttermilk campfire cake, **244–245**
  apple crumble, **246**
  applesauce-pecan cake, **250**
  apple spice cake, **251**
  Aunt Bett's butter cake, **245**
  biscuit bread pudding with lemon sauce, **260–261**
  buttermilk coffee cake, **158–159**
  in cowboy diet, 112–115

double crust apricot cobbler, **241–242**
lone star gingerbread cookies, **258–259**
Mexican wedding cookies, **257**
mocha pecan layer cake, **252–253**
overnight coffee cake, **156–157**
peach and bourbon cobbler, **242–243**
raisin long cake, **247**
spiced prune cake, **248–249**
spotted pup rice pudding, **261**
Texas chocolate sheet cake, **254–255**
dessert topping, **156**
  mocha pecan layer cake frosting, **252–253**
  Texas chocolate sheet cake frosting, **254–255**
devil's rope (barbed wire), 56–58, 67
Diamond-A Ranch, stove table–chuck box invention of, 42
Diamond K Ranch, 233
diarrhea remedy, 34
Dickey Ranch, festivity on, 74
diet, cowboy, 92–95, 99
  food-processing industry effect on, 48
  meat in, 80, 81–83
  postwar changes in, 60
  staples of, 16, 46
  starch in, 99
  vegetables in, 92
  vitamin deficiencies, in, 52
dinners, campsite, 26, 27, 39
dip, cowboy beefy cheese, **134**
dishware, 37
Dobie, J. Frank, 49, 102
doctors, cooks as, 66
double crust apricot cobbler, **241–242**
Double X Wagon, 234, 260
doughbellies, dough punchers, 70
dressing, ranch, **135**
dried chile peppers, 129
drinking, 66
drovers, 22
drying, of fruit, 95–96
dry rub, Cookie's, **168**
  beer-basted barbecued brisket, **172–173**
  sourdough chicken-fried steak with cream gravy, **176–177**

duck:
  in cowboy diet, 88
  roast, with sweet and sour grapes, **194–195**
dude ranches, 60
dumplings, corn, herbed beef stew with, **212–213**
Dutch ovens:
  and chuck wagon cooking, 31–32, 105–107
  modern cooking in, 202–203

Eatons' Ranch, 156
egg(s):
  in cowboy diet, 112
  huevos rancheros, **217**
  nog, old-fashioned, **275**
electric fire starters, 167
electricity:
  at corporate ranches, 53
  static, 43–46
Ellis, George, 67
embalmed beef, 81
enameled dishware, 37
Epsom salts, 66
Espuela Land and Cattle Company, 52
etiquette, campsite, 70, 76
expenses:
  coffee, 119
  food, 16, 52
  railroad freight, 48
  sharing of, 23
  utensils, 31, 32
  wages, 65, 68
  wagons, 22

Fant, Dillard, 68
Far East smoked pork chops, **183**
farmers, 56–57, 98
farm produce, and cowboy diet, 92
fence posts, as fuel, 37
Ferguson, Nancy E., 156
fiddlers, 74
Figure 3 Ranch, 151, 182
firearms, 40, 66, 74
fires, cooking, 29
  for barbecuing and grilling, 166–167
  for Dutch ovens, 203
fires, prairie, 35
fish:
  citrus-marinated grilled swordfish, **197**
  in cowboy diet, 87–88
  pan-fried trout with lemon-mint drizzle, **198–199**
  seviche San Juan, **199**

fishing, 87–88
flunkies, 67
fly bait, 113
flying angel trademark, 120, 121
food-processing industry, 96
  and coffee, 119–121
foremen, 64, 65
Francis, Christine L., 137, 230
Francis Hat Creek Ranch, 137, 230
Franklyn Land and Cattle
  Company, 98
freight rates, 48
freight wagons, 17
French, William, 98
French dish, 113
frijoles (pinto beans), in cowboy
  diet, 92
frosting, dessert:
  mocha pecan layer cake, **252–253**
  Texas chocolate sheet cake, **254–255**
fruit:
  apple buttermilk campfire
    cake, **244–245**
  apple crumble, **246**
  apple spice cake, **251**
  apricot nut bread, **154**
  canned, 95, 96–98
  citrus-marinated grilled
    swordfish, **197**
  for cobblers, 114–115
  in cowboy diet, 92
  double crust apricot cobbler,
    241–242
  dried, 32, 95–96
  orange and pecans, sweet
    potatoes with, **232**
  peach and bourbon cobbler,
    242–243
  peach and citrus chutney, **273**
  railroad transport of, 98
  raisin long cake, **247**
  spiced prune cake, **248–249**
  sweet and sour grapes, roast
    duck with, **194–195**
Frying Pan Ranch, and
  disposition of cooks, 70
fuel:
  for campfires, 34–37
  wagons for transport of, 42
furnishings, winter camp, 52–53

gambling, 39–40
game:
  in cowboy diet, 80
  curing of, 83
  hunting of, 87

gardening, 98
Garland, Hamlin, 40
garlic-stuffed pot roast, **179**
gas grills, 167
geese, in cowboy diet, 88
gelatin, in cowboy diet, 113
Gerloff, Cecil R., 141, 154, 178, 216
German bacon and potato salad, **139**
Gillette, Guy and Pipp, 261
Gillette Ranch, 261
ginger:
  Jamaica, 34
  peach and citrus chutney, **273**
gingerbread cookies, lone star, **258–259**
glaze, jalapeño, grilled quail with, **196**
glazed ware, 37
goat stew, in cowboy diet, 87
Goodnight, Charles, 17
Goodspeed, Decie, 245
granite ware, 37
grapes, sweet and sour, roast
  duck with, **194–195**
Graven, Fred, 101
gravy-fed irrigation, 98
gravy, 84
  cream, sourdough chicken-
    fried steak with, **176–177**
greasy sack outfits, 16
Great Depression, 58
Great Western trail, 22
green chile peppers, *see* chile
  peppers
grilling, 166–167, 203
Griswold Manufacturing
  Company, 31
ground coffee, *see* coffee
grub boxes, 17–21
grub-spoilers, 70
guacamole, **266**
  huevos rancheros, **217**
Guercio, Lucy Angie, 232, 252
guns, 40, 66, 74
gyp holes, 34

Haley, J. Evetts, 72, 102
Hamner, Laura V., 98
Harcourt, Donna, 194
hardtack, 102, 108
Hastings, Frank, 77
Hatfield, Horace, 162
Hat X Ranch, sanitation standard
  at, 76
healers, cooks as, 66
health problems, *see specific
  ailments*

Hearst Ranches, 180, 188, 214, 254, 268
hearty beef pie, **220–221**
heat level, of chile peppers, 128
Heinz, H. J., 96
herbed beef stew with corn
  dumplings, **212–213**
herb marinade, grilled vegetables
  with, **236–237**
herb rub, Clyde's, **170**
hibachis, 203
high-altitude cooking, 93, 240
Hildreth, Marion, 107
Hirschy, Ann and Jack, 188
Hispanic cooks, 68
historical societies, 61
*Historic Sketches of the Cattle Trade
  of the West and Southwest*
  (McCoy), 41
hoecakes, in cowboy diet, 102–103
hoe men, 56–57
Holden, William Curry, 52
holiday festivities, 54, 56, 88
Holleyman, Eva M., 209, 235, 257, 265
homemade beef jerky, **181**
Home Ranch, 130, 132, 155,
  158, 160, 161, 183, 190,
  197, 227, 236, 269, 271, 272
home remedies, 66
hominy:
  and chicken chili, **210–211**
  in cowboy diet, 92–93
honey sauce:
  bourbon, **190–191**
  pecan-chicken breasts with,
    190–191
hoodlums, 67
hoodlum wagons, 42, 58
horses:
  in trail drives, 22
  wagons drawn by, 17
  watering of, 34
horse wranglers, 22, 29, 67
hot chile peppers, *see* chile
  peppers
hot rolls (bedding), 41–42
houn' ears, 115
huevos rancheros, **217**
Humphreys, Jimbo, 234, 260
hunting, 87, 88
hush puppies, in cowboy diet, 103
hygiene, 76, 107

Indian Territory Ranch:
  cooking supplies of, 25

Indian Territory Ranch (*continued*)
  food shortage at, 22
  potatoes cooked at, 94
Ingerton, Harry, 96
irrigation, 98

Jack Hirschy Livestock Inc., 188
jackrabbit meat, 87
Jackson, Nancy, 199, 228
Jacques, Mary, 56
jalapeño peppers, 128
  Cecil's smothered steak, **178**
  cheesy corn bread, **161**
  chicken and hominy, **210–211**
  chile con queso, **132–133**
  chile salsa, **264**
  corn pudding, **233**
  cowboy beefy cheese dip, **134**
  glaze, grilled quail with, **196**
  guacamole, **266**
  porky pinto beans, **226**
  seviche San Juan, **199**
  spicy pecan pinwheels, **133**
  tomato and rice soup, **143**
  tropical pineapple salsa, **272**
JAL Ranch, rabbit meat
      consumed at, 87
Jamaica ginger, 34
JA Ranch:
  beef consumed at, 82
  female callers to, 40
  wagons run by, 58
jerky, 83–84
  homemade beef, **181**
Jesus (chuck wagon cook), 108
jewelry chests, 21
John Chinaman (rice), 94
johnnycakes, in cowboy diet,
      103

Kansas City fish (salt pork), 81
kegs, 21
Kenedy Ranch:
  campsites struck by, 29
  food quantity required by, 83
kid stew, in cowboy diet, 87
kindling, 35–37
King Ranch:
  beans served at, 97
  campsites struck by, 29
  fresh beef at, 83
  mealtimes at, 27
  sourdough cooking at, 108

lamb, in cowboy diet, 87
Lambshead Ranch, 242
language and behavior, 40

La Parra Ranch, coffee drinking
      at, 121
"lasagne," Mexican, **218–219**
Las Animas Leader, on cowboy
      life-style, 47
Las Tablas Creek Ranch, 194
layer cake, mocha pecan, **252–
      253**
layered salad, **137**
layout boxes, 19, 37
leaveners, 103
leftovers, 39
lemon:
  -mint drizzle, pan-fried trout
      with, **198–199**
  peach and citrus chutney, **273**
  sauce, biscuit bread pudding
      with, **260–261**
  and wine, chicken with, **192**
Lerma, Juan, 29, 108
Lewis, Meriwether, 202
LFD Ranch:
  and Curley the Crow, 68
  fuel stored by, 37
  and molasses as cowhand bait,
      113
lick (sorghum molasses), 112–113
lighter fluid, 167
lima beans, in cowboy diet, 92
lime and avocado salad, **141**
literacy, among cowboys, 74, 98
Llano Estacado (ranch), brushfire
      on, 35
log rafts, for river crossings, 23
lone star gingerbread cookies,
      258–259
Long S Ranch:
  daily provisions required by,
      24
  entertainment on, 74
long sweetnin' (sorghum
      molasses), 112–113
Long X Ranch, 150, 248
LS Ranch, canned goods at, 96
Luman, Abner, 73
lumpy Dick pudding, 113
LX Ranch:
  desserts brought to, 40
  and disposition of cooks, 70
  fish consumption at, 87–88
  hygiene at, 76

macaroni salad with tomatoes
      and corn, ranch, **140**
McCauley, James Emmit, 114
McCoy, Joseph, 41
Mackay, Alexander, 107
McKee, Liz, 251
mackerel, in cowboy diet, 88

McSpadden, Clema and Donna,
      134, 136
maize, as coffee bean substitute,
      122
Majoribanks, A. J., 48
Mangum, Hal, 118
Manhattan Club, 65
maple syrup, cowboy valuation
      of, 113
marinade:
  Asian-grilled chicken breasts,
      188
  barbecued chicken, **189**
  citrus, grilled swordfish in, **197**
  herb, grilled vegetables with,
      236–237
marketing, of coffee, 121
married cowboys, 77
marrow guts (calf entrails), 85
Masterson, R. B., 88
Matador Ranch:
  bed tents at, 43
  and Bellyache Charley Colic,
      70
  campsites struck by, 29
  Christmas dinner at, 56
  coffee coupons collected at,
      121
  farming at, 98
  utensils at, 37
  wagons run by, 58
  workday pace at, 27
Mead Creek, 53
meal bran, as coffee bean
      substitute, 122
meal preparation, 37
  food quantities required for,
      24, 48, 82, 83, 99, 118
  and fresh meat, 84–87
  regional variation in, 46
  time allotted for, 33
  see also specific techniques
meat:
  baked short ribs, **180**
  beefy beans, **228**
  beer-basted barbecued brisket,
      172–173
  brisket chuckwagon stew,
      204–205
  Cecil's smothered steak, **178**
  in cowboy diet, 84–87
  Far East smoked pork chops,
      183
  garlic-stuffed pot roast, **179**
  German bacon and potato
      salad, **139**
  green chile stew, **208–209**
  grilled beef tenderloin, **170–
      171**
  hearty beef pie, **220–221**

herbed beef stew with corn dumplings, **212–213**
homemade beef jerky, **181**
Mexican "lasagne," **218–219**
New Mexican red chili, **209**
old-fashioned oxtail stew, **206–207**
smoked and rubbed prime rib roast, **168–169**
sourdough chicken-fried steak with cream gravy, **176–177**
sweet and spicy ribs, **182**
taco salad casserole, **214–215**
tamale casserole, **216**
T-bone steaks with Perini's steak rub, **174–175**
utensils for roasting of, 32
venison pot roast, **184–185**
meat hooks, 21
medicines, 66
Memphis, Tenn., 31
mesquite, 34, 43
mess call, 25–26
mess chests, 17, 22
mess halls, 54
mess tables, 42
Mexican cookery, 46, 86
Mexican "lasagne," **218–219**
Mexican wedding cookies, **257**
milk, in cowboy diet, 112
Miller 101 Ranch:
   coffee consumed at, 118
   economizing of food at, 24
   and river crossings, 23
milling, of coffee beans, 119
mineral salts, 34
mint-lemon drizzle, pan-fried trout with, **198–199**
"Mississippi Lawyer" (fiddle tune), 74
mocha pecan layer cake, **252–253**
Mom's cloverleaf rolls, **159**
Montgomery Ward, 31
Mooar, J. Wright, 83–84
Moore, J. Ealy, 32
Moore, Kent, 233
Mora, Joe, 72–73
morale, 68
mountain oysters (calf testicles), 85
mule trains, 16–17
Munger Ranch, irrigation on, 98
music, 40, 74
Musselshell range, stingy rationing on, 48
Mustang liniment, 66
mutton, in cowboy diet, 87

National Cowboy Hall of Fame, 61
navy beans, in cowboy diet, 92
Neff, Boss, 74
Nelson, Clyde, 130, 132, 155, 158, 160, 161, 183, 190, 197, 227, 236, 269, 271, 272
Nelson, Oliver, 72, 122
neutralizing of alkaline water, 93, 97
New Mexican red chili, **209**
New Mexican zucchini and corn, **235**
New York Times, 112
nicknames, cowboy, 68–70
nut(s):
   applesauce-pecan cake, **250**
   apricot bread, **154**
   buttermilk coffee cake, **158–159**
   Mexican wedding cookies, **257**
   mocha pecan layer cake, **252–253**
   panhandle pecan pie, **256–257**
   pecan-chicken breasts with honey sauce, **190–191**
   pecans and orange, sweet potatoes with, **232**
   spicy pecan pinwheels, **133**

oatmeal berry pancakes, **163**
occasions, special, 54–56, 84, 88
off season, 52–54, 64, 67
old-fashioned egg nog, **275**
old-fashioned oxtail stew, **206–207**
"Old Mother Blair" (fiddle tune), 74
"Old Rough and Ready" pudding doorstop, 114
Old Time Chuck Wagon Trailers, 60
onions, in cowboy diet, 92
open-range roundups, 23–25
orange:
   peach and citrus chutney, **273**
   and pecans, sweet potatoes with, **232**
   -spice raisin sourdough rolls, **151**
outfitting centers, 22
overland trout, *see* bacon
overnight coffee cake, **156–157**
Owens, Oak "Colie," 67
ox-drawn carts, 17
oxtail stew, old-fashioned, **206–207**

pack trains, 16–17
pancakes, berry oatmeal, **163**
pan gravy, 84
panhandle pecan pie, **256–257**
Parr, Virgil, 58
pasta:
   chicken with lemon and wine, **192**
   Mexican "lasagne," **218–219**
   ranch macaroni salad with tomatoes and corn, **140**
Patton, Uncle Johnnie, 108
Pattullo, George, 118
peach:
   and bourbon cobbler, **242–243**
   and citrus chutney, **273**
pecan(s):
   -applesauce cake, **250**
   apricot nut bread, **154**
   -chicken breasts with honey sauce, **190–191**
   Mexican wedding cookies, **257**
   mocha layer cake, **252–253**
   pie, panhandle, **256–257**
   pinwheels, spicy, **133**
Pecos River, 24, 34, 42–43, 93
Pecos strawberries, 92
peddlers, 52
People, Drew, 33
pepper and cabbage slaw, **138**
peppermint candy, in coffee marketing, 121
peppers, hot chile, *see* chile peppers
peppery beans, Buck's, **224**
Perini, Tom, 174, 204
Perini's Steak House, 174, 204
Perry, Jim, 68
pets, 74
pewter dishware, 37
Philadelphia, Pa., 17
Philmont Scout Ranch, 153
picket ropes, 21
pickles, in cowboy diet, 92
pickup trucks, chuck wagons replaced by, 57
pie:
   in cowboy diet, 114–115
   hearty beef, **220–221**
   panhandle pecan, **256–257**
Piebiter (cook), 70
pineapple:
   Asian-grilled chicken breasts, **188**
   avocado and lime salad, **141**
   salsa, tropical, **272**
pinto beans:
   beefy, **228**

pinto beans (*continued*)
  buckaroo saucy, **225**
  Buck's peppery, **224**
  in cowboy diet, 92
  porky, **226**
  sweet and tangy, **227**
Pitchfork Ranch:
  beef consumed at, 83
  chuck wagons abandoned at, 58
  and evolution of meal quality, 59–60
  food quantities required by, 99
  gourmet chef at, 74
pit roasting, 84
plumbing, 53, 58
poblano chile peppers, 129
  chuckwagon tomato sauce, **269**
  green chile stew, **208–209**
  quesadillas ricas, **130–131**
  see also chile peppers
poetry, campsite, 26, 40, 74
Polk, Cal, 94–95
pooch (chuck wagon meal), 97
pork:
  baked short ribs, **180**
  chops, Far East smoked, **183**
  in cowboy diet, 80, 81
  German bacon and potato salad, **139**
  green chile stew, **208–209**
  pinto beans, **226**
  sweet and spicy ribs, **182**
Postal Service, U.S., 120
postwar cowboys, 58–61
potato(es):
  and bacon salad, German, **139**
  cattlemen's club twice-baked, **230–231**
  in cowboy diet, 92, 93–94
  and vegetable bake, cowboy, **229**
  see also sweet potatoes
pot liquor, 93
pot racks, 29–31, 42
pot-rasslers, 70
pot roast:
  garlic-stuffed, **179**
  venison, **184–185**
Potter, Jack, 42
poultry:
  Asian-grilled chicken breasts, **188**
  barbecued chick, **189**
  chicken and hominy chili, **210–211**
  chicken with lemon and wine, **192**
  in cowboy diet, 88

grilled quail with jalapeño glaze, **196**
pecan-chicken breasts with honey sauce, **190–191**
roast duck with sweet and sour grapes, **194–195**
wide open spaces turkey, **193**
practical jokes, 75–76
prairie coal, 34–35
Prairie Lane and Cattle Company, 97
prairie oysters (calf testicles), 85
prairie whistles, 92
Price, Betty, 133, 256, 258
Price, Con, 70
price gouging, 52
prime rib roast, smoked and rubbed, **168–169**
Proctor, Lee, 113
prune(s):
  cake, spiced, **248–249**
  in cowboy diet, 92–93
pudding:
  biscuit bread, with lemon sauce, **260–261**
  in cowboy diet, 113–114
  jalapeño corn, **233**
  rice, spotted pup, 40, 113, **261**
punishment, 70

quail:
  in cowboy diet, 88
  grilled, with jalapeño glaze, **196**
quesadillas ricas, **130–131**
quinine, 66

rabbit meat, in cowboy diet, 87
railroad, 56
  and food transport, 22, 48, 98
railroad cross ties, as fuel, 37
Rainy Valley Ranch, 162
raisin(s):
  long cake, **247**
  -orange spice sourdough rolls, **151**
  peach and citrus chutney, **273**
  sweet and tangy beans, **227**
Ramsey, Bette, 206
ranch dressing, **135**
ranchero sauce, **270**
  huevos rancheros, **217**
ranch macaroni salad with tomatoes and corn, **140**
raspberry oatmeal pancakes, **163**
rationing, 16, 22
Rawhide (television show), 60–61
Rawhide Bill, 70

Reams, Robert L. "Buck," 179, 244
recipes, ranch cooks' use of, 72
Red River, 52
red snapper seviche San Juan, **199**
refrigeration, 53, 58, 99, 112
Reid, Chalma Pitts, 59–60
reloading tools (tableware), 37
revivals, roundup, 61
rheumatism, remedy for, 66
ribbon cane, 113
ribs, sweet and spicy, **182**
  see also pork
rice:
  chicken with lemon and wine, **192**
  chile and tomato soup, **143**
  in cowboy diet, 94–95
  pudding, spotted pup, 40, 113, **261**
Rickety Bob, 70
Riley, Mitzi, 218, 250, 275, 276
Riley Ranch, 218, 250, 275, 276
Rincon Ranch, wages at, 68
ristra (rope of chiles), 129
river crossings, 22–23
roasting, of bell peppers, 129
Rocking Chair Ranch, rotten supplies at, 48, 270
rodeos, 60
Rollinson, John K., 40
root cellars, 98
RO Ranch, irrigation at, 98
round pans, 39, 70
roundup drawers, 19
roundups, 23–24
  campsite locations of, 29
  food consumed at, 24–25
  modern-day revivals, 61
  provisions for, 16
Round-up Wagon, 22
rubs:
  Clyde's herb, **170**
  Cookie's dry, **168**
  Far Eastern, **183**
  Perini's steak, T-bone steaks with, **174**
Rude, Cleo, 225
rum, in old-fashioned egg nog, **275**
Russell, J. E., 121

saddle blankets (pancakes), 108
"Saddle Old Spike" (fiddle tune), 74
salad:
  avocado and lime, **141**
  corn bread, **136**

German bacon and potato, **139**
layered, **137**
taco, casserole, **214–215**
salad dressing:
  ranch, **135**
  smoky tomato vinaigrette, **271**
salsa:
  chile, **264**
  tropical pineapple, **272**
salt horse, salt junk, saltpeter, in cowboy diet, 81
salt pork, in cowboy diet, 80, 81
sangria, **276**
Saratoga chips, 94
sauce:
  beer moppin', **172**
  California-style barbecue, **268**
  Caribe, **265**
  chicken stock, **194–195**
  chile salsa, **264**
  chuckwagon tomato, **269**
  Clyde's moppin', **170**
  cowboy barbecue, **267**
  cream gravy, sourdough chicken-fried steak with, **176–177**
  guacamole, **266**
  honey, pecan-chicken breasts with, **190–191**
  honey bourbon, **190–191**
  lemon, biscuit bread pudding with, **260–261**
  ranchero, **270**
  tropical pineapple salsa, **272**
scorpions, in coffee, 122
sea biscuits, in cowboy diet, 102
sea level, cooking above, 240
Sears and Roebuck, 31
seeds, chile pepper, 129
Selmon, John, 77
serrano peppers, 128
seviche San Juan, **199**
Shakespeare, William, 74
Shardleman, Frank, 86
Shaw, Nell, 159, 229
sheet cake, Texas chocolate, **254–255**
shinnery, as fuel, 34
ship's bread, in cowboy diet, 102
shiverin' Liz (gelatin), 113
short ribs, baked, **180**
sidearms, 40, 66, 74
signatures, in coffee marketing, 121
Silver Creek Ranch, 199, 228
simmering, technique for, 203
Simpson, Bob, 74
Simpson, Frank, 23
Sims, Bill, 76

six-shooter coffee, 121
skillet and lid (Dutch oven), 31–32
slack lime, 66
Slaughter, C. C., 74
slaughtering, 81–83
Slaughter Ranch, size of roundup at, 24
slaves, 68
slaw, cabbage and pepper, **138**
sleep accommodations, 70
slow-bake technique, 203
Smith, Frank, 107, 121
smoked and rubbed prime rib roast, **168–169**
smoky tomato vinaigrette, **271**
snuff, as cinnamon substitute, 72
social routines, 39–41
soda crackers, in cowboy diet, 102
softshell turtle meat, in cowboy diet, 87
Soggy (ranch cook), 76
son-of-a-bitch-in-a-sack pudding, 113–114
son-of-a-bitch stew, 25, 85–87
sorghum molasses, in cowboy diet, 112–113
soup:
  chile, tomato, and rice, 143
  chuckwagon, **142**
sourdough bread, **148–149**
  biscuits, **152**
  cowboy's Dutch oven delight, **150**
  orange-spice raisin rolls, **151**
sourdough chicken-fried steak with cream gravy, **176–177**
sourdough cooking, 102
  vs. baking soda cooking, 108
  in Dutch ovens, 105–107
  fermentation in, 104
  kneading in, 105
  leaveners for, 103
  modern methods of, 146
Sourdough Jack, 70
sourdough starter, **147**
South Bend, Ind., 22
South Canadian River, 23
sow belly, 81
Spade Ranch:
  special dishes of, 94, 97, 113
  wages at, 65
spareribs, sweet and spicy, **182**
  see also pork
special occasions, 54–56, 84, 88
spice cake, apple, **251**
spiced prune cake, **248–249**
spicy pecan pinwheels, **133**

splatter dabs (pancakes), 108
spotted pup rice pudding, 40, 113, **261**
Spur Ranch:
  food quantities required by, 48, 82
  ranching begun by, 98
Square and Compass Ranch, 54
stakes, 21
static electricity, 43–46
Steagall, Red, 244
steak:
  Cecil's smothered, **178**
  sourdough chicken-fried, with cream gravy, **176–177**
  T-bone, with Perini's steak rub, **174–175**
stew:
  brisket chuckwagon, **204–205**
  green chile, **208–209**
  herbed beef, with corn dumplings, **212–213**
  old-fashioned oxtail, **206–207**
stock farms, 56
storage boxes, 17–21
storytelling, 40
stoves, 42, 44, 53
stray men, 23–24
Stuart, Granville, 103
Studebaker Brothers Manufacturing Company, 22
sucamagrowl (pudding), 113
sugar, in cowboy cooking, 112
suggans (bedding), 41–42
supper, 26, 27, 39
supply centers, 22, 48–52
sweet and sour grapes, **194**
sweet and spicy ribs, **182**
sweet and tangy beans, **227**
sweet potatoes:
  as coffee bean substitute, 122
  with orange and pecans, **232**
Sweetwater Chuck Wagon, 60
Swenson SMS Ranch, married cowhand hired by, 77
swordfish, citrus-marinated grilled, **197**

tableware, *see* utensils
taco salad casserole, **214–215**
Tailgate Ranch, 251
tamale casserole, **216**
tasso, *tasajo* (jerky), 83–84
Taylor, Abner, 81
T-bone steaks with Perini's steak rub, **174–175**
tea, in cowboy diet, 122
Teinert, Cliff, 150, 248

television westerns, 60–61
Tennyson, Alfred, Lord, 74
tents:
  bed, 59
  cook, 42–44
Texas butter, 72
Texas chocolate sheet cake, **254–255**
Texas Cowboy Reunion, 60
Texas Land and Cattle Company, 25
T5 Ranch, 66, 107
  coffee drinking at, 122
  coffee quantity required for, 118
Thai peppers, 128
Thanksgiving feasts, 88
theft, of coffee coupons, 121
thirst quenchers:
  canned tomato juice, 97
  Jamaica ginger, 34
Three C cowboys, etiquette among, 76
tin cans, 96
tin dishware, 37
T. Morris Perot Company, 17
tomato(es):
  canned, in cowboy diet, 96–97
  chile and rice soup, **143**
  and corn, ranch macaroni salad with, **140**
  sauce, chuckwagon, **269**
  vinaigrette, smoky, **271**
tool boxes, 21
topping, dessert, **156**
  mocha pecan layer cake frosting, **252–253**
  Texas chocolate sheet cake frosting, **254–255**
tortillas:
  in cowboy diet, 102
  huevos rancheros, **217**
  quesadillas ricas, **130–131**
  spicy pecan pinwheels, **133**
  taco salad casserole, **214–215**
trade catalogs, 31
trading cards, 121
trail boss:
  status of, 64
  wages of, 65
trail driving, 22–23
transportation, of farm produce, 22, 48, 92, 98
tremblin' jelly (gelatin), 113
tropical pineapple salsa, **272**
  citrus-marinated grilled swordfish, **197**
trout, pan-fried, with lemon-mint drizzle, **198–199**

trucks, chuck wagons replaced by, 57
True, Jean, 192, 247
True Ranch, 192, 247
turkey:
  in cowboy diet, 88
  pit-roasted, 84
  wide open spaces, **193**
"Turkey in the Straw" (fiddle tune), 74
Turkey Track Ranch, coupons collected at, 121
turpentine, as medicine, 66
turtle meat, in cowboy diet, 87
22 Ranch, food quantities overestimated by, 94
Twin-K Enterprises, 203
Two Bar Ranch, 40

underground cooking, 84
utensils:
  for cooking, 16, 25, 167
  cost of, 31–32
  for eating, 37

vegetable(s):
  chuckwagon soup, **142**
  cowboy demand for, 92, 99
  grilled, with herb marinade, **236–237**
  and potato bake, cowboy, **229**
  railroad transport of, 98
  see also specific vegetables
venison:
  jerky, 83
  pot roast, **184–185**
vinaigrette, smoky tomato, **271**
vinegaroons, in coffee, 122
vitamin deficiencies, 52

wages, 65, 67, 68
Waggoner Ranch, persistence of old school cooking on, 59, 105–106
wagons, 17
  bed or hoodlum, 42
  chip, 35
  construction of, 21–22
  drivers of, 67
  evolution of, 17
  as replaced by cars and trucks, 57
  and river crossings, 22–23
  in roundups, 24
  storage in, 17–21
Walden, Frank, 74
wallets, 16

Walsh, Paddy, 74
Warren, Joseph Bailey "Cap," 59, 105–106
washtubs, 39
water:
  alkaline, 34, 93, 97
  barrels for, 21, 34
  shortages of, 33–34
  tanks for, 58
  wagons for, 42
W.B.G. cowboy cooks:
  bread cooked by, 107–108
  disposition of, 71
weapons, 40, 66, 74
wedding cookies, Mexican, **257**
well water, 98
Western Chuck Wagon Association, 61
Western Heritage Center, 61
westerns, television and movie, 60–61
wheat, as coffee bean substitute, 122
wheat flour, 102
Wheeler, Clyde and Barbara Dodd, 212
whippings, 70
whirlups, 115
whiskey:
  in coffee, 121
  for medicinal purposes, 66
Whistling Jake, 70
Whitlock, H. V., 68
wide open spaces turkey, **193**
windbreaks, 29
wine:
  and lemon, chicken with, **192**
  sangria, **276**
winter camps, 52–54, 64, 67
Wishbone (*Rawhide* cook), 61
Withers, Mark, 23
women:
  cowboys alerted to presence of, 40
  dessert contributions of, 115
  male cooks replaced by, 76–77
  on stock farms, 56–57
wood-burning stoves, 42
wood campfires, 203
wood chips, for barbecuing and grilling, 167
workday hours, for cowboys, 25, 27, 65–66
World War II, ranching affected by, 58–59
wreck pans, 39
WS cowboys, and gardening, 98

X-G Ranch, 141, 154, 178, 216
XIT Ranch:
African-American cook at, 68
beef consumption at, 82
bread baking at, 100
canned goods banned by, 96
farming at, 98
husband and wife cooks at, 77
progressive provisions of, 42

slaughter of beef at, 81
supplies list of, 32
visitors to, 54
XT Ranch, English pudding
cooked at, 114

"yaller bread," in cowboy diet,
103

yeast, in bread baking, 103
Yokley Ranch, firearms at, 74
Young, John, 108

Zimmer, Stephen, 153
zucchini and corn, New
Mexican, **235**